Sermons On The Gospel Readings

Series I

Cycle A

Susan R. Andrews
Richard E. Gribble, csc
Stephen M. Crotts
Stan Purdum
George L. Murphy

CSS Publishing Company, Inc., Lima, Ohio

Copyright © 2004 by
CSS Publishing Company, Inc.
Lima, Ohio

Scripture quotations are from the *New Revised Standard Version of the Bible*, copyright 1989 by the Division of Christian Education of the National Council of the Churches of Christ in the USA. Used by permission.

Scripture quotations marked (RSV) are from the *Revised Standard Version of the Bible*, copyrighted 1946, 1952 ©, 1971, 1973, by the Division of Christian Education of the National Council of the Churches of Christ in the USA. Used by permission.

Library of Congress Cataloging-in-Publication Data

Sermons on the Gospel readings : series I, cycle A / Susan R. Andrews ... [et. al].
    p. cm.
    ISBN 0-7880-2323-3 (perfect bound : alk. paper)
    1. Sermons, American. 2. Bible. N.T. Gospels—Homiletical use. I. Andrews, Susan R.,
1949-. II. Title.

BV4241.S426 2004
252'.6—dc22
                                                                    2004012405

For more information about CSS Publishing Company resources, visit our website at www.csspub.com or e-mail us at custserv@csspub.com or call (800) 241-4056.

ISBN 0-7880-2323-3   PRINTED IN U.S.A.

Table Of Contents

**Sermons For Sundays
After Pentecost (First Third)
Hidden In Plain View
by Stephen M. Crotts / Stan Purdum**

Sermons For Sundays
After Pentecost (Middle Third)
The Incomparable Christ
by Stephen M. Crotts / George L. Murphy

Sermons For Sundays
After Pentecost (Last Third)
Rendering To God
by Stephen M. Crotts / George L. Murphy / Stan Purdum

Sermons On The Gospel Readings

For Sundays In Advent, Christmas, And Epiphany

The Offense Of Grace

Susan R. Andrews

For the members of
Bradley Hills Presbyterian Church,
who have taught me how to preach

Advent 1
Matthew 24:36-44

Swept Away!

It's the same year after year. On this most somnolent of American weekends when it takes three days to recover from one day of gluttony, this lazy weekend when some people sleep in for four days in a row — it is this Sunday that the church decides to defy the culture and catapult us into a new year — smacking us first with judgment and then with demand. It is this weekend that the liturgical calendar tells us to "Wake Up!" Life as we know it will eventually end. Get up! The world as we experience it will surely change. Watch! The God we think we know is about to become for us a God we have never met. Yes, my friends, today is the first Sunday of Advent — the season of moving toward a God who will invade our predictable world and shake us up.

Strangely enough, this year I am ready for Advent. I am ready to burrow into its purple shadows. I am ready to wander through its murky mysteries. I am ready to embrace its open-ended darkness. I am ready to hear the stories and learn the lessons which this season has to teach us — stories about how to wait, lessons about how to repent, teachings about how to endure in the middle of the night, when burdens weigh down and anxiety overcomes. Yes, I am ready to figure out how to be a faithful Christian at times when Jesus seems far away and the world seems ready to fall apart.

We can always count on apocalyptic language this first Sunday of Advent. Echoing the phantasmagorical language of Revelation, the bizarre visions of Ezekiel and Daniel, on this New Year's Day of the Christian year, the gospel writers always greet us with images of cosmic catastrophe and jolting judgment — stories that warn us that all that is predictable and all that is comfortable in our lives will be swept away. And, they tell us, there is nothing we can do to stop it.

Matthew's predictions this morning were written to a complacent and lethargic community — Christians who had lost the expectation of the Second Coming — lost the vision of God's rich and peaceable kingdom on earth. After all, the church in Jerusalem had been waiting for eighty years and nothing had happened. And so their faith and their commitment and their connection to God had cooled off. The believers in Jerusalem had become lukewarm — sort of like us — middle-class agnostics living in one of the most affluent counties in America, cushioned by so much comfort, programmed by so much self-importance, that we, too, manage to keep God at a safe distance. When we first hear it, this apocalyptic language, this scary language, this urgent language doesn't really speak to our situation. Or does it?

My friends, if we open our eyes to the world around us, catastrophe surrounds us. The devastation in Iraq and Afghanistan and the Sudan has killed thousands of people. Talk about being swept away! Our barbaric regime has given way to lethargic occupation and sporadic guerrilla warfare.

And what about the former Soviet Union? Poverty and anarchy reign in a vast land of hungry and miserable people. Soldiers are paid with hunting licenses because there is no money for salaries. Alcohol consumption is skyrocketing, while democratic reformers are murdered. And in the midst of it all, in the midst of all this chaos and dysfunction, Russia's vast nuclear stockpile sits inadequately monitored.

And what about Africa and the Middle East and Ireland, where religious persecution and suspicion and warfare boil and bubble in deep cauldrons of ancient hatreds? A few years ago in Egypt 1,000 Coptic Christians were manacled to doors, beaten, and tortured with electric shocks to their genitals. All the while, teenage girls were raped, babies were beaten, and men were nailed to crosses. All in retaliation for the unsolved death of one Muslim.

And what about Washington, D.C., where patterns of street violence, and poor education, and drug addiction, and single-mother

16

families struggling just to greet each morning — where all these patterns are escalating? Where one third of young men in their twenties are in prison, and where the death rate for young black men has risen 700 percent in the last ten years? Yes, my friends, the shadows of apocalypse are all around us if we have eyes to see and ears to hear.

And not only out there in the unpredictable patterns of our chaotic world. These words also echo in here in the carefully circumscribed worlds of our souls. Despite our presentable masks of stability, despite our filled-up calendars and carefully managed stock portfolios, despite our alarm controlled homes and our computer controlled communication, despite our lists and our voice mail, despite our mission statements and our goals and objectives, we all live in worlds we cannot control. And if we are honest, an apocalypse of anxiety often eats away at us in the middle of the night. What if the stock market tumbles again? How will we pay for college — and for that second home? What if that cyst turns out to be malignant? How many years do we have left to live? What, we wonder, will be the next crisis with our aging parents or our children? And how will we find the time and the energy and the wisdom to meet the needs of all those who depend on us — the kids and the spouse and the friends and the parents and the people who lean on us at work? And, when all is said and done, what difference does any of it make anyhow? What is the point of it anyhow? If scripture is right, it will be in the midst of our marrying and working, in the midst of our eating and drinking, there will come a moment, an unexpected moment, when each one of us will be swept away — and there is not one thing we can do about it.

William Willimon tells the story of a funeral he attended when he was serving a small congregation in rural Georgia. One of his members' relatives died, so Willimon and his wife attended the funeral held in an off-brand, country Baptist church. He writes: "I had never seen anything like it. The preacher began to preach. He shouted; he flailed his arms. 'It's too late for Joe. He's dead. But it ain't too late for you. People drop dead every day. Why wait? Now is the day for decision. Give your life to Jesus.' "

17

Willimon goes on to suggest that this was the worst thing he had ever seen. He fumed and fussed at his wife Patsy, complaining that the preacher had done the worst thing possible for a grieving family — manipulating them with guilt and shame. Patsy agreed. But then she said: "Of course the worst part of it all is that what he said is true."[1]

My friends, each one of us lives in the shadow of the apocalypse — the dark reality of the end of our time and the end of the world's time. That is the warning of Advent. But there is also good news. There is also the promise of Advent — the promise that in the darkness, in the shadows, in the unpredictable anxiety of our unfinished lives, God is present. God is in control, and God will come again. With each candle we light, the shadows recede a bit, and the promise comes closer. With each candle we light, we are proclaiming that the light shines in the darkness and the darkness will never overcome it. The promise is that wherever there is darkness and dread in our lives, wherever there is darkness and dread in the world around us, God is present to help us endure. God is in charge, and hope is alive. And as long and as interminable as the night seems, morning will come — in God's good time and God's good way.

And so we have a choice. We can wither away with anxiety. Or we can wait expectantly. We can bury our fears in the deep valleys of sleep. Or we can wake up and watch the horizon. We can crawl into caves of dread and despair. Or we can find our way into the hallowed halls of hope. We can give up and settle for little. Or we can work diligently for the salvation of the world — trusting that God will complete our work with wholeness and abundance.

In her novel *Animal Dreams*, Barbara Kingsolver introduces us to two sisters — Codi and Hallie — whose mother died in childbirth and who were raised by a cold and autocratic father. The two sisters react very differently to the emotional impoverishment of their childhood. Codi becomes a drifter, unable to find roots in work or love or relationship — suspicious of the world — scared of passion — cynical about this crapshoot called life. But Hallie makes a different choice. Somehow she is able to embrace life and discover passion and decide in the unfinished world of which she

18

is a part that she can and must make a difference. She ends up going to Central America as an agricultural specialist — determined to lose her life in order to find it. In a letter to her mystified sister, Hallie writes:

> *Codi, here's what I've decided: the least you can do is to figure out what you hope for. And the most you can do is live inside that hope. Not admire it from a distance but live under its roof ... Codi, I wish you knew how to squander yourself (for hope).*[2]

My friends, this Advent season, we are called to embrace the darkness, to trust the Presence, to watch for the flickers of light, to wait for the sure coming of God in new ways. And — while we wait and while we watch — we are called to squander ourselves for hope, proclaiming that God is in charge and that one day the kingdom will fully come.

May it be so — for you and for me. Amen.

---

1. Source unknown

2. Barbara Kingsolver, *Animal Dreams* (Boston: G. K. Hall and Co., 1991), p. 299.

Advent 2
Matthew 3:1-12

Road Rage

When our children were small, a nice church lady named Chris made them a child-friendly creche. All the actors in this stable drama are soft and squishy and durable — perfect to touch and rearrange — or toss across the living room in a fit of toddler frenzy. The Joseph character has always been my favorite because he looks a little wild — red yarn spiking out from his head, giving him an odd look of energy. In fact, I have renamed this character John the Baptist and in my mind substituted one of the innocuous shepherds for the more staid and solid Joseph. Why this invention? Because, over the years, I have decided that without the disconcerting presence of John lurking in the shadows of our manger scenes, the Jesus story is mush — nothing but child's play, lulling us into sleepy sentimentality.

Woe to a world that tries to silence John the Baptist! Woe to a world that muffles the voices of those crying in the wilderness — crying above the desolation and the despair and the disillusionment of the mess that we have created! Woe to us if we ignore the voices of Ralph Nader and Susan B. Anthony, Mahatma Gandhi and Mother Teresa, Ed Murphy and Elizabeth St. John! Dietrich Bonhoeffer said it well — the promises and the predictions of Advent are frightening for anyone who has a conscience.

We need to know that when John shows up in that barren desert outside first century Bethlehem, what the people see is a spitting image of Elijah — the wild hair and the wild robe and the wild words of *the* greatest prophet who ever lived. Elijah was the first big voice to name the failures of God's people. He was the man

21

who dared to tell the truth — about their greed, about their cold-heartedness, about their timidity in the face of evil. And Elijah was the one who predicted that, because of their spiritual sloth, the people of God would crumble into oblivion — losing their land, losing their soul, losing their way in the seductive wilderness of the world. And, of course, everything that Elijah predicted came true — the bloody battles, the arrogant arguments, the social decay, the humiliating exile of Israel's story.

And so, centuries later, when John the Baptist shows up in the shadows of that remnant, he is speaking to a people who have no holy spirit, no holy hope, no holy guts. *But*, as a mirage from the past, he simply electrifies the crowd. His urgency, his energy, his truth — yes, even his anger — tantalizes their apathy. And, the text tells us, lots of people come to hear him. They intentionally come and subject themselves to a kind of verbal road rage. They open their lives to be judged and scared and harassed — to be driven right off the comfortable, boring highways of their lives. Why? Why do they come? Because maybe, just maybe, in the midst of rebuke — they will repent. Maybe they will be reborn. Maybe they will remember — remember who God is and remember who they are. Maybe, just maybe, John's blunt blast will become a bold blessing.

Repent! This ancient, angular word echoes awkwardly in our feel-good world. And yet, my friends, *Repent!* is the only kind of preparation called for in scripture during these days and weeks before Christmas. *Repent!* for the kingdom of God is at hand. *Repent!* for the moment of travail and birth is at hand. And as with any birth — the birth of Jesus, the birth of vision, the birth of justice, the birth of honesty, the birth of compassion, the birth of a new age, the birth of our own embryonic souls — as with any birth, the old must pass away and the startling, demanding, difficult new must come. But fear not. According to John, God will be our mid-wife — coaching our birth, and easing the radical changes that squirming new life always brings.

And so, my friends, John's voice crying in the wilderness of this sanctuary is first and foremost a voice of accountability. To the scribes and to the Pharisees, to the conservatives and to the liberals, to the peasants and to the powerful, to the Jews and to the

22

Gentiles, to the believers and to the skeptics, to the people back then and to us gathered here — to all the odd and varied people who gather in the wilderness, John demands moral and spiritual accountability.

Yes, John is raging at us today. In our me-and-my-Jesus kind of faith, in our me-and-my-clan kind of politics, in our me-and-my-happiness kind of world, John rages at our self-absorbed narrowness. Christmas, Christianity, spirituality — none of this is about me and mine. It is not even about us and ours. It is about God and God's vision. John takes what we have personalized and sentimentalized — and he rips it open, politicizing and socializing the good news of the gospel. The kingdom of God is not contained within the comfortable walls of this sanctuary. It is not contained within the ordered structures of denominationalism. It is not contained within the proud patriotism of America. It is not even contained within the sanctimonious bubble of Christianity. Just because Abraham, or Calvin, or Jesus is our ancestor — this does not mean that only *we* are chosen — that only *we* are precious — that only *we* matter. John tells us that God is even able to turn stones into faithful people. In God's imagination, everyone matters. In God's sovereignty, everyone belongs at the kingdom table. And in God's economy, everyone will be judged — judged as to how passionate we are about seeking justice for all.

As amused as I was by the recent anti-SUV campaign, I know in my heart that John the Baptist would have approved. I think the answer to the question, "What would Jesus drive?" is clear. The answer is: "Jesus wouldn't drive at all — he would only take public transportation!" Which, of course, judges all of us — those who drive Chevy Cavaliers and those who drive SUVs. Brothers and sisters, anything we do that separates us by power or privilege from other children in God's world, anything that abuses creation or oppresses people or substitutes the comforts of stuff for the comforts of soul, yes, anything that puts our puny selves above the desperate cries of a wounded creation — all of this is contrary to the kingdom of God. And all of this must change if Christ is to be fully incarnated in this world. Far from being hyperbolic, John the Baptist is simply telling the truth.

And so, John's voice crying in the wilderness of a weary world is a booming voice of accountability. And I believe that most of us are here today partly because, like those restless people of long ago, we want to be held accountable. We *need* to be held accountable. But the good news of our Advent faith is that John's voice of accountability is also a loud voice of hope. "Prepare ye the way of the Lord. Make his paths straight." John is quoting Isaiah who first spoke these words to the hopeless people of Israel who had shriveled up in the catastrophic captivity of Babylonia. And yet, Isaiah reminds these homeless exiles that God has not abandoned them — that indeed God is preparing right now a way for them to return to Israel, to return to life, to return to God, to return home. In echoing Isaiah's words this morning, John is speaking to the faithful remnant who have returned to the land, but have not returned to the vision. He is saying to them — he is saying to us — that God is building a new highway, a new path, a new way right here in our wilderness — preparing for us a straight path amid the crooked and the confused ways of this world.

In the New Testament the word for "road" and the word for "way" is the same. And of course, we know that for us, who call ourselves Christians, the Way, the Truth, and the Life is Jesus. And what a way it is — this journey straight through and with and in Christ. This Jesus is the mighty one who topples the proud and the powerful. But he is also the gentle one who cradles his lambs and tenderly carries us home. This Jesus is the angry prophet who turns over tables of greed. But he is also the Savior, who unconditionally forgives the prodigal son and the prostitute daughter. This Jesus is the demanding teacher who confronts us with our hatreds and our prejudices and our selfishness. But he is also the healer, who casts out our demons and opens our blind hearts and feeds us with the very bread of life. Yes, Jesus is the Way, the straight and promising path through the treacheries and the disappointments of this world. And he reminds us that daily repentance and daily renewal and daily commitment is what the journey of faith is all about.

A few weeks ago I was part of a clergy gathering at the Bryn Mawr Presbyterian Church in Pennsylvania. A 4,000-member congregation, the Bryn Mawr church includes some of the wealthiest and most powerful people in the Philadelphia area. Part of that experience was listening to a panel of men and women from the business community — all of them elders in the church. They had been asked to tell us, the pastors of this world, what they, the movers and shakers of the world, need to hear from the church. It was a sobering experience. Contrary to what I had expected, these people do not want only to hear words of comfort; instead what they most want to hear are words of confrontation and truth. They want to be reminded in clear ways what the values and responsibilities of our faith really are. They want to be held accountable for the rich gifts and privileges they have been given. Yes, week in and week out, they want to be called to repentance — so that when push comes to shove, in the boardrooms of America, they will find the wisdom to be faithful and the courage to be honest. They want to be able to resist the seductions and the lies that have corrupted the Enrons and the world.coms and the Halliburtons of this world.

One woman on the panel summarized it all. She said, "I come to worship to pray and to sing and to listen. But most of all, I come for the benediction. Because that is the moment that I am reminded who I am. That is the moment when, one more time, I am pushed by God out into the world to be the very presence of Christ." This is the benediction which is used every week at the Bryn Mawr Presbyterian Church:

> *Go out into the world in peace;*
> *have courage;*
> *hold onto what is good;*
> *return no one evil for evil;*
> *strengthen the fainthearted;*
> *support the weak, and help the suffering;*
> *honor all people;*
> *love and serve the Lord,*
> *rejoicing in the power of the Holy Spirit.*

This, of course, is just an elegant way of echoing John's very tough, very good news: "Repent! for the kingdom of God is at hand."

May it be so. Amen

25

Disappointed In Jesus

It was a painful experience for both of us. Jane was a young mother about my age. She had been on the pastor nominating committee that called us to New Jersey. And we had shared much laughter and friendship through the years. She also was on the session — and that cold November night she seemed edgy and distant. I soon found out why. Following the meeting, she waited for me out in the parking lot. And after I locked the church door, she simply lit into me. "How dare you!" she said. "How dare you push your own political viewpoints down our throats, and abuse your privilege as a pastor! And most of all how dare you play partisan politics on the lawn of church property!"

You see, it was election time, and I had put a placard supporting my presidential candidate on the front lawn of the church manse. Obviously it was not Jane's candidate. And she was furious. Of course, she was right. It *was* inappropriate for me to put a partisan placard on church property. And since that day I have never put political propaganda — stickers, buttons, placards — anywhere outside or inside church property — other than that which is the official position of our Presbyterian denomination. But Jane's outburst went much deeper than campaign posters. She was — all of a sudden — deeply disappointed in me — and angry that I had let her down, that I had not met her expectations, that I turned out to be human, after all. Well, after a few days of cooling down, I went and talked with Jane, admitting my error, but also encouraging her to think about what was beneath her outburst. And together we were able to understand that her disappointment with me was also

27

a projection of her disappointments in general — her disappoint-ment in a life that wasn't always clear cut, her disappointment in the church that — surprise! surprise! — is full of sinners, and her disappointment in God who didn't seem to be making the world turn out right.

This morning we meet John the Baptist in very odd circum-stances. And what we discover is his deep disappointment with Jesus. If you remember back to last week, we first met John in the wilderness — a wild man with a hairy shirt and a locust diet — a passionate prophet who was ranting and raving about the wrath of God. Calling those of us in the crowd and in these pews a brood of vipers, he made it clear that the wrath of God Almighty will de-vour all of us who do not confess and change our ways. And if we don't repent, the consequences will be clear. The ax of God's judg-ment will cut us down and we will be thrown into the torture of unquenchable fire. Now, what I can't figure out is that, rather than walking away, according to the third chapter of Matthew, the crowds of people just kept coming back for more — more of John's verbal abuse.

Jesus, of course, was one of the crowd. Why? Because God, in human disguise, was living and feeling and yearning just like all the rest of us. But, scripture tells us, when John saw Jesus, he immediately knew that Jesus was the One — the One all of Israel had been waiting for. And he, John, did not consider himself wor-thy to carry the sandals of Jesus. "No," John shouts: "Jesus is about to baptize with fire. And then with a winnowing fork, this mighty Messiah will separate the chaff from the wheat. And all unrepen-tant sinners will be cast into the furnace of hell." Not a very com-forting scene, is it?

Now, fast forward two years to today's text. John is in prison because, with his usual offensive audacity, he has spoken truth to power. Yes, John has told Herod that it was wrong for him to com-mit adultery. It was wrong for him to steal his brother's wife and then sleep with her. Such judgment has gotten John in deep trouble, and today he languishes in a prison cell awaiting his death. And while he sits there, he begins to hear all the things that Jesus is doing. And he has lots of time to think. Yes, John has lots of time

28

to begin to realize that Jesus is not acting the way the Messiah — according to John — should act. Rather than blazing with the fire of indignation, Jesus seems to be telling stories and playing with children. Rather than railing against the sins of the world, Jesus is eating with tax collectors and prostitutes and poor people. Rather than tossing people into the blistering cauldron of hell, he is listening to them, forgiving them, and changing them from the inside out. Our Bible study group came up with a wonderful image. What John expected in a Messiah was a rottweiler, growling and attacking the sinners of the world. But what he got was a puppy, changing hearts with warmth and affection. No wonder John has started asking the question: "Is this the one who is to come, or are we to wait for another?"

Now, in order to figure out this passage, we need to digress for just a minute into the world of the prophets. Contrary to popular opinion, prophets in the Bible are not primarily fortune tellers who predict what is going to happen in the future. They are much more social commentators who accurately describe what is going on now — and usually in ways that people don't want to hear. In the Hebrew Scriptures, the prophets were those men and women who experienced the mystery of God in some deep and personal way, and then felt called to articulate what they had seen and heard for others. Marcus Borg defines the Hebrew prophets this way: "I see them as God-intoxicated voices of radical social criticism, and God-intoxicated advocates of an alternative social vision. Their dream is God's dream."[1]

According to this definition, John the Baptist was a true-blue prophet — a God-intoxicated dreamer who passionately advocated for God's alternative social vision of *shalom*. But passionate as he was, in the long run, John wasn't very persuasive.

Walter Brueggemann has made a very helpful distinction between *prophetic criticizing* and *prophetic energizing* — both of which appear in abundance in the Hebrew Scriptures. Prophetic criticizing takes a laser-sharp look at the world and lifts up all the blatant sin and selfishness of the world. Prophetic criticizing proclaims God's dream and desire for creation and then attacks each one of us in the heart of our apathy and our greed. Prophetic criticizing drops bombs of honest judgment and leaves us writhing in the ashes of guilt and failure, with radical repentance the only hope for survival. Prophetic criticizing has its prominent place in scripture, as John the Baptist can attest to. And God has the right to put it there. But there is very little good news in prophetic criticizing.

The other form of prophetic activity is *prophetic energizing*. And it is equally prominent in scripture. This form of proclamation is centered in hope. Despite our sin and our failures as God's people, God has not given up on us or the world. And God is about to do a new thing with and for the world that we have desecrated. When those disciples come back to Jesus and ask him John's question, Jesus responds with classic prophetic energizing. Is he, Jesus, the Messiah, or should John — should we — look for another? Quoting Isaiah, Jesus presents his positive messianic vision, his description of the new social order that God *is* bringing about: The blind receive their sight, the lame walk, the lepers are cleansed, the deaf hear, the dead are raised, and the poor have good news — not bad news — brought to them. And then knowing that John will be very disappointed in these words, Jesus adds a wistful benediction: "Blessed is anyone who takes no offense at me."

It is clear that in his preaching and teaching, Jesus combined prophetic criticizing with prophetic energizing. He railed at the legalistic religious authorities of his day, calling them "hypocrites" and "broods of vipers." He gently criticized Martha for her anxious busyness and the woman at the well for her promiscuous lifestyle. But he constantly forgave the ones he criticized and then energized them with visions of new chances, new beginnings, new opportunities for abundant living. I believe that Jesus took the prophetic vocation and carried it one step further. He combined prophetic criticizing and prophetic energizing by embodying them both. Through *prophetic actualizing*, Jesus became the incarnation of the dream, the embodiment of the new social order, the one who walked the walk and lived the vision. And, brothers and sisters, as the Body of Christ, we are called to do the same.

There is a wonderful parable that tells us what "prophecy actualized" might look like in our lives. There was once a woman who was disappointed, who was disillusioned, who was depressed. She wanted a good world, a peaceful world, and she wanted to be a good person. But the newspaper and television showed her how far we were from such a reality. So she decided to go shopping. She went to the mall and wandered into a new store — where the person behind the counter looked strangely like Jesus. Gathering up her courage she went up to the counter and asked, "Are you Jesus?" "Well, yes, I am," the man answered. "Do you work here?" "Actually," Jesus responded, "I own the store. You are free to wander up and down the aisles, see what it is I sell, and then make a list of what you want. When you are finished, come back here, and we'll see what we can do for you."

So, the woman did just that. And what she saw thrilled her. There was peace on earth, no more war, no hunger or poverty, peace in families, no more drugs, harmony, clean air. She wrote furiously and finally approached the counter, handing a long list to Jesus. He skimmed the paper, and then smiling at her said, "No problem." Reaching under the counter, he grabbed some packets and laid them out on the counter. Confused, she asked, "What are these?" Jesus replied: "These are seed packets. You see, this is a catalogue store." Surprised the woman blurted out, "You mean I don't get the finished product?" "No," Jesus gently responded. "This is a place of dreams. You come and see what it looks like, and I give you the seeds. Then you plant the seeds. You go home and nurture them and help them to grow and someone else reaps the benefits." "Oh," she said, deeply disappointed in Jesus. Then she turned around and left the store without buying anything.[2]

Friends, I believe that our passage for today speaks to us about our calling as Christians in a world of violence, in a world of increasing poverty, in a world of terrorism and intolerance. As disciples of Jesus, our text for today is calling us to follow him as those who embrace his prophetic vocation. Yes, we are called to criticize when necessary. We are called always to energize with hopeful visions of a new social order. But most of all, we are called to actualize Jesus' passionate dream of a whole and healed world. We are called to *actualize* God's creative plan by the way we live our daily lives.

So, my friends, let's pick up those packets of seeds. And let's plant them — for the sake of our children and all the children of the world.

May it be so — for you and for me. Amen.

---

1. Marcus Borg, *Reading the Bible Again for the First Time* (San Francisco: Harper, 2002), p.127.

2. As told in *Spiritual Literacy: Reading the Sacred in Everyday Life*, F. and M. Brussat, editors (New York: Scribner, 1996), p. 359.

The Power Of Positive Dreaming

According to tradition, Joseph was the strong, silent type —
an older carpenter who willingly submitted to impotent fatherhood
— a second-string player in the drama of God's human birth. But
according to scripture, none of this is true. All that is actually recorded in the Bible is that Joseph was a dreamer — a righteous
man who transformed the meaning of righteousness by taking seriously his dreams.

To be righteous, according to Torah, is to be law-abiding. And
so, as a law-abiding Jew, Joseph could have had Mary stoned to
death — the punishment commanded in the twenty-first chapter of
Deuteronomy for betrothed women who slept with other men. But,
to be righteous, according to Torah, also means to be merciful —
so Joseph, a man of compassion, decided, instead of stoning, that
he would dismiss Mary as his wife, quietly. What never occurred
to Joseph is that there is yet another way to be righteous — the way
of mystery, the way of surprise, the way of acceptance and forgiveness and grace. Joseph, all on his own, couldn't imagine how
God could be present in so difficult and embarrassing and dangerous a situation as Mary's pregnancy. And so, God had to help him.
In the deep darkness of sleep, God came to Joseph, God spoke to
Joseph in a dream, God brought truth into the irrational depths of
Joseph's intuition. In ways deeper and more magnificent than the
mind can imagine, God changed Joseph. And because God changed
Joseph, Joseph became a channel of God's grace in the world.

Seventy times in scripture, God becomes real and present
through dreams — sleep dreams, day dreams, intuitive dreams,

vision dreams. Seventy times in the Bible the forgotten language of God bubbles up out of the depth of the human soul. Adam, Noah, Moses, Jacob, Joseph I, Isaiah, David, Daniel, Elizabeth, Joseph II, Paul, Ananias, John — these earthy, needy, confused people become the mouthpieces of God. How? By listening to and honoring their dreams. How? By moving beyond the controlled rationality of their minds.

In recent years, scientists have been able to establish the presence of dreams in the sleep of every single human being. The movement of the eyelids and brain waves during sleep has uncovered the certainty that each one of us dreams an average of an hour and a half each night — that our inner worlds spin six or seven dreams every time we sink into our pillows. Whether we remember them or not, dreams are truth for us, because they uncover the world of our unconscious self — the memories, feelings, needs that our mind rarely acknowledges. Psychologists now know that if this unconscious material is ignored, if it is not acknowledged and integrated in some way into our experience of living, then we will suffer great mental and emotional distress. We will experience persistent anxiety about the meaning and dependability of life. Dreams, visions, hunches are the way we compensate for the spirit and truth we have cut out of our lives. Dreams are the way we discover the full image of God that rests deeply within each one of us. Our dreams — waking dreams and sleeping dreams — these are spiritual windows into our souls.

And so Joseph dreamed. And what he discovered was that Mary's baby was not a disgrace, not an embarrassment, not a problem, but instead the very possibility of hope for himself and for the world. Joseph dreamed, and what he discovered was that he could behave in a new way, that he *must* behave in a new way — that is if he wanted the God in him, the God in Mary, the God in the world to survive. Joseph's dream did not give him rational explanations or scientific facts or detailed instructions — the how, what, where, why of Mary's pregnancy. Instead, Joseph's dream gave him inspiration. His dream invited him, practical, solid Joseph, to become a partner with God in mystery. Not understanding, but believing, Joseph woke up. In faith, Joseph responded.

With courage, Joseph risked new behavior. And excited by hope, Joseph assisted in giving birth to God — a new God for a very old world. Such is the power of dreams.

Recently I was talking to a man in his mid-forties — a good man, a righteous man, a bored man. All his life he's done what is right — worked hard, been faithful in his marriage, been responsible to his children. But life for him has become stale. His marriage is stale, his mind is stale, most of all, his imagination is stale. A few months ago this man had a dream. In the dream he was cleaning his house and unintentionally pushed against the wall in the living room. A secret door opened up showing him a room in his house he had never discovered. The room was an adult play room — complete with fireplace, sofas, and glass windows open to the beauty of the world. This dream has helped my friend to take stock, to realize what is missing in his life, to help him know that there is newness waiting for him in the marriage and the life he already has.

Where are your dreams and visions, needs and intuitions this day? Is the unconscious voice of God whispering to you in your heart, in your sleep, in your feelings, in your hunches? What is the restlessness which is stirring you up and echoing in your emptiness and bubbling within your fears and anxieties? What is it that God is trying to say to you in the undiscovered parts of who you are? How is God pushing you to give more life to the world? How can you this day, this year, sink into your dreams, trusting them and following them, so that God can be born in you, so that God can be born *through* you into this world of woe?

The story of the angels and the shepherds, the star and the wise men, the peasant mother and the stoic father — this ancient tale about a baby God finding a home in our world — none of it makes much sense. And historians and scientists find delight in the illegitimacy of this tale. But God persists anyway. You see, my friends, Christmas is not about fact or fiction. Christmas is about incarnation. Christmas is God's dream becoming flesh. Christmas is God's invitation to each one of us to experience in our most inner selves the coming together of the human and the divine, to sense the possibilities of our own living, to sense the possibilities of the world's healing. Christmas is our opportunity to believe that beneath the predictable patterns of practical living there is the imagination of God's love — an imagination that can make all things new.

Frederick Buechner has written: "If the Christmas tale is true, it is the chief of all truths. What keeps the wild hope of Christmas alive in a world notorious for dashing all hopes is the haunting dream that the Child may be born again in us — in our needing, in our longing for him."[1]

My friends, my prayer this holy season is that this may be so — for you and for me. Amen.

---

1. Frederick Buechner, *A Room Called Remember: Uncollected Pieces* (San Francisco: Harper & Row, 1984), pp. 55-56.

Vital Vulnerability

At the risk of putting you to sleep, I'd like to ask each one of you to close your eyes. Right now, for just a minute. Please close your eyes. And now imagine with me. Imagine that you are holding a newborn baby. Imagine how this baby feels — skin touching skin, curves touching curves — harmonious heartbeats as life surges between you. Imagine the smell — the earthy sweetness of breath and body perfuming the air. Imagine the sound — the silent melody of sighing, stretching, settling. Right now, for just a minute, let your imagination go. Feel the baby. Smell the baby. Hear the baby. And rejoice! This very night the baby you hold in your arms is God.

Now as you open your eyes, as you come back to this warm womb of worship, let us think for a minute about the utter absurdity of it all. God — as a baby. Mighty, majestic God, powerful, passionate God, omnipotent, omniscient God — as a baby. God — giving up all the grandeur — coming down — here — crawling inside our skin — vital but vulnerable — resting in our arms. How can this be? It is a mystery. But it is God's mystery, and it is God's startling choice.

I was fortunate enough to give birth to my babies in the good old days when mothers were allowed to stay in the hospital and recover. And since I had two Caesareans, my stays were luxuriously long, five days in each case. The first birth was a bit traumatic, so I needed all that time to heal medically. But the second birth was much easier, and so I had five days to sleep, to eat, to ponder, and to hold my daughter — just to hold her in utter wonder and amazement. The touch and the smell — the satin skin and the greedy mouth and the tiny toes — it was moment after moment of miracle. I agree with Anne LaMott when she writes: "This is in fact what I think God may smell like — a young child's slightly dirty neck."[1] My friends, holding a baby is the most human of activities, and yet it may be the holiest moment some of us ever get. Utterly ordinary — achingly awesome — how can such a paradox exist?

In her book *For the Time Being*, Annie Dillard weaves an utterly bizarre collage of images. One image she keeps coming back to is Nurse Eisberg, an obstetrical nurse in a large urban hospital. Reminding us that 10,000 American babies are born each day, Dillard describes the nurse's work:

> *Here on the obstetrical ward, is a double sink in a little room ... This is where they wash the newborns like dishes ... Nurse Eisberg lifts them gently, swiftly, efficiently ... She wipes white lines of crumbled vernix from folds in his groin and under his arms. She holds one wormy arm and one wormy leg to turn him over; then she cleans his dorsal side, and ends with his anus. She diapers him ... and gives the bundle a push to slide it down the counter....*[2]

A baby assembly line, day after day, week after week — babies processed like canned hams — clean, compact, utterly ordinary. I wonder, would Nurse Eisberg even recognize Jesus if he was born in her hospital and dunked in her sink? Probably not. When you've seen one baby you've seen them all. And so, my friends, either each baby is holy, or none of them are holy at all. I believe that the Christmas story proclaims loudly that every child is holy — that each one of us is holy.

The two ends of the Christian story are what sets our spiritual saga apart from all other world religions. God as a tiny, helpless baby — God as a crumpled, bleeding corpse, God as utterly vulnerable — God as utterly helpless, God as one who embraces the fullness of human experience in order to sanctify it all. My friends, if you want an ethereal, otherworldly, cosmic religion, then

Christianity is not your bag. Because, if we don't touch it, if we don't smell it, if we don't live it and experience it and become it, well, then, the Christian story is dead. God chooses to become like us so that we can become like God. The most amazing and distressing consequence of this whole crazy night is that God needs us. God cannot be God without us. Quite simply, without us, this newborn baby God cannot survive.

As any parent sitting in this sanctuary knows, vulnerable babies drastically change our lives. They disturb, they delight, and ultimately they demand. Sleep is disrupted forever, anxiety develops angles never before imagined, feelings of inadequacy become daily companions, and waves of sadness can, at times, overwhelm us. We become totally, completely enmeshed in the fabric of a baby's life, and we are changed forever. Babies are gifts, but they are costly, exhausting gifts.

And so it is with the baby God of this night. Tonight God chooses — purposely chooses — to come in simplicity and vulnerability to disturb us, to delight us, and to make strong demands upon us. God comes to enmesh us in the sacred story. And if we choose to pick up this baby Jesus, our lives will never be the same. Self-absorbed ambition and success can never again be our main reason for being. The world is no longer just a backdrop for our own personal agenda. When this baby interrupts our lives, we must begin to think about someone, something, some purpose beyond our own.

And so, when all is said and done, what is being born this night is not only a new image of God, but also a new image of our own self — more mature, more responsible, more compassionate, more emotional, more physical, more ethical, more spiritual than any self we have ever known. Yes, this baby God has come to disturb us and to delight us, and to make demands upon our very souls. And if we fail to respond, well then we will be neglecting, even abusing, this God whose survival depends upon us.

The great writer Martin Buber believed that God gives each one of us a speck of the world to redeem — an infant spark of creation to nurture into fullness of life. My friends, the baby God who is being born this night within each one of us is a fragile burst

39

of creation that is only ours to redeem. What is the particular spark in you? Is it a relationship that is ripe for commitment? Is it a vocational dream that is waiting to be realized? Is it a moral decision that is ready to be claimed? Is it a creative instinct waiting to be expressed? What is the holy in you — vital and vulnerable — yearning to be born? This infant holiness, gestating within your soul, will come when it is time to come, and then you, then I, then we must respond. This God spark within you will be totally dependent upon you to survive.

The writer Max DePree tells of an early experience with his granddaughter Zoe. She was born prematurely, weighing only one pound seven ounces. Zoe was so small a wedding ring could slide up her arm to her shoulder. Her doctor said she had a five to ten percent chance of living three days. When Max visited Zoe, she had two IVs in her navel, one in her foot, a monitor on each side of her chest, and a respirator tube and feeding tube in her mouth. Zoe's biological father had left. Consequently, the nurse told Max that he must come to the hospital every day and rub her body, her legs, and her arms with the tip of his finger. While doing that, he was to say to her how much he loved her. It was essential that his voice be connected to his touch.[3]

Tonight God comes to us as a vital, vulnerable child — perhaps a bit premature for automatic survival in our secular world. With lusty voice we sing the carols, we read the story, we proclaim the joy and hope of this season. But, my friends, if our voice does not connect to our touch, if our singing does not connect to our service, well, then, this fresh presence of a fragile God may not survive the night.

The Church of the Nativity in Bethlehem is the traditional site of Jesus' birth, and is, in good times, the destination of many faithful pilgrims. There is only one door into the church — only one way to get inside this holy spot. And this door is so low and so small that each visitor must bend low — in some cases, even crawl, in order to enter. Such is the story of this night. God bends low to come as one of us — a baby blessing us — calling us to be nurturers of life. If we have the courage to respond, the courage to stoop low and pick up the child, this baby will fit perfectly into our arms.

And we can become participants in God's maturing presence in the world.

Can you feel the baby? Can you smell the baby? Can you hear the baby? This is Emmanuel — God-With-Us.

May it be so — for you and for me. Amen.

---

1. Anne LaMott, *Traveling Mercies* (New York: Pantheon Books, 1999), p. 102.

2. Annie Dillard, *For the Time Being* (New York: Alfred A. Knopf, 1999), pp. 36-38.

3. Source unknown.

41

The Rest Of The Story

Just five days later, the needles are falling, the poinsettias are drooping, and the cookies are stale. How do we hold onto the feeling? How do we hold onto the warmth, the wonder, the welcome of Christmas?

- Christmas letters — offering graceful glimpses of old friends;
- That rare mother/daughter afternoon, creating the most perfect Christmas of our lives;
- American soldiers sharing Christmas with war-scarred children;
- Virginia neighbors sharing love with a Pentagon widow;
- A Christmas pageant, so full of joy and giggles and energy, that I *know* God was smiling;
- A rippling harp lifting human voices to heaven;
- That sea of candles, shimmering with hope and memory, in the dark womb of this sanctuary.

Yes, my friends, if we try, we can hold onto the feelings, the images, the memories. But we will need to struggle to let this fresh incarnation, this tangible, touchable God carry us through the rest of the year. For the way things really are has already come crashing down upon us. This morning, before the baby has even digested his first decent meal, the gospel writer has us running — fleeing from danger and death and despair. Yes, Matthew forces us to deal with the rest of the Christmas story. And the reality is that

43

the incarnation of good, of God, leads quickly to the incarnation of evil — not only 2,000 years ago, but today, here, now.

The slaughter of the innocents is one of the most unsavory stories in all scripture. In fact, for years the appointed lectionary passage for this first Sunday after Christmas intentionally left out verses 16-18, the actual murder of all the baby boys under two who lived near Bethlehem. The lectionary scholars assumed that our delicate Christian constitutions just couldn't deal with the raw evil of Herod. But, let's face it. Since our daily newspapers regularly report the slaughter of innocents all over the world, why should we pretend that Jesus is immune from such terror? Just substitute the name Hitler or McVeigh or bin Laden or Hussein for the name Herod, and you have a thoroughly modern tale of murder and slaughter and hatred.

Several years ago, in Bethlehem, the following version of "O Little Town Of Bethlehem" was sung (written by an American from Littleton, Colorado, and circulated on the internet):

> O little town of Bethlehem, how still we see thee lie;
> Above thy deep and restless sleep, a missile glideth by;
> And over dark streets soundeth, the mortar's deadly roar;
> While children weep in shallow sleep, for friends who are
>   no more ...
>
> O sing for wholly innocents, who hurled a hopeless stone.
> Who ran from tank, who, wounded, sank in gutters all alone.
> Their eyes by bullets blinded, their lungs by gasses burned
> In sad exile, the Holy Child knows Herod has returned.
>   — Don Hinchey

Of course, such pain and destruction and despair could also be echoed by Jewish teenagers bleeding in Tel Aviv, by children rendered fatherless in the ashes of Ground Zero, by starving Christians dying in the Sudan, by hungry, haunted mothers, homeless in Afghanistan or Liberia. Refugees and victims of violence do not wear just one political brand, or bear one national identity. They speak every language. They worship every name of God. They bleed out of every color body. For we human beings are imperfect

44

creatures; no country or creed or political system is completely righteous; all corners of God's fragile world are broken and incomplete. And it is into *this* reality — this brokenness and imperfection and sin — that Jesus has been born. He comes not to escape the tribulation, but to enter it with us, and to love us and this world into wholeness.

In his eloquent oratorio "For the Time Being" the poet W. H. Auden has a section called "The Flight to Egypt." Amid leftovers and dismantled trees, broken ornaments and bored children, Auden remembers "... the Stable where for once in our lives / Everything became a You and nothing was an It." Yes, he remembers those moments just a few days ago when the ordinary was suffused with divine glory — and God and creation were one. Auden, then, goes on to bemoan our lack of imagination, for "... we have seen the actual Vision and failed / To do more than entertain it as an agreeable Possibility." Instead, we are left with the Time Being — the in between time — between the birth of Christ and the completion of Christ — which "... Is, in a sense, the most trying time of all ... a tired, tawdry, tedious time, where the streets seem narrower, the office more depressing ... a time when we must pay the bills, repair the machines, learn irregular verbs." And the challenge is clear. We, as the remnant of God's grace on earth, must figure our how to redeem this Time Being — this present time, how to "redeem it from Insignificance." Yes, when the Herods of this earth strike terror, when danger and anxiety drive us into the exile of Egypt, when the birth has turned from wonder into hard work, when, according to Auden, our "souls must endure God's Silence," how do we hold onto the star, the promise, the holy innocence of God, alive and fresh, in our midst?

As is so often the case, the ordinary folk in scripture are the ones who show us the way. And today, it is Mary and Joseph and an ancient matriarch named Rachel, who model faithfulness for us. They invite us to weep. They invite us to dream. And they invite us to trust. Yes, first they invite us to weep. For it is in our emotion and our empathy that we feel God's heart beat. Then they invite us to dream. For it is in the intuition and imagination of our minds that we most clearly hear God speak. And, finally, they invite us to trust, for it is in the offering of our lives, unfettered by anxiety, that we find the grace of God.

The allusion to weeping in Matthew's story is an obscure one. Tradition suggests that Rachel, Jacob's second wife who died long ago in childbirth, was buried near Bethlehem. And centuries later, when the people of Israel were dragged into exile — refugees cut off from all that was precious in their lives — it was then that Rachel was heard weeping from her grave, mourning the pain of loss and failure and despair, which seems to be at the heart of every human story. And so it is today as Jesus, the embodiment of the new Israel, is again exiled, dragged into oblivion and danger by the very real evil of a very real world. Again Rachel weeps and invites us to weep with her, acknowledging the way things really are and discovering a God who holds us while we weep — a God who holds us and comforts us and yes, weeps, inconsolably, with us.

Sometime in the 1980s, a group of psychotherapists were meeting in New York to learn about Carl Jung's theory of dream analysis. As part of the symposium, real dreams were described, and then a panel of experts, including Carl Jung's grandson, dissected and discussed the meanings of the dreams. One of the horrific dreams described that day was a recurring image in which the dreamer was stripped of all human dignity and subjected to Nazi atrocities. Immediately, the audience began to formulate their own theories and symbolic explanations of the dream, while waiting for the experts to respond. But the response of the panel was unexpected. Instead of analyzing the dream, Jung's grandson asked the audience to stand. And then, he invited them to remain standing in silence. As one analyst explained, "... there is in life a suffering so unspeakable, a vulnerability so extreme that it goes far beyond ... explanations and even beyond healing. In the face of such suffering all we can do is bear witness so no one need suffer alone."[1]

So, the first thing we are invited to do today is to weep — to weep for all the innocents of all times who are slaughtered in God's world. We are called to honor their pain with the pain of our own hearts. But the second thing we are invited to do is to dream — to listen to our dreams of life as well as our dreams of death. Yes,

46

after we weep for the way things really are, we can, we must, imagine the way things can be. We, like Joseph, must pay attention to our dreams, for dreams, like tears, are the voice of God. It was in a dream that God explained to Joseph the importance of the baby that Mary was carrying. It was in a dream that Joseph was warned to go to Egypt — fleeing from the infamy of Herod's sword. And it was in a dream that Joseph was told that it was time to return — to return to the familiarity of his hometown of Nazareth.

Which leaves us with some questions. Today, in the dangers, the deserts, the dreary places of your life, where are *your* dreams? *What* are your dreams? And *who are you* in those dreams? Not just the dreams of deep sleep, but the daydreams that dance around the edges of your daily life? Learn this day from Joseph. Learn to listen to your dreams. To honor your dreams. To trust your dreams. To follow your dreams. To make your dreams come true. For the very life and innocence of our living God depends on it. Yes, the rest of the Christmas story depends on you and depends on me — depends on all of us — weeping and dreaming and trusting, returning to life as usual but with a hope that is unusual — returning to the way things really are, but with the courage to redeem this Time Being from insignificance.

Years ago King George V sent this New Year's blessing to his British subjects:

> *I said to the man who stood at the Gate of the Year*
> *Give me a light that I might go safely out into the darkness.*
> *And he replied, Go out into the darkness and put your hand*
> *   into the hand of God.*
> *That shall be more to you than a light and safer than a known*
> *   way.*[2]

Weeping. Dreaming. Trusting. With our hands in the hand of God. My friends, this is the safe way — the known way — the way to redeem this time — to redeem our time for significance and for salvation in God's name.

May it be so — for you and for me. Amen.

1. R. Remen, *My Grandfather's Blessing* (New York: Riverhead Books, 2000), p. 105.

2. *Ibid.*, p. 376.

Christmas 2
John 1:(1-9) 10-18

Demonstrating The Divine

For almost fifty years I have lived comfortably within the church. And for almost fifty years I have loved the church. I still remember sitting in the pew, a small child of three or four — dwarfed by big shoulders embracing me on every side. I loved the music — the grand soaring chords of the organ. I loved the windows and the colors, the flowers and soft cushions. I loved the warm, full voice of the preacher and I loved the hushed silence — a silence that made me feel like I was part of something special — something that I didn't understand with my mind but which I already savored in my heart. Most of all, I loved the offering plates — those shiny brass bowls, lined with deep blue velvet, and filled with holy money. As ushers carried those plates forward, with my dime tucked into all those big bills, I sometimes imagined that I was curled up in that offering plate, that I was being offered to God. Perhaps, then, it is not strange that this church which I have loved for over fifty years is also the church that I have served as a Minister of Word and Sacrament for almost thirty. During all this time my love for the church has not diminished. But the quality of that love has had to change. Like most of us, I have had to learn that to love the church does not always mean to like the church — and that moments of soaring will always be matched with messy moments of slogging through the mud.

After all, the church is made up of people — people like you and people like me — with our peculiarities, with our stubborn opinions, with our self-inflated egos, with our anguished anxieties. And so, if we are to love the church, we need to start by loving each other and by loving the church as it really is. In her book, *Holy the Firm*, Annie Dillard writes: "There is one church here, so I go to it ... We had a wretched singer once, a hulking blonde girl with chopped hair. Nothing could have been more apparent than that God loved this girl, nothing could more surely convince me of God's unending mercy than the continued existence of the church."[1]

Yes, my friends, it is only by God's mercy that all of us, or any of us, exist. But exist we do with great variety and texture. When I served as Moderator of National Capital Presbytery, it was a pleasure to wander through the churches across the metro area — big churches and little churches, churches with fancy choirs and churches with slightly out-of-tune organs, churches with velvet cushions and stained glass, and churches with clean, clear windows and with worn wooden pews. Every congregation was wonderful. And no congregation was perfect.

The energy and joy was palpable at a merger service of two congregations — a sanctuary filled with hope and possibility. But afterward, when folks were munching their cookies and being real, their anticipation was clearly mixed with anxiety, and feelings of sadness and resentment easily crept into the language of hope and joy. The ordination of a new pastor at a Korean church took place in a packed sanctuary where the number of teenagers and children almost outnumbered the adults; a bursting, growing congregation, where the feast afterward could have fed the whole Presbytery. And yet, nothing is perfect. When the laying on of hands took place, the only female hands were mine as our Korean brothers and sisters continue to struggle with a gospel of inclusivity.

In congregation after congregation, earnest, hopeful, joyful faces watched as promises were made and covenants were sealed with new and eager pastors — and yet, in almost every instance, the average age of the congregation was way over the median age of the communities in which we live and serve. I have learned that there are a lot of Presbyterians in our metropolitan area who love the church — just as it is — warts and all. And I am encouraged. But, my friends, we are called not just to love the church as it is. We are also called to love the church as it might be, as it is called to be, as with the power of God it still can be.

Believe it or not, our *Presbyterian Book of Order* actually contains some inspirational language. Nowhere is that more apparent than in chapter 3, where the purpose of the church is described. In stark, strong language our constitution tells it like it is. "The Church of Jesus Christ is the provisional demonstration of what God intends for humanity." Note it does not say "can be" or "should be." It says "is." The church is the provisional demonstration of what God intends. Unlike some famous people we know, you and I don't have the privilege of quibbling over what the meaning of the word "is" is. Through baptism we are called to demonstrate the divine, and discipleship demands that we respond. The big question is, "How?" How are we to "demonstrate the divine"? How are we to embody Christ?

John, with elegant electricity, gives us an answer. The Word became flesh and dwelt among us, full of grace and truth. God's holy flesh pitched a tent in our midst — and in contrast to human flesh, full of self-promotion and deceit — this holy flesh was full of grace and truth. As always, biblical language about God is paradoxical: truth *and* grace; confrontation *and* caring; judgment *and* mercy; honesty *and* compassion; gracious generosity *and* harsh, demanding trustworthiness. John 1:14 defines the incarnation, the human/divine reality of Jesus. But it also defines us — the church — the resurrected Body of Christ on earth. Yes, John tells us how we are to "demonstrate the divine." We are called to embody a paradox — the paradox of grace and truth.

The fact that the Christian faith is paradoxical is a challenge. If opposite things are true, then the trick is to hold that opposition in balance — the truth of God with the grace of God. I think it is our inability — or perhaps our unwillingness — to struggle with this balancing act that has gotten our beloved Presbyterian church into so much trouble; that has prevented us from being that "provisional demonstration of what God intends for all of humanity."

Some of us weigh far too heavily in the direction of truth. In reaction to a world growing more diverse and more complex and more pluralistic, we have pulled in our horns and cracked down, drawing narrow boundaries, putting a straight jacket on the Spirit of the law in order to preserve the letter of the law. Forgetting that

51

Jesus defied the law in order to fulfill the law, we all too often deify the law. Think about it. Jesus healed on the Sabbath, he touched menstruating women, he put the needs of children before the needs of adults, he preferred the companionship of sinners over saints. Jesus fulfilled the law by redefining the law — by turning rules into relationships. Jesus flexibly figured out in each situation how holy virtues and values could best be embodied — values of compassion and covenant and faithfulness and wholeness and justice and kindness and joy. But we, in a changing, chaotic world, are often too scared to follow him.

More than anything else, I believe that the struggle about ordination of gays and lesbians is about this balance, or lack thereof, between grace and truth. Legislation to forbid ordination focuses on rules instead of values and virtues — defining sin as an act rather than condition. And as such we have begun to worship truth at the expense of grace. Let me give you another example. If two healthy, humble, faithful people want to make a covenant before God to be faithful to one another until death do them part — how can we prevent them just because they are homosexual? Is this focusing on law or "truth" at the expense of the Spirit or "grace"? Is this failing to honor the paradox of the Word who becomes flesh?

Yes, some of us weigh too heavily in the direction of truth. But, my friends, others of us weigh far too heavily in the direction of grace. In an effort to be open-minded and open-hearted, in our passion to be inclusive and welcoming, we have made God's grace gooey. The truth embodied in the Living Word has become emaciated. Rather than becoming an alternative community embodying an alternative vision, we have become a rubber stamp for the confused and chaotic world around us.

Now, we can — and must — authentically argue about whether homosexuality is a sin or a healthy sexual expression. But we must never argue about the absolute necessity of fidelity and monogamy and covenant faithfulness before God. We can authentically argue about how much of scripture is fact and how much is poetic metaphor. But we must never argue about the ultimate authority of scripture in our lives. We can authentically argue about the relative wisdom of Democratic or Republican public policy. But we must never argue about the centrality of honesty and integrity, account-ability and trust as the rock bottom foundation of an ethical political system.

My friends, to "demonstrate the divine" means to embody the paradox of grace and truth. Truth without grace is cold and empty. But grace without truth is shapeless warmth that just dribbles away. Rita Snowden tells a story from World War II. In France, some soldiers brought the body of a dead comrade to a cemetery to have him buried. The priest gently asked whether their friend had been a baptized Catholic. The soldiers did not know. The priest sadly informed them that, in that case, he could not permit burial in the church yard. So the soldiers dug a grave just outside the cemetery fence. And they laid their comrade to rest. The next day the soldiers came back to add some flowers, only to discover that the grave was nowhere to be found. Bewildered, they were about to leave when the priest came up to speak to them. It seems that he could not sleep the night before, so troubled was he about his refusal to bury the soldier in the parish cemetery. So early in the morning he left his bed, and with his own hands he moved the fence in order to include the body of the soldier who had died for France. My friends, truth demands that we build fences. But grace demands that the shape of those fences be flexible.

As faithful Christians, we will continue to disagree about what defines truth and what defines grace. But we must not disagree that balancing the two is what we are called to do. In order to be "the provisional demonstration of what God intends for all humanity," we, as the church of Jesus Christ, are called to continue to enflesh God's Word with powerful truth and generous grace. This is our challenge within our individual lives, within the congregations we call home, and within this wonderful, imperfect body called the church of Jesus Christ.

May it be so — for you and for me. Amen.

_____

1. From *Holy the Firm* by Annie Dillard in *Cries Of The Spirit*, ed. by Marilyn Sewell (Boston: Beacon Press, 1991), p. 199.

Epiphany 1
(Baptism Of The Lord)
Matthew 3:13-17

God's Delight

Once upon a time a student approached his teacher and announced that he was ready to assume the office of ministry.

"And what are your qualifications?" the teacher asked.

"I have mastered the art of physical discipline," the student replied. "I am able to sleep on the ground, to eat nothing but raw grains, and I can carry huge loads on my back."

The teacher took the young man by the arm and led him toward a field. "Do you see the mule? He too sleeps on the ground, eats nothing but grains, and can bear large burdens on his back. Up to this point you may qualify to be an ass, but you are not yet ready for ministry."[1]

Today we celebrate the ministry which we all share as the people of God. Today we also set apart for particular ministries seven of our brothers and sisters through the historic laying on of hands. Now these folks that we are setting apart have already demonstrated their discipline and their ability to work hard. Otherwise they would not have been elected by you to serve as elders in this congregation. But like the student in our story, it is wise for us to remember that discipline and hard work are not the most important marks of ministry. Instead, what is moving in the lives of these candidates for ordination — and what is at work in the lives of us all — is the power, God's power, to shape and create the reign of God on earth — the power, God's power, poured into our lives at the moment of baptism and confirmation and ordination, and then sustained daily by the living grace of God.

55

Now, in these pre-inaugural days, the very word "power" both excites us and disgusts us. There is so much lust for power running through the fax machines and telephone lines and mailboxes of Washington that one wonders if the finite human ego can survive it all. As Christians we have always tended to frown on the word "power," and have focused instead on Jesus' special concern for the powerless. And yet, my friends, power, which comes from the Latin word *posse*, means simply "to be able." It is the birthright and need of every human being to be powerful, to be able, to experience both significance and influence. And power, when rightly understood, is at the very heart of the Christian gospel. Following the resurrection and before the ascension, the apprehensive disciples ask the risen Lord, "What will become of us when you are gone?" And Jesus, predicting the Day of Pentecost, answers, "You will receive power when the Holy Spirit comes upon you; and you will be my witnesses ... to the ends of the earth." It was only after these words that Jesus was able to leave the disciples, confident that his power to save would continue to be expressed through the faith and ministry of a living church.

Our New Testament lesson for this morning is Matthew's account of Jesus' baptism. It is nothing more and nothing less than a public affirmation of Jesus' very personal and very potent power. It is important to note, for all of us who are not being ordained this morning, that Jesus was never ordained to ministry either. Instead, his baptism served as his ordination. It was the single moment when he was named and set apart, so that he could use God's power in him in very particular ways.

When John pulls Jesus, drenched with the waters of the River Jordan, out of the water, the skies open and the voice of God is heard: "This is my Son, the Beloved, with whom I am delighted." These words are taken straight from the most hopeful prophesies in Hebrew Scripture — words straight from the Isaiah text which we also read this morning. Jesus' baptism then is a baptism of public power — publicly witnessed and corporately experienced every time we baptize, every time we commission and ordain within our own community of faith. Yes, the hands of the community become the hands of God, passing on the power of the Holy Spirit, passing on the gifts and the ability to use these gifts, passing on the power to become God's presence on earth — yes, hands blessing us so that we can become a blessing to others.

By quoting Isaiah 42, Matthew indicates just what kind of power Jesus is receiving — what Christian power was and is and continues to be. Let us now look and listen and hear so that we can recognize this power in our own lives.

First and foremost, Christian power is *servant power* — power fully and emphatically embraced so that it can be fully and emphatically given away. Isaiah's words were first penned when Israel was still in exile — without land, without influence, without hope. It would have made sense for Isaiah to pump the people up with images and encouragements of a superpower future — a vision of military and political might when the enemies of Israel would be crushed and destroyed. Instead, the image of power that the prophet presents is an image of service — the gracious and life-affirming power of justice and liberation and freedom given away to others. God says, to Israel as well as to each of us, "You are my servant, I chose you, I will uphold you, I will put my Spirit upon you. And, when you embody my power through servanthood, then you will become my delight."

There has been much talk and worry recently about the evolving role of the United States — the one remaining superpower in the world. In this post-Cold War period, when fanaticism and nationalism are causing violent outbursts all over the globe, just what should be the military and political role of our country? Should we have gone into Somalia? Were we wrong to invade Iraq and wipe out Saddam Hussein? How should we respond to the horrors of rape and murder in Africa? One columnist put it this way:

> *Should America act more or less with others, or should it act ... more on its own? Should the large idea of the United States be collective security which involves a readiness to find a common policy with other countries and with international institutions, especially the United Nations? Or should the large idea be national self-assertion (and self-interest), resting on a determination*

to keep the selection of means as well as ends mostly in American hands?[2]

Purely political considerations may well lead us to answers grounded in American self-interest, but a Christian answer to this dilemma is different. Christian power is only given to us so that it can build up the common good of all. It is servant power used to serve the needs of a united and interdependent world. It is power used *with* and *for*, not power used *over* and *against*.

And so Christian power is servant power. It is also *gentle power*. The servant described in Isaiah "does not cry or lift up his voice, a bruised reed he will not break, a dimly burning wick he will not quench." The servant uses strength and authority not to control the other, but to heal gently and release the power of life around him. Father Timothy Healy, who for a decade was President of Georgetown University, was, in the last few years of his life, head of the troubled New York Public Library system. Before his sudden death several years ago, this commanding and influential priest was the confidante of several United States presidents, a valued guest at the most exclusive dinner parties, a towering intellect who could intimidate the most famous scholars in the world. And yet, as one friend said at his memorial service: "(though) Tim was bigger than life, he was also gentle as anything. I don't know anybody who didn't feel bigger in his presence." Timothy Healey was a transparent channel for the vigorous and transforming power of God, but it was a gentle power — used to touch and encourage and bless the individual lives of thousands of people.

Finally, Christian power, as embodied by Jesus and described by Isaiah, is *persistent power* — power that does not grow faint, cannot be crushed — power that even a cross and a tomb cannot destroy — power that even 2,000 years of troubled, fainthearted Christianity has not been able to extinguish. It is power that permeates and inspires and nourishes life long after one's personal power is gone.

There is a folk tale from India that summarizes our thoughts this morning. It seems that there was a good king who ruled wisely and who ruled well. One day the king called his three daughters

58

together and told them he was leaving on a long journey. "I wish to learn about God, so I will need to go away and spend a long time in prayer. In my absence I will leave the three of you in charge. Before I leave I would like to leave each of you with a gift; a gift I pray will help you learn how to wisely use your power to rule." Then he placed in each of their hands a single grain of rice.

The first daughter tied a long golden thread around her grain of rice and placed it in a beautiful crystal box. Every day she looked at it and reminded herself that she was powerful. The second daughter took one look at the common grain of rice, and threw it away, thus squandering her father's mysterious gift. The third daughter just looked at her grain of rice for a long, long time — until she finally understood what to do with it. She went outside and planted it in the ground. And it became a seed, giving life beyond itself, eventually turning into vast fields of hope and nourishment for others.

When the father returned years later, he asked his three daughters what they had done with their grains of rice. Though he was polite to his first two daughters, he did not respond to their explanations with much enthusiasm. It was only after the king saw the fields of grain resulting from his third daughter's wisdom that he responded with delight. Taking the crown off his head, he placed it on hers, saying, "Beloved, you alone have learned the meaning of power." From that day forward, the youngest daughter ruled the kingdom. She ruled long, and she ruled wisely, and she ruled well.[3]

Brothers and sisters, this day as we remember the blessings and power of our baptism, as we set apart brothers and sisters for particular tasks of ministry, I pray that all of us will continue to be God's delight — powerful servants — pouring out our power for the hope and nourishment of the world.

May it be so — for you and for me. Amen.

---

1. William R. White, *Stories For The Journey* (Minneapolis: Augsburg Press, 1988), p. 24.

2. Stephen S. Rosenfeld, *Washington Post*, January 8, 1993.

3. White, *op. cit.*, p. 71, adapted.

Call Waiting

Chaim Potok was an intensely religious man; a Jew who explored the dimensions of faith in our lives. From an early age, Potok knew he wanted to be a writer. But his mother wasn't so sure. When he went away to college she said, "Son, now I know you want to be a writer. But I want you to think about brain surgery. You'll keep a lot of people from dying. And you'll make a lot of money." To which Potok responded, "No, Mama, I want to be a writer."

But, "No," is not what Mama wanted to hear. So, every vacation break for four years she would repeat her comments about his becoming a brain surgeon and keeping people from dying and making a lot of money, and always his response was the same. Finally the son had enough, and, when the same mantra began, he cut off his mother with exasperation, and with great passion he told his mother, "Mama, I don't want to keep people from dying, I want to show them how to live."[1]

This morning's Gospel Lesson from John is a "call" story, but unlike so many call stories in scripture this one is not crisp, dramatic, or decisive. Today there is no flashing light, no booming voice, no clear instructions as to what the disciples are to do. Instead, what we hear is Jesus asking a question — a strange, penetrating question. But it is *the* question that forms the foundation for understanding "call" for understanding vocation. The question is: "What are you looking for?"

Now, please note what the question is not. It is not what do you want to do? What do you want to produce or achieve or prove?

It is not what do others expect you to do? No, the question is: "What are you looking for? What is important? What is it that will fill your life with purpose and joy and meaning?" After struggle and discernment, the writer Chaim Potok was able to answer this very particular question. What was he looking for? He was looking for life — for abundant life for himself and others. Writing novels just happened to be the means for him to find it.

There are a couple of interesting details in today's Gospel Lesson. When the disciples are "called" by Jesus, they are already doing something else. They are already serving as disciples of John — probably invested in the pecking order, comfortable with their job description, dependent upon their compensation package, and not terribly anxious to upset the apple cart by shifting gears in mid-stream. But, there was *something* about Jesus and something about his question that hooked them. You see, Jesus invites them into their imaginations. Jesus invites them into their curiosity. Yes, Jesus invites them into God's world — not through a sense of duty, but through intuition and passion. And so in midlife, Andrew and Simon jump ship. They start moving in a new direction.

The second interesting detail in this story is the disciples' response. The person and the question of Jesus stops them in their tracks, and, like those disciples on the road to Emmaus in the Gospel of Luke, the hearts of these disciples seem to burn within them. Yes, my friends, there is something about Jesus, something about God, something about the deep question of life that can stop us in our tracks, that turns us around, that changes us — when and if we listen.

Andrew and Simon respond to Jesus' question with a question of their own: "Where are you staying?" They feel so immediately drawn to the spiritual power of this man who asks them the most important question of their lives, they feel so connected to him, that they want to be with him, not in a geographical place, not in an architectural place, but in a spiritual place. "Where do you stay, where do you abide, where do you rest your spirit and your body?" they ask. "And can we come and stay, can we come and abide, can we come and remain with you?" To which Jesus responds immediately, "Come. Come and see. Come and be. Come and abide with me. It's not important what you do. Just come and see — and then the doing will follow. Like water from a fountain. Like waves billowing out of the depth of the sea. The doing will follow the seeing."

At the beginning of my senior year of college I didn't have a clue what I was going to do when I grew up. My goal when I started college was to be a career diplomat, serving in some exotic place in the world. But I quickly discovered that I am anything but diplomatic — and my skill with foreign languages is nil. As for getting married and having a family, well, there were no prospects on the horizon. And so I panicked. What was I going to do with my life, and more concretely, how was I going to pay off my college loans? It was at that point that the college chaplain suggested seminary — not in order to become a pastor, but as a place where I could ask the question, "What am I looking for?"

It was, serendipitously, while I was working as a seminarian with a group of junior highs in a Congregational church in Newton, Massachusetts, that I began to receive the answer to that all-important question. Those adolescents painfully reminded me of myself — with my restless energy, my peripatetic mind, my mercurial sense of self-esteem, my desire to be good and to see good and to do good in the world. What was I looking for? I was looking for a balanced life — where truth and passion could give voice to the God in me and the God in others — where justice could join hands with joy, and where grace would abound. What finally happened, among those fifteen thirteen-year-olds, was that after 24 years of hearing the *story of Jesus*, I finally discovered the *person of Jesus*. I discovered the One who models that balanced and joyful and passionate life. And then I knew that I was called to abide with Jesus, to stay with Jesus, to become like Jesus in whatever fragile and finite ways I could. For me, the way to do that was in parish ministry. And marriage. And motherhood. And writing. And just being. But abiding with Jesus can just as easily happen in the classroom or the kitchen or the boardroom or the courtroom or the laboratory or the studio. The call is not to a particular job. It is to a particular relationship — and to a particular vision — and to a particular answer to the all-important question: "What are you looking for?"

My friends, all of us as Christians are called — called through our baptism to be God's person in the world. But the call is not a digital voice from heaven giving us a printout with specific directions. Rather the call is a lifelong question, burning in our hearts, given to us by the One who encourages curiosity, and models risk, and offers commitment — given by the One who invites us to journey with him and abide with him through all the questions and curves of life. The vocation of Christians is above all a vocation to imagine — to imagine seeing what God sees when God looks at the world; to imagine abiding with God in the passionate places where God lives; and to imagine sharing that passion by being God's presence in the world.

Barbara Brown Taylor writes: "One midnight I asked God to tell me as plainly as possible what I was supposed to do. 'Anything that pleases you.' That is the answer that came into my sleepy head. 'What?' I said, waking up. 'What kind of answer is that?' 'Do anything that pleases you,' the voice said, 'and belong to me.' "[2] After that things became much simpler for Taylor. She could pump gas or clean out latrines. But as long as she remembered whose she was, her "calling" was a true one. And she realized that God calls us not once, but many times.

My friends, some times the call is stunning, clear: loud, dramatic, and specific. And that makes it easier for our answer to be equally loud and clear and dramatic. But most of the time the call is much more subtle and much more vague than that. And so, we are left shy, confused, and curious — tentative and tongue-tied — pilgrims on a journey toward the unknown. But, please know that whether you are clear or whether you are confused, God is calling you — wrapping warm grace around your restlessness. God's call gives voice to that ancient prayer of the church: "Lord, we know that our hearts are restless until they find their rest in thee."

More than forty years ago there was a man who heard a call from God and answered it. He heard God ask him, "What are you looking for?" and he was able to answer: "I am looking for freedom and justice for all of God's people." And so, Martin Luther King,

Jr., was able to give voice to the voice of God through the voice of his own passion.

"I have a dream that is deeply rooted in the American dream ... I have a dream that my four children will one day live in a nation where they will not be judged by the color of their skin but by the content of their character." And then all of us will be "free at last."

My friends, what are you looking for? What are you looking for? It is by asking and answering that question, with Jesus as your companion, that you will hear God's "call" to you. And then, you, too, will be free at last.

May it be so — for you and for me. Amen.

---

1. Eugene Peterson, *Under The Unpredictable Plant* (Grand Rapids, Michigan: Eerdmans, 1992), p. 46, adapted.

2. Barbara Brown Taylor, *The Preaching Life* (Cambridge, Massachusetts: Cowley Publications, 1993), p. 23.

Kairos Commitments

One snowy day a few years ago, after I had declared the church a "nonessential" business and closed the office for the day, I experienced a luxury I often dream of, but rarely do. I climbed back into bed to read. But dare you think I was totally decadent, what I chose to read was our congregation's Annual Report. It turned out to be more enjoyable than any novel could have been. What a remarkable document — and what remarkable disciples you all have been! Some reports were lyric in their poetry. Some were bursting with compassion and urgency. Some were laced with delightful humor, others warm and gracious in their tone of gratitude. And the final pages were the icing on the cake — healthy financial figures — based on the generous giving and wise management of our financial resources.

I was struck with how little I've had to do with most of what is described in these pages — and how much we are all letting the Spirit of God shape and mold us into a community of faithfulness. There is not much about today's scripture passage that you don't already know as a community called to discipleship in the name of Jesus Christ. But lest we become complacent about the radical nature of God's call, let us hear once more who and what God wants us to be.

In Matthew's Gospel, Jesus' call to ministry through his baptism and his temptation is immediately followed by his call to others — to Simon and Andrew, to James and John. What is clear is that Jesus cannot and does not redeem the world alone. God-in-flesh means God-in-all-of-us.

67

Just before these first disciples are called, Jesus makes an astounding announcement. "The kingdom of God — the rule of God — is at hand." The time, my friends, is *now*. This announcement is astounding for two reasons. First, the Jews had always believed that the kingdom would only come at the end of time — as the culmination of all God's work. And the kingdom would mean perfection — the wholeness and integration of all things — immediately. But today Jesus says something very different. The kingdom is not only a vision in the mind of the Creator and a reality at the end of time. The kingdom is also immediately tangible and available in the person, the values, the behavior of those who follow Jesus. In other words, the kingdom is now, here, in this sanctuary — in and among those of us who dare to follow Jesus.

The second astounding thing Jesus says is this: The time which is now is a special time. The word used is not *chronos*, the Greek word for the steady progression of seconds and minutes, days and weeks, years and decades. Instead the word used is *kairos*, God's time — a particular moment of God's inbreaking Spirit — a time to accomplish through us what we cannot accomplish ourselves.

"Call" language is hard language to understand. We clergy types are expected to understand it, for we have to articulate our "call" in order to earn the title "Reverend." But that does not let the rest of you off the hook. As our scripture story suggests today, all those who bear the name of Christ are "called" into ministry.

H. Richard Niebuhr has broken down the concept of *call* into four different categories. First, there is the *common call*: the invitation to ministry which is central to our baptism — the sense that once we are grafted into Christ through the graceful power of the Holy Spirit, we inevitably get swept up in the ministry of the church. But there is more. A second kind of call, available to all of us, is the *providential call*, the ministry given to us through our unique talents and abilities. It is by doing what we do best that we honor and serve God, whether it is within the church or out there in the world. The third kind of call is the *secret call*, that private, personal connection with God's Spirit that is offered to all of us but recognized by only some of us, that *kairos* moment, when God's need and our willingness meet in an electric moment of commitment. Finally, there is the *ecclesiastical call*, a call to minister within the offices of the church as a minister of the Word and Sacrament, as a deacon, or as an elder. This kind of call is the only one of the four that not everyone receives. This does not mean that the ecclesiastical call is any better than any other kind of call. It is just more visible, for it places us in a position to be a role model and a witness to all the other disciples of Christ.

For me, the hardest part of Matthew's call story is the speed with which the call is answered. To be a disciple means to *learn* — that is the literal translation of the Greek word. To be a disciple means to *love* — according to scripture to "catch people" in the wide reaching net of God's unconditional love. But, in today's text what being a disciple means most is to *leave* — to abruptly change that which we have been in order to become that which we can still be. In today's scripture story, all four of the fishermen, comfortable middle-class workers like us, respond immediately, leaving job security, family security, turning their backs on previous commitments and responsibilities, letting go of all that is dependable and familiar in order to respond to Jesus. Personally, I much prefer the Old Testament call stories: Moses, Samuel, Isaiah, Jeremiah, all of whom hemmed and hawed, made excuses, moaned about their unworthiness and unsuitability for the tasks at end — all of whom had to be wined and dined by a patient God until they reluctantly said, "Yes!" But not so James and John, Simon and Andrew. For them the urgency of the moment and the authority of the call wiped out any ambivalence or inadequacy they might have felt. It was a *kairos* moment. God was in charge — and they obeyed.

Kairos moments come to us, too — moments when, instead of counting the cost, we accept the challenge and the risks involved — moments when by saying yes to something new, we are also saying no to something old. I was struck by the comment a few years ago, that of the four men picked up by *Time* magazine to be Men of the Year, Arafat, Rabin, Mandela, and de Klerk, only de Klerk was going to lose power and prominence by the risks he had taken. De Klerk's vision of the kingdom for South Africa meant the loss of white power, but it also meant the fulfillment of justice. It was his vision that led him to make a *kairos* commitment — a willingness to give up personal gain for the fulfillment of God's reign.

Several years ago, God broke into the comfort of this community in a *kairos* moment. By raising the reality of the pain of the children of Anacostia, a call to commitment was made. Twenty people responded to that call and formed an Urban Mission Team. Adding to our already established suburban outreach projects, these folks created ten new hands-on mission opportunities for people to bring about the kingdom of God in the city — through tutoring, through care for the elderly, through a Saturday morning enrichment program for children, through office skills training. Those who responded at that moment had to give up precious time and some sense of physical security in order to venture into the bowels of the city. But for them, at that particular point in their lives, the call was irresistible.

Several of our elders being ordained and installed today said yes immediately, whereas in years past they said no to other invitations to serve. Though external circumstances in their lives may not have changed that much, something in their internal landscape has changed, and any mountains of resistance they might have had have been brought low by the pervasive power of God. Such is the nature of the call; such is the nature of *kairos* commitments. And they can happen to any of us within any of the arenas of our living — homes, work, church, or community.

The clearest *kairos* moment in my life — when God's vision and possibility most neatly coincided with my willingness to respond — was years ago when the Pastor Nominating Committee of this congregation first contacted me. It made no sense for this church to risk calling as pastor a young mother who was serving a 250-member, blue-collar congregation, with no experience in a sophisticated metropolitan community — to call me to serve a church as complex and convoluted as this congregation was back then. But then again it made no sense for me to uproot my family, drag my husband away from a job he enjoyed, in order to come to a conflicted, debt-ridden flock that some clergy told me not to touch with a ten-foot pole. Rationally, it didn't make a lot of sense. But spiritually, it felt absolutely right. I knew that the possibilities

70

in me and the possibilities in this gifted, ripe community of faith were being connected by the inbreaking power of God. And in a dim, small way, I felt that for me, and for us, the kingdom of God was at hand. I still feel that way today.

I once read an excellent paper interpreting several call passages. One line jumped out at me. "Leaders within a Christian context are those people who are willing to be led." Leaders are those who are willing to follow — to follow the call, to follow heart and intuition and vision, to follow the prompting and the inbreaking of God's Spirit. My friends, you have been a community of leaders that has answered God's call vigorously and creatively — in many times and in many places. Let each one of us recommit ourselves today and in the days ahead to listen, to respond, to risk, and to follow as we continue looking for the *kairos* moments of our living.

May it be so — for you and for me. Amen.

Epiphany 4
Ordinary Time 4
Matthew 5:1-12

Rejoicing In Reality

Our text says that Jesus "went up to the mountain" and, oh, what a beautiful mountain it is! The Mount of the Beatitudes is not all that high, but in Galilee it is the equivalent of Mount Everest. Stretched out below is the most fertile agricultural land in Israel, intricately laid out next to the jeweled sea, that breathtaking, blue prism reflecting the hot beauty of the Middle Eastern sun. A few years ago, after wandering around on the hilltop for a while, our pilgrim group decided that this was the place we wanted to celebrate communion — that here, on this mountain, we would share the Living Bread just as Jesus shared the Living Word.

The nuns who take care of this holy site told us where the best spot would be — right on the edge of the hill, with the sea shimmering below. There was, however, one catch. The nuns made it very clear that no woman was allowed to officiate at a communion service on this sacred hill. A bit stunned, I was somewhat at a loss as to what to do. There *was* a male pastor in our group, but he had taken no spiritual leadership during the trip and didn't particularly want to. And, besides, I had been longing to speak the words of institution on this spot so central to the ministry of Jesus. Finally, we agreed that *all* of us would say the familiar words consecrating the bread and cup — not really what the nuns had in mind, but technically honoring the request that a man officiate at the sacrament.

And it turned out to be a holy, simple moment. The wind picked up as we prayed and sang. It was as if the Spirit was surging and singing, stirring and stinging us, clearly and cleanly claiming us.

Yes, the Spirit was connecting us to the past and freeing us for the future — sending us as the Word of Jesus to be spoken through the ministries of our lives. It was a grace moment — God breaking into the narrowness of our human experience and blessing us with lavish love.

Today's Gospel Lesson is one of the grace moments in scripture, stirring us, stinging us, clearly and cleanly claiming us. But it is rarely heard that way. Instead we hear it as a list of shoulds and oughts — calling us to a kind of life we are not able or willing to live. After all, who willingly wants to be poor, meek, mournful, persecuted? As much as we need to be comforted and filled, as much as we want blessing and mercy, as much as we yearn to be the precious children of God, we're not sure it is worth the cost. Or is it?

Some commentators call this passage the "ordination address to the twelve." Matthew makes it clear that when Jesus saw the crowds, he made a beeline for the mountain, moving away from all the curious people in order to have conversation with the serious people. Just prior to this passage, we hear about the call to the disciples, those twelve bewildered fishermen and tax collectors who have all of a sudden been claimed, dragged, invited, beguiled into living and learning and leaving with Jesus. As captivated as they are by this call however, these recruits still aren't sure what it means. So this morning Jesus takes them away on retreat — to the mountaintop — to teach them. These words, then, these familiar beatitudes, aren't for everybody. They are for disciples, for those of us who are serious about following Jesus, captivated but still confused by what the call means. If we don't begin there, in the heart of committed discipleship, then the words will make very little sense at all.

Now, let us be sure we know what the words are about. They are not about shoulds and oughts. Not about working and doing. They are about blessing. Jesus begins with the blessings that are already ours. This passage, this prologue to the Sermon on the Mount, is not about what *will* be. It is about what *already* is. This passage does not tell us that God *will* be good to us. It tells us that God is *already* good to us. It does not suggest that the kingdom *will* come — some day. It proclaims, with great joy, that the kingdom of God is *already* here. This passage does not say that we have to act in certain ways in order to be blessed; instead it celebrates the reality that because we are already blessed, we are empowered to act in certain ways.

Right here in the reality check of our imperfect lives, God is blessing us and loving us. Despite our titles and our public smiles, despite our bank accounts and the length of our resumé, despite all the acquired riches of the world, we know, if we are really honest, at a deep level, that we are very poor in spirit. That our lives are filled with sadness. We know that, as much as we want to be in charge, we are utterly dependent upon the grace of God to make it through the night. Yes, we know that our meager efforts to find peace in a violent and turbulent world make little difference. We know that when we really stick up for what we believe and what we value, the power brokers of this world will laugh at us and pass us by. My friends, if we can see ourselves as that small band of disciples mysteriously pulled out of the crowd, gathered at the feet of Jesus, learning to be an alternative melody of grace in a graceless world — if we can see ourselves that way — then we are already the broken, needy, vulnerable people described by the beatitudes. And it is because of that brokenness, because of that neediness, that we are blessed. This, believe it or not, is the good news of the gospel.

Some time ago on National Public Radio, there was an editorial about inspirational calendars. The commentator suggested that the very same people who are caught up in the spinning cycles of secular success are also the people watching *Touched by an Angel* and reading *Chicken Soup for the Soul.* And they — we — are the ones buying all those tear-off inspirational calendars with daily pithy quotes, so that when we hit rock bottom today, we can tear it off and find something tangible to keep us going tomorrow. As tough and together as we appear to be to others, we are as needy and impoverished of spirit as any of the people taught and touched by Jesus. And it is that very neediness that invites and receives God's blessings. It is that very neediness that provides the fertile soil for our spiritual life to grow. And if we can accept and rejoice

75

that it is in our neediness that God's blessings are bestowed, then we can begin to embrace the neediness of others and become a blessing to them.

I recently heard about a woman who spent her life educating brain-damaged children. Now if there is any group of people whom the world rejects more than brain-damaged children, I do not know about them. Oh, we're nice to them. We're charitable to them. But we don't really value them. And so we keep them at a distance.

But this woman spent her whole career working with these children, so much so that her values were transformed. Not only were these children *not* worthy of being rejected, they became, to her, chosen and precious. They became to her a blessing — the poor in spirit, the clean of heart, the sad and persecuted ones who somehow reflect the joy of God's grace.

One year she decided to have her class put on a production of *My Fair Lady*. It never occurred to her not to give the lead part to a girl whose motor system had been damaged to the point that she was confined to a wheelchair. It never occurred to her not to give her the part. It also never occurred to her on the night the curtain opened on that first performance and that girl wheeled herself out on the stage and sang, "I could have danced all night. I could have danced all night," that the audience would weep. They had been confronted with the values of the gospel. That which the world rejects is in God's sight chosen and precious.[1] That which is needy is blessed and becomes a blessing to others.

The beatitudes are actually translated wrong in most of our Bibles. The Greek does not read "Blessed are ..." but instead, "O the blessedness of...."

O the blessedness of our utter dependence on God, for that dependence ushers us into God's heart.

O the blessedness of our deep, deep sadness, for it is in that sadness that God can touch and fill and comfort us.

O the blessedness of our finite earthiness, for it is in humility that we find abundance.

O the blessedness of our yearning for the good, for that hunger can be fed by God's grace.

O the blessedness of our generosity, for generosity is the sweetness of God's love.

O the blessedness of whatever justice and harmony we can create, for peace is the reflection of God's face.

O the blessedness of suffering and struggle, for joy is the fruit of adversity.

Rejoice and be glad in the reality of our living, for it is in that reality that God is building a kingdom of love.

One preacher has summarized the beatitudes very simply. "You are loved. Go, therefore, and act like it!"[2]

May it be so — for you and for me. Amen.

1. From a sermon preached by Dr. Thomas Long at the 1989 Westminster Worship and Music Conference.

2. Barbara Brown Taylor, The Preaching Life (Cambridge, Massachusetts: Cowley Publications, 1993)

Lite — Or Light?

There is, in this congregation, a running conversation as to what to call this structural wonder that rises above my head. Is it a dome? Or is it a lantern? The answer, of course, is both/and, depending on your perspective. It is a modern dome — the 1960s version of those elegant Byzantine basilicas that grace much of Europe, reminiscent of glittery mosaics and luminous paintings proclaiming the powerful promises of God. But functionally, architecturally, it is also a lantern, transparently receiving and then sending forth the light of God's creative and healing Spirit. In either case, it is beautiful; it is unique to this space, and it defines who we are called to be in this community and in God's world.

Almost fifty years ago the forebears of this congregation made the decision to build a church on a hill — actually on the slight rise of ground called Bradley Hills. They then proceeded to build a building that would be a beacon of light in the neighborhood, not hidden under a bushel, but set on a hill for all the world to see. Last year, the session decided to recommit to that identity. They voted to install high-powered lights facing out toward the street, and then put them on a timer, so that every evening between 8 and 11 this colorful prism will burn brightly, as beacon, as witness, as invitation to receive the love of God. Yes, this lantern is a powerful physical symbol of who we are. The question must always be raised, however: How accurately does this physical symbol reflect the spiritual health and vitality of this congregation?

I have always resisted preaching the Gospel of Matthew, and this morning I am reminded why. This is not "Christianity Lite"

— a low calorie version of the faith that can somehow remove some of the weight of the gospel. No, this morning's passage, particularly when coupled with Isaiah's political and provocative prophecy, is the real thing: a full course, full-bodied text that fills and transforms all of who we are. This is not gourmet food set out on fine china with attractive presentation. This is the oatmeal, the vegetable soup, the soul food of the Christian faith. And it reminds us of the powerful privilege, the awesome responsibility of being Christ's disciples in the world.

According to Genesis, light was the very first work of creation — God's basic, elemental gift of salvation. As the years have unfolded within the Jewish tradition, the first five books of scripture, the Torah, have come to be considered the light of God's truth. The Gospel of John takes this image one step further by making clear that Jesus is the light of the world — the Torah personified and embodied — God's salvation in flesh and blood. But Matthew goes all the way. He brings all of this home with a practical, terrifying, wonderful suggestion. He says that you — I — we are the light of the world. Not maybe! Not some day! But now! You — I — we *are* the light of the world. *We* are the salvation of God in the daily rhythm of creation.

Now, this light that we are needs to be understood in a couple of ways. First, and most importantly of all, this light comes from the *outside in*. It is God's light first and our light second. Physicists tell us that the diffusion of light in the world is caused by the reflection of the rays of the sun off particles in the air, off the clouds, off the earth. If it weren't for this dispersion of light, there would only be the sun and darkness. But because of the miracle of how light works, each particle of matter becomes a miniature sun. Likewise, in the Christian faith, the light of God's love is dispersed and reflected off each one of us, so that we become miniature gods in the world.

When our two new windows were being designed, the artist made it clear that the beauty of the windows would be dependent upon the whim of the light — the sun hitting the color and angle of the glass and dispersing it into our midst. And so the message, the power of these windows cannot be controlled. They are dependent upon the light, upon the mercurial glow of God, to create that which is new and fresh at every moment of each day. And so it is with us. When we are angled and colored just right, then we are transparent to the grace and glory of the Creator.

Some of you know that I carry a glass oil lamp with me almost everywhere I go: to session meetings, to spiritual retreats, to confirmation class sessions, to daybreak devotions. This lamp is, to me, a concrete reminder of God's presence and power in our midst. In the mundane business of our life together, we light this lamp first to remind ourselves who we are and whose we are. Lately, this lamp has been smoking terribly, filling the room with an unpleasant odor and clouding up the glass of the lantern. God has become dysfunctional, or so I thought. That is until Mike Werner suggested that I trim the wick, a necessary discipline of oil lamp ownership that I had never been taught. Well, now that the wick is trimmed, my lamp doesn't smell or smoke, it uses fuel much more efficiently, and the glass is clear and clean, allowing God to shine sharply, warmly in our midst. Ah, yes, the dysfunction wasn't with God. It was with me.

The disciplines of the Christian faith are the ways we trim our wicks and polish the glass of our lives. Developing habits of prayer, study, silence, stewardship, and service — these are the ways we become transparent, ready to receive and return the light of the God who burns inside us, in the well-trimmed wicks of our souls. It is then that we can move to a deeper level of understanding — realizing that though light comes from the outside in, it only serves its purpose if it burns brightly and pervasively from the *inside out*.

The painter Rembrandt, a strong and committed Christian, used light to reflect his spiritual understandings. Some of his most powerful characters appear to emanate light from within themselves, embracing those around them with warmth and energy. Even in his sketches, like *Christ Preaching*, the inner radiance of Christ gives definition to the sick, to the children, and to all the others who gather around him. In contrast to this, in Rembrandt's painting *Descent from the Cross*, there is no inner light anywhere. A lone torch in the distance casts lifeless shadows of death on Christ's tortured body, showing a dead world without the life and light of

God. And so it is with us. The light within us, which is the power and grace of God, is life for and to the world. And without the God in us shining in the good deeds of our lives, the world will surely die.

During the last blizzard, our family had the opportunity to build a blazing fire, and then sit back and enjoy it. I have learned over the years that it takes work to get a fire just right: the wood needs to be carried and stacked a certain way with just enough air circulating around it. And of course, the damper has to be open. But once the fire is going, it is wonderful just to sit back and enjoy — to relax, to nap, to sink into the rhythm of the dancing flames. The danger is to relax too much, for then the flames die down, the fire turns to embers, the embers turn to smoke, and the fire dies out.

Several years ago, this congregation entered into a remarkable period of revitalization. With the capital campaign, the vision task force, several years of restructuring, the assimilation of the forty percent of you who are new in the last seven years, the blossoming of dozens of new programs in the area of education and mission, God — and you — have built a strong and vigorous fire in this special place. And the light of these flames has been wonderful to behold. But we must be careful, my friends, that we don't sit too long just enjoying the blaze, for the fire will surely die down. The session and the members of Task Force 2000 believe that it is now time to stoke our fire with fresh wood, to give some vigorous pumps with the bellows of our lives to ensure that the dancing flames of our life together will not turn to embers.

Friends, church is like a warm and comfortable fire for many of us — helping us to reflect and enjoy God's gift of life. But it is now time to trim the wick, to polish the glass, to fuel the flames so that our fire, our light will burn brightly, for years to come, not only for ourselves, but for that world out there which God calls us to serve.

May it be so — for you and for me. Amen.

The Embassy At 6601[1]

The year was 1967. Vietnam was exploding. The Nuclear Arms Race was escalating. The Women's Movement and the Civil Rights Movement were agitating the soul of our nation. And the Presbyterian church was trying to figure out how to witness to Jesus Christ in the midst of all this cultural chaos.

1967 was also the year I turned eighteen and graduated from high school. Though vaguely aware of all the political and global tumult swirling around me, I was much more concerned about my prom dress, my SAT scores, and the looming adventure of attending college 3,500 miles from home. But, even as self-absorbed as I was, I *do* remember the Confession of 1967 (C67), the first contemporary statement of faith crafted by the Presbyterian church since the seventeenth century. And, I remember the heat, the anger, the venom that my father took because he boldly preached the gospel embedded in the words of this historic confession.

In true Presbyterian fashion the Confession of 1967 was written by a committee, and so it took ten years to complete! Historical records tell us that the members of the committee understood the cataclysmic timing of their task. And, according to the chair of the committee, the words from 2 Corinthians 5:17-20 that I just read, "irresistibly imposed" themselves upon the group. Paul's image of reconciliation — this centerpiece of Christian theology — simply permeated the hearts of those men and women. And they were converted to a new image of the church. They came to understand that we, as the Body of Christ, are not power brokers, but peacemakers, not a self-absorbed community of comfort and

83

convention, but an embassy of ambassadors, sent to represent God's reconciling love in a foreign and alien world. And so, rather than pontificating about distant, dusty doctrine, the C67 folk called the church to a new task: to the prophetic task of probing and proclaiming a gut-level ethic of grace. They called the church to address the real issues of real people in a real world. And they named the demons of the day: war, poverty, sexual confusion, racial prejudice.

The core sentence in this fairly lengthy document is really pretty simple: "to be reconciled to God is to be sent into the world as his reconciling community." In other words, the church — *this* church — is a spiritual embassy for God. And we are called to be the ambassadors, ambassadors for Christ entrusted with God's message of reconciliation. Quite simply, God is making God's appeal to a broken world through us. And if we do not re-present the vision, God's kingdom will not come.

As I have reread the words of C67, I have been struck by how relevant they are today, 35 years later. Reconciliation is still the crying need in our world. And the ethical issues of our day are still vexing and horrific — not just war and weapons of mass destruction, not just poverty and the unresolved pain of sexual conundrums — but also issues of science and faith, cloning, environmental destruction, terrorism, consumerism, and the devastating divide that separates rich from poor. And we as Presbyterians are still called to be ambassadors, to be peacemakers, to be proclaimers of a hopeful vision. But how do we start? How do we get our arms around this huge task? How do we come to terms with our puny power amidst all the overwhelming evils of our day? The answer comes in our Gospel Lesson for today where Jesus speaks to our heart, where Jesus appeals to our personal integrity and to our personal power.

These tough words from Jesus come as part of the Sermon on the Mount — the three chapters of ethical teaching that form the core of Matthew's Gospel. Just before these words today, Jesus has told the crowd that he has come not to abolish the law, but to fulfill it. Now this does not mean that he is replacing or belittling or watering down the law. Instead Jesus is embodying the law, putting flesh on the law, and digging underneath the law in order to find God's deeper values and vision which the law points to. And then Jesus takes this abstract idea and makes it concrete, giving six examples of how the word becomes flesh in the realities of our everyday lives. And as usual Jesus is neither polite nor politic. He takes on murder, adultery, divorce, lust, legal game playing, and political revenge. And he tells us that if we cannot embody love and reconciliation in our personal lives, well, then, reconciliation in the world is doomed.

Today's particular words focus on anger and they are addressed to the bickering, resentful, bitter parts inside us, as well as inside those early crowds. As a good Jew, Jesus starts with the Ten Commandments — Thou shalt not kill — but then he digs even deeper. He suggests that each one of us is a murderer. Each one of us is a killer of life and love when we harbor anger and contempt toward anyone. And he makes it clear that the hard part of reconciliation must start with us — with our decision to be reconciled to God and to neighbor. And we are to do this no matter who is at fault.

Plato once imagined the spiritual journey as a chariot moving through the wilderness of life, with the soul as the charioteer trying to rein in two powerful horses: the horse of anger or passion, and the horse of reason or order. Plato understood that both passion and reason can be life-giving, but only when they are held in dynamic tension, only when each power neutralizes the potential destruction of the other. This morning Jesus tells us that we must balance the passion of anger with the discipline and reason of love. And he tells us that the law of love can best be fulfilled, not through rules, but through relationships.

The word that Jesus uses means a particular kind of anger. He is not talking about short bursts of annoyance or frustration. Rather he is talking about the brooding, pervasive kind of animosity that can eat away at us — a kind of leprosy of the soul. This toxic poison destroys relationships and leads to malicious gossip, to character assassination, and to the destruction of lives and reputations. Now lest we are tempted to excuse ourselves from such ugly behavior, I ask you to reflect on your own lives for a minute. Who was the last person you gossiped about or maligned? How frequently do you label or stereotype others who may disagree with you? How willing are you to savor animosity and bitterness toward a friend or family member in order to hold onto your own hurt, your own self-righteousness, your own brokenness and pain? I love to tell the story of the conservative Presbyterian who just a few weeks ago called me a heretic, a harlot, and a wicked teacher of apostasy. And yet how easy it is for me to retaliate — to label *him* and to put *him* in a box. How easy it is to turn other people into a category, rather than seeing them each as a beloved child of God who just happens to see things differently than I do.

What Jesus is suggesting this morning is that all our political convictions and theological pontifications about reconciliation mean absolutely nothing if we are not committed to healing and forgiveness in our own political lives. I was awe-struck with an article in the *Washington Post* about Aaron Miller, who has been one of the chief United States negotiators for peace in the Middle East. Mr. Miller recently changed the venue of his work. Rather than operating at the global, political level, he decided to work at the local, personal level. He has become President of Seeds of Peace, a non-profit organization that tries to enable reconciliation between Arab and Israeli teenagers through one-on-one encounters. Mr. Miller is convinced that the only hope left is at the grassroots level.

Miller quoted a young participant in the Seeds for Peace program, who said, "In order to make peace with your enemy, you have to make war with yourself."[2] In other words, we must battle our own hateful instincts. Or, to paraphrase Jesus, before you offer your peace plans on the altar of world opinion, first go and be reconciled to your brother or your sister. For love, according to scripture, is not irritable or arrogant or boastful or rude. Love does not insist on its own way, but bears all things, believes all things, hopes all things, endures all things.

There is a true story abut two farmers in Canada. One day the dog of one farmer got loose and mauled to death the two-year-old child of his neighbor. The devastated father cut off all relationship with his neighbor, and the two men lived in cold, defiant enmity for years. Then one day a fire devastated the property of the dog-owning farmer, destroying his barn and all his equipment. He was unable to plow and plant, and so his future appeared doomed. Except that the next morning he woke up and found all his fields plowed and ready for seed. Upon investigation, he discovered that his grieving neighbor had done this good deed. Humbly the rescued farmer approached his neighbor and asked him if he had plowed his fields — and, if so, why. The answer was clear: "Aye," the former enemy said. "I plowed your fields so that God can live."[3] My friends, hard-core Christian love is not about affection and friendship. It is about forgiveness and reconciliation. It is about a law deeper than litigation. It is about the law of grace and the power of resurrection.

This day, if any of us feel estranged from God, it is not because God has moved away from us. It is because we have moved away from God. We have become distanced by all the anger and brokenness and disappointment in the relationships of this world. In a wonderful speech celebrating the thirty-fifth anniversary of C67, pastor John Wilkinson says this:

> In the "Little Gidding" T. S. Eliot writes:
>
> > "And all shall be well and
> > All manner of thing shall be well
> > When ... the fire and the rose are one."

Yes, when ...

> all manner of creatures are one. And all manner of Christians are one. And the broken and fearful world and its creator are one. And the church and its Lord are one. Thank God for that ever present and not-quite-yet gift of reconciliation, in the name of the one in whom such reconciliation is found, and no other, even Jesus Christ.[4]

This is the good news of the gospel. May it be so — for you and for me. Amen.

1. The address of Bradley Hills Presbyterian Church is 6601 Bradley Boulevard.

2. From the *Washington Post*, 1/31/02, p. A20.

3. As told by William P. Barker.

4. John Wilkinson, in an address given at the Covenant Network of Presbyterians Conference, Minneapolis, Minnesota, November 2002.

The Offense Of Grace

Victor Hugo begins *Les Miserables* with the story of Jean Valjean. He is an ex-convict who has just been released from nineteen years in prison for stealing bread to feed his sister's children. As he reenters society, no one will house him or give him work because of his criminal record — that is until he stumbles into the bishop's house. Much to Valjean's bewilderment, the bishop treats him with kindness and hospitality. Seizing the moment, Valjean steals the bishop's silver plates and, then, flees into the night.

The bishop's reaction to Valjean's treachery is not what we might expect. Instead of being angry and offering condemnation, the bishop examines his own behavior and finds himself lacking in charity. "I have for a long time wrongfully withheld this silver; it belonged to the poor. Who was this man? A poor man evidently," he reasons to himself. So when the police arrive with the captured Valjean, the bishop's silver in his possession, the bishop calmly greets the thief and says, "But I gave you the candlesticks also ... why did you not take them along with the plates?" The police, surprised and confused, reluctantly let the thief go.

Like Joseph's brothers cowering in fear before the one they have wronged, Jean Valjean expects blame and condemnation for his actions. Instead, he receives forgiveness and mercy. He expects hatred, and, instead, he receives love, and at that moment evil is transformed into good.

Our story today is a true story of grace, and as such it is God's story. In fact, it summarizes the gospel — the good news which we have received, and the good news which we are called to live.

Though Jesus' words and Joseph's words focus on how we are to treat others, they are based upon the way God treats us. Loving enemies, forgiving negative experiences, giving and expecting nothing in return, offering mercy instead of blame and condemnation — this is God's story. After all, God put a rainbow promise in the sky, even though we hadn't earned it. God made manna to fall from heaven, even though the wandering Israelites had done nothing but complain and whine. In Jesus' most difficult parable, the vineyard owner, who is God, pays the one-hour workers the same as the eight-hour workers, and thus gives them — and us — not what we deserve but what we need. And in the archetypal tale of the Prodigal Son, we meet a God who rejoices when a sinner comes home.

Yes, again and again and again, God gives us grace instead of grief. God gives us blessing instead of blame. God gives us comfort instead of condemnation. And in the serendipity of those surprising moments *we* are changed. Yet, it is one thing for God to be gracious to us. After all, that is what God is for. It's quite another for us to do the same. After all, we live in the real world, and we must be practical, cautious, and sensible. Loving our enemies and turning the other cheek is dangerous business — foolhardy and contrary to our best interests. No, we need to be right, to be safe, to be number one, always to be in control of the situation — this is the only way to preserve one's skin. And so we, the worldly people of the twenty-first century, live not in a world of grace, but instead in a world of hostility. We live in a world where if we get robbed or mugged, we press charges. We live in a world where, in order to maintain national superiority, we can never admit that the United States is wrong. We live in a world where eighty percent of Americans believe in legalized revenge — better known as capital punishment. We live in a world where, after parents die and sibling rivalries turn into warfare, millions of dollars and thousands of emotional hours are spent contesting wills and fighting over family heirlooms.

Yes, resentment and retaliation, judgment and blame are tightly woven into the fabric of our human nature. This negative reaction to the bad things in life is learned behavior in a world where self comes first. It is part of the original sin of seeing ourselves as the center of the universe. And it is the disease of the soul which Jesus comes to heal. When he eats with Zacchaeus, when he forgives and empowers the woman at the well, when he breaks bread with Judas, and when he gives authority to faithless Peter, Jesus gives them — and gives us — grace. He gives us the benefit of the doubt, the gift of a second chance, the lavish and generous blessing of unconditional love. And then Jesus asks *us* to do the same — to take the risk, to make the decision, yes, to follow him. He asks us to be foolish enough to spurn the ways of the world, and to do things in a new way.

The writer and surgeon Bernie Siegel tells the story of Wild Bill, an inmate of a concentration camp, who after six years of serving the enemy as an interpreter, was still full of energy and physical health and a gentle positive spirit. To the other prisoners, he was a beacon of hope, an agent of reconciliation, one who was constantly urging them to forgive each other and the enemy. This man's positive spirit was all the more amazing because of the horror which he himself had experienced at the beginning of the war — watching his own family: his wife, his two daughters, his three little boys, shot before his very eyes by Nazi soldiers in Warsaw.

When asked to explain his lack of bitterness, Wild Bill responded, "I had to decide right then whether to let myself hate the soldiers who had done this. It was an easy decision, really. I was a lawyer. In my practice I had seen too often what hate could do to people's minds and bodies. Hate had just killed the six people who matter most to me in the world. I decided then that I would spend the rest of my life — whether it was a few days or many years — loving every person I came in contact with."[1]

A new ethic — to love our enemies, to turn the other cheek, to forgive and love no matter what — it is what Jesus asks. But does it make sense? And does it work? Or is it an offense in our dog-eat-dog world? Is it realistic to expect the families of Timothy McVeigh's victims to forgive him and to love him? Is it appropriate to ask a battered wife to pray for the one who abuses her, to offer the other cheek to the husband who has struck the first one? Yes, God sends sun and rain on the righteous and the unrighteous alike — but are *we* called to love and be merciful to people who take us for granted and use us for their own advantage? These selfless, idealistic values may be fine for a Messiah, but for those of us who are victims and victimizers in the real world, they are offensive and dangerous.

Unless, of course, we look at them in a new way. Years ago I read a book about Christian assertiveness, and these puzzling words from Matthew were offered as guidelines for healthy assertive behavior. You see, to love our enemy is to take charge of the situation, to refrain from just reacting as a victim of their behavior. To love our enemy is to *change* the situation, to take the initiative to relate to our victimizers in a new way — literally to take the power out of their hands and to put it in ours in a positive way. To *love* the enemy does not mean to *like* the enemy. Instead it means to understand them as human beings — troubled and sinful human beings who have hurt us because they themselves hurt inside. It means to make a decision to respond to them in ways which will benefit them and perhaps lead to healing.

This is not to suggest that we passively sit back and ask for more abuse. It does not mean that the abused wife continues to live with the husband who beats her. No, the loving thing to do, the thing that is in the best interests of the one who is doing the hurting, may be to blow the whistle, to press charges, to get help for a sickness that is out of control. You see, to do good, to love and forgive those who offend us, is to refrain from hurting them in the same way they have hurt us. It is to initiate a new form of confrontation and healing that will lead to the well-being of *all* the parties involved. An ethic of grace — far from being an offense — is an invitation to take the offensive, to live positively instead of negatively, to stop playing the role of victim, and to start living a life of proactive discipleship.

Martin Luther King, Jr., once wrote:

> *Forgiveness does not mean ignoring what has been done. It means, rather, that the evil act no longer remains as a barrier to the relationship ... We must recognize that the evil deed of the enemy neighbor, the*

thing that hurts, never quite expresses all that he is. An
element of goodness may be found even in our worst
enemy.[2]

King concludes that when Jesus asks us to love our enemies he is pleading with us to offer understanding and creative good will to all people. This is the only way we can truly be children of a loving God.

My friends, an ethic of grace is different from an ethic of justice. Instead of reacting to the sin of others, instead of basing our response on reward or revenge or reciprocity, we can, instead, initiate a new relationship based on love and hope. And, by taking the high road, we can become fertile ground for abundant life to grow, both for our enemy and for our selves.

I was once offered the gift of grace from an enemy, and it was a transforming moment in my life. Years ago, when my husband and I were called to be co-pastors of a church in New Jersey, the pastoral nominating committee was split. Seven members of the committee were favorable to our candidacy, but four members were opposed. Though it is usually a bad idea to accept a call to a church when there is that kind of split, we were assured that the committee itself was so conflicted that no candidate could have fared better. One of the members who was opposed to us was Pearl, a strong-minded, fairly conservative elder who also happened to be clerk of session. She didn't like our theology, she didn't like the idea of a clergy couple, and she definitely didn't like the idea of a clergywoman. Fortunately, the congregation voted overwhelmingly to call us as their co-pastors, but that still didn't convince Pearl. She just didn't like us, and she wasn't about to accept us as her pastors.

A few weeks after we moved and started our ministry, I was feeling particularly low. Though the congregation had been welcoming, I was still feeling like a stranger, still feeling like people were suspicious, still feeling like my husband was the more acceptable pastor. In fact, I was feeling like we had made a terrible mistake, when all of a sudden the doorbell rang. I went to open the door, and there stood Pearl, holding a broom, a loaf of bread, and a shaker of salt. She smiled at me and said, "I come from German stock, and there is an old tradition in our family. Whenever someone moves into a new home they are given three gifts: a broom to sweep away the evil spirits, a loaf of bread to make their house into a home, and a pinch of salt to bring good luck. I want to welcome you to your new home — and to welcome *you* as my new pastor."

Well, Pearl and I never saw eye to eye on theology. But that day Pearl took the offensive and changed a relationship of hostility into a relationship of grace. That day she decided to love her enemy, and I felt like I had finally come home.

These words in Matthew are not spoken to the world at large. Jesus knew that secular people could neither understand nor honor such a difficult ethic. No, these words in Matthew are spoken to the disciples, to believers who have decided to follow Jesus. These words are spoken to us, people who have chosen to be the yeast in a world that needs the fullness of grace. This day may we hear these words, and do them, all to the glory of God.

May it be so — for you and for me. Amen.

---

1. Bernie Siegel, *Love, Medicine, and Miracles* (New York: Harper and Row, 1986), p. 195.

2. Source unknown.

Worry And Wonder

Well, the orange alert has finally been lowered to yellow. The purported organizer of the 9/11 attacks is now under arrest. And this week, rather than protecting us from biological or chemical poison, it seems that duct tape is being promoted as the perfect cure for warts! Perhaps, just a bit of our terror has subsided.

And yet unsettling news is still around us. Tens of thousands of our troops are still in Iraq. Contrary to the wisdom of most religious leaders, including the Stated Clerk and Moderator of our Presbyterian General Assembly, and ignoring the sentiments of most of God's global community, our country has toppled Hussein and devastated a country, the very first time our nation has ever engaged in preemptive strikes against an enemy. And post-war Iraq is a tinderbox. All the while, in news that is truly terrifying, North Korea has nuclear warheads that can reach the shores of California. And Kim Jong-il has restarted North Korea's plutonium producing reactor.

A friend that I met in Louisville this past weekend told me that in her sixty years of living, both here and in the Middle East, she has never experienced such chronic anxiety, such persistent low-grade depression about the state of the world.

Brothers and sisters, we live in nerve-wracking times. And how does Jesus respond? "Don't worry," he says. And then he asks a really good question: "Do you think that any of you by worrying can add one single hour to your span of life?"

But worry we do. Think about it. When we are pushed out of the dark, warm, welcome of the womb, our very birth is a descent into anxiety, into the uncertainty of that which we can't under-stand and can't control. And we quickly pick up the anxiety of our parents, those big, hovering people who want the best for us, who want us to be the best, who project all their unfinished anxieties onto us. Who can forget the anxiety of crying in the night? The anxiety of being abandoned that first day in nursery school or kin-dergarten? The anxiety of our first spelling test or our first time up to bat? Who wants to repeat the waiting game for SAT scores and college acceptances? Or what about that first job interview? Or children who wander and squander and eventually meander out of our lives? And what about the anxiety of that inconclusive mam-mogram? Or the elevated PSA levels?

And these are just the anxieties buried in our personal lives. What about the anxieties of that uncontrollable world out there? A turbulent stock market? Remember the anxiety of Y2K, the Unabomber, Timothy McVeigh? The anxiety of 9/11 and anthrax, of the sniper, of Osama bin Laden, and yes, despicable Saddam Hussein? Saturated by a world of worry, it's no wonder we re-spond irrationally — buying duct tape and plastic sheets to en-tomb us in breathless, hopeless tombs of anxiety, devising careful plans about where and how we are to meet our loved ones when the world blows up, when there probably won't be time to go and meet our loved ones, anyway.

Now, at first glance, Jesus seems to be psychologically naive, if not downright dangerous. "Do not worry," he says, as if this is really possible. He might as well be saying, "Don't be human." After all, psychologists tell us that anxiety is central to human ex-istence. And far from being debilitating, anxiety can be fertile ter-ritory for growth and change and maturity. Actually the Greek word which Jesus uses is not referring to the garden-variety worries of the day. No, it is the word for extreme angst — for anxious worry-ing — for being so full of care for oneself and one's survival that the world shrinks to me, myself, and I. The anxiety Jesus is talking about is the exact opposite of faith. The exact opposite of trust and hope in the providence of a dependable and gracious God.

In his famous book, *The Courage to Be,* twentieth-century theologian Paul Tillich gives a theological definition of anxiety.

"Anxiety," he says, "is the state in which a being is aware of its possible nonbeing. Anxiety is finitude, experienced as one's own finitude."[1] And then Tillich suggests three kinds of anxiety — the threat of three kinds of non-being — all of which feed into what we have been experiencing in the last few weeks and months. There is the anxiety of death. Today a terrorist could drop a dirty bomb and we, and our children, could be asphyxiated by lethal chemicals. Then there is the anxiety of meaninglessness. If we are fragile targets of insanity, then what really is the meaning of our lives, the meaning of God, the purpose of creation? And finally, there is the anxiety of guilt. If I can't stop Osama bin Laden, if I can't protect my family, then what am I worth, how relevant am I, how effective am I as God's image in the world?

What Jesus is suggesting this day is that this awareness of our possible non-being, this acknowledgment of our finitude, is a part of the reality of God's creation. And it is only through grace that God can make happen what we cannot make happen ourselves. Then, in order to teach us how to submit our worries to God, Jesus asks us to do two things.

First of all we are to look at the lilies of the field, which, as weapons of mass destruction loom over us, seems like a preposterous suggestion. But again, word study is important. Jesus is not describing some kind of Buddhist bliss. The word is "look, study, scrutinize" the patterns of nature around you. Look and learn. The lilies he refers to are generic wild flowers, bright poppies that flourish and dazzle for just one day and then are thrown into the oven as fuel for the fire. These flowers have one spectacular shot at living their lives, and in that fleeting flash there is beauty and meaning and joy. Each one of them is unique and irreplaceable, but they are part of something much bigger than themselves. In other words, Jesus is suggesting that by comparing ourselves to the lilies of the field, we are looking at our own finitude, looking at our own puny but precious particularity. We are facing our anxiety about death and meaninglessness, and we are seeing it for what it is. And by facing our fears, and moving through them, our anxiety will immediately lose its power to immobilize us.

Early in my ministry, I discovered that I was crippled by a pervasive sense of anxiety. Performance anxiety: how can I possibly do my ministry well? And another anxiety: how could I possibly bear and nurture children without destroying them? I was fortunate to be led by the Spirit to a nurturing psychotherapist, and through several years of conversations, I learned to face my fears and to understand them. And I found the courage to take the risks of ministry and motherhood, because I trusted that God was with me in the risk taking.

Soon we will go with Jesus into the wilderness of Lent. With the waters of baptism still dripping from his brow, Jesus is immediately driven by the Spirit into the desert. And there he is tempted by Satan. Both beasts and angels are with him. It is perfectly clear that God *wanted* Jesus to struggle — to struggle intensely, with both the inner and the outer beasts of his life. God wanted Jesus to face his fears, to face his doubts, to face his weaknesses, to face his temptations, to face the deep ambiguities and anxieties of being human. And, my friends, God wants us to do the very same.

So, the first thing Jesus asks us to do today is to look, to study, to scrutinize, to acknowledge our finitude and our feelings and our fears, to admit the inevitabilities of life and of death, to embrace both the bane and the blessing of exquisite, ephemeral existence.

Then the second thing that Jesus asks us to do is to live — just live. *But* to live in a particular way. He asks us, out of the very depth of our anxiety, to live for God and like God, anyway. He asks us to strive first for the kingdom of God and God's righteousness, and then, Jesus promises, all these things we worry about will be given to us as well.

Death is facing you or a loved one? Live fully and deeply anyway. War is hovering over the world? Live generously and faithfully anyway. Poverty and injustice and political paralysis seem to be gripping the world? Creeping old age is diminishing your power and your energy? Live prayerfully and thankfully anyway. The relationships and dreams that have grounded your life are crumbling and disappearing? Live with hope and expectation for the new thing God is doing anyway. My friends, the only antidote for anxiety is trust. The only answer to despair is hope.

If you have not seen the Oscar-winning movie *The Pianist*, I encourage you to do so. Unlike most Holocaust films this one does not focus on the concentration camps, but on the life of a Polish Jew who, through grace, escapes boxcars and spends years hiding out in the shadows of Warsaw. Since childhood, this man has been gifted as an expressive pianist. And so he has a purpose that transcends his own life and feeds the soul of a whole people. Through horrifying scenes of torture, hunger, loneliness, and spiritual abandonment, we watch this wraithlike refugee survive. Why? Because his love of life is stronger than his anxiety about death. And through it all are the scores in his head, the melodies in his soul, the silent music in his fingers that constantly, pervasively, magically sustain him. Yes, we watch his soul striving for the vision, the kingdom of God beyond his Jewishness, beyond the evil of Hitler. Yes, he lives — spiritually and emotionally — in an inner place of trust and hope that no anxiety can control.

The Apostle Paul writes: "It is a terrifying thing to fall into the hands of the living God." But the terror he talks about is not the terror of anxiety. It is the terror of awe. Worry replaced by wonder. Fear replaced by faith. Trembling replaced by trust. "Do not worry," Jesus says. "For who of you can add one hour to your life by worrying?"

This is the good news of the Christian faith.

May it be so — for you and for me. Amen.

---

1. Paul Tillich, *The Courage to Be* (New Haven, Connecticut: Yale University Press, 1952), p. 35.

**Transfiguration Of The Lord
(Last Sunday After Epiphany)
Matthew 17:1-9**

Visions And Voices

I don't know about you, but I envy Moses and Peter and James and John. I envy Joseph and Mary and Abraham and Sarah and Paul and Jacob — all the biblical folk who see visions and dream dreams and are swept into the palpable presence of God. And I particularly envy the many parishioners I have known over the years who have shared their holy experiences with me. Jeanne Grimm's blinding moment of light when a dazzling Jesus stood by her death bed. A widow's glimpse of her beloved after his death, once again whole and healthy by her side. A young man's incredulous tale of his father's voice affirming him after death in a way he had never affirmed him in life. It seems to me that such dramatic epiphanies must certainly make faith a whole lot easier to swallow.

This morning, if we allow our imaginations to sweep us up the mountain, we may experience an inkling of visionary magic. But beware. If you try to understand this story with your mind, you will most certainly be disappointed. It is only if you try to see it with your soul, that you may find your heart strangely warmed. In this pivotal story in the gospels we are midway through the story — halfway between the birth and the death — teetering between the baptism and the resurrection. And as midlife, midpoint travelers we are still trying to find Jesus. Up until now this Jesus story hasn't been all that hard to swallow. As a baby, as a teacher, as a preacher, as a moral example, even as a healer, Jesus has inspired us, but he hasn't yet mystified us. Until today — when we hit a brick wall of magic. All of a sudden the earthy Jesus with his dusty feet and tired eyes becomes the ethereal Jesus — robe glowing and face shining — a shimmering window into pure, unadulterated divinity. This isn't just a "thin place" where hints of the holy seep into the ordinary. This is a ripping of the barrier between God and us — and God comes flooding into our midst.

An intriguing detail of Matthew's version of the Transfiguration is that the disciples do not seem all that amazed when Jesus suddenly turns into a pulsing light show, when all of a sudden he stands in the august company of Elijah and Moses. All of this they seem to take in stride. That is, until they hear the Voice, until they hear God repeating once again the words of baptism. "This is my Son, the Beloved; with whom I am well pleased; listen to him." Yes, my friends, it was the Voice and not the vision that knocked the disciples to the ground. It was the Voice and not the vision that blanketed them with fear.

In the mid-'50s Martin Luther King, Jr., was a 26-year-old rookie, fresh out of divinity school, a young father, an inexperienced pastor just trying to figure out how to manage the details of parish ministry. The last thing he was prepared to do was to pick up the mantle of a massive grassroots movement to abolish racism in America. And yet after Rosa Parks decided to rest her weary body in the front of a bus, all hell broke out in Montgomery, Alabama. And King was thrust into leadership almost without his consent. He quickly felt the grip of angry resistance as he was jailed for driving five miles over the speed limit, and as he received threatening phone calls: "Nigger, we're gonna blow your brains out."

One late night he sat in his kitchen, his wife and young daughter asleep in the next room. And he found himself wrestling and murmuring with God. King was unsettled, scared, angry, and he felt very distant from God. And then he found himself praying: "Lord, I think what I am doing is right. But I'm weak. I'm faltering. I'm losing my courage." And at that point — a moment of brutal honesty and need — King heard a voice. He heard The Voice: *Martin, stand up for righteousness. Stand up for justice. Stand up for truth. And lo, I will be with you even until the end of the world.* It was the crystallizing moment of his life. And even three nights later, when a bomb exploded on his front porch, Martin never forgot the power of those words, the reassurance of that Voice, a Voice that echoed again and again and again in his soul through all the dark days of his crusade. God had promised never to leave him, never alone, never to leave him alone.[1]

What are the voices, ethereal and otherwise, that murmur in your soul, in your conscience, in your memory this day? What are the voices that have called you to your truest self — cutting though fear, demolishing inadequacy, dueling with doubt, lifting laziness? What are the voices that have given you focus and given you courage for the living of your days?

I remember the voice of my father, his warm, firm preaching voice, lulling me and shaping me as a child, week after week, in worship, spinning out the stories of our faith, providing the foundation, the safety net of good news that has grounded my life for over fifty years.

I hear the voice of my mother, every Good Friday, singing, "He was despised and rejected — a man of sorrows acquainted with grief." And in the rich melancholy of that voice she captured all the forlorn pain of the world, reminding me that there is no sorrow and no affliction that Jesus does not share with me and with you.

I hear the voice of the college chaplain suggesting that I go to seminary, suggesting that I do something to rise above my tedious, self-absorbed, young adult angst.

I hear my husband's voice teaching me how to pay attention to the exquisite details of life: the shape of a tree, the shadows of a painting, the soft satin of a baby's skin, the small ordinary "visions" that reveal the holy, day in and day out.

I hear the voice of John Adams calling me on my fortieth birthday, telling me that Bradley Hills wanted me to be their pastor — to hear the voice and be the voice that nurtures all the voices of this amazing congregation.

And I hear the voice of my man-child calling from the heart of South America and in a light moment of affection calling me "Mama," a reminder that 23 years ago, for some kind and crazy reason, God empowered me to be a mother, even though I was more terrified by that calling than anything else God has ever asked me to do. Yes, it has been voices — and not visions — that have slowly opened my life to God.

The Voice in today's story reassures and empowers Jesus just before he turns his face toward Jerusalem, toward the cruelty of the cross. It reassures and empowers the disciples who have just been told to deny themselves and pick up *their* crosses. And it reassures and empowers us as we embrace our own Christian journey, a journey which demands that we regularly wrestle, in the wilderness of temptation, in the wilderness of repentance, in the wilderness of suffering, in the wilderness of commitment.

The Voice says several important things. First of all it says, "Remember your baptism." Remember, my friends, *your* baptism — that *you* are the Beloved — that *you* are uniquely created, named, blessed, and set apart by God for holy purpose in the world. That alone is all we really need to know in order to get through whatever the world hands us. God tells us, like he tells Martin Luther King, Jr., that we will never be alone. Never alone. God will never ever leave us alone. And that promise is reiterated every time we listen, every time we listen for the voice of Jesus, first and foremost in the voice of scripture, but then echoed in the newsroom, in the dining room, in the sanctuary, in the boardroom, in the bedroom, in the classroom — a voice that echoes if we have ears to hear and the heart to respond.

A few months ago I read the best-selling novel *Lying Awake* by Mark Salzman. I loved it for its vivid prose. And I hated it for its disappointing ending. It is the story of Sister John, a cloistered nun, who is slowly drawn into the intimate presence of God through stunning, dazzling, disintegrating visions. An ordinary woman becomes a quivering mystic, disappearing into "pure awareness."

> *She became an ember carried upward by the heat of the invisible flame ... until the vacuum sucked the feeble light out of her. A darkness so pure it glistened, then out of the darkness ... nova.... More luminous than any sun ... all that was her ceased to exist. Only what was God remained.*[2]

Unfortunately for Sister John, there is a complication. Along with her visions come excruciating headaches, which demolish her for days at a time, making her unavailable for the work of the cloister and causing her to be a great burden to the other nuns. Finally, a doctor diagnoses her with epilepsy, a condition that will get worse unless she chooses an operation — an operation that will relive the pain, but most likely destroy the visions. What should she do? After an intense wrestling match, Sister John chooses the operation. Why? With great reluctance, she denies herself, for the health and well-being of the larger, convent community. And sure enough the debilitating pain disappears. But so, too, does the exquisite passion — those intimate, ecstatic encounters with God. She goes back to the ordered, plodding life of the community where she is but one of many, serving God in the mundane moments of daily discipleship. I'm not sure I could have made that choice. I'm not sure that I would have been willing to give up all those visions and voices. What about you?

In a final moment of wisdom in the book, the Mother Superior offers Sister John words that sustain her after the mountain moments have disappeared, when her daily faith journey seems dull and tentative:

> We stretch out our emptied hands to take hold of the Light. We may feel that our prayers are arid, or that God has abandoned us. Although we suffer deeply, those become our most precious hours, because only in complete darkness do we learn that faith gives off light.[3]

My friends, in the long run, it is not the dazzling moments of transfiguration that connect us to God. It is the slow plodding — through the daily trenches of faithfulness that truly connect us to God. Our gospel story today ends with a very human Jesus — the glow completely gone. Once more he stands alone, his feet still dusty, his eyes still tired. Gently he touches the disciples and encourages them to rise up. The Greek word here is "resurrection." Yes, Jesus gently resurrects the disciples *this* side of the grave, so that they can travel with him down into the valley — down into the reality of the way things really are. Jesus resurrects us *this* side of the grave, so that together with God's low, steady wattage simmering quietly within us, we can turn our faces toward Jerusalem. So that together we can do what needs to be done.

If voices and vision come your way, treasure them and savor them for all the joy they can bring your way. But remember. The true light of God's presence is in the trust of your heart and in the daily faithfulness of your lives.

May it be so — for you and for me. Amen

---

1. As told by Philip Yancey in *Soul Survivor* (New York: Doubleday, 2001), pp. 20-21.

2. Mark Salzman, *Lying Awake* (New York: Knopf, 2000), pp. 5-6.

3. *Ibid.*, pp. 177-178.

Sermons On The Gospel Readings

For Sundays In
Lent And Easter

Building Our Foundation
On God

Richard E. Gribble, csc

These homilies were written during a time in my life when I was greatly inspired by the positive attitude, friendliness, genuine good nature, and strong Christian faith of a dear friend who, during this same period, made her special commitment to God through religious life as a Sister of Divine Providence. This work is most appropriately dedicated to my dear friend, Sister Tania.

Preface

The Christian community celebrates God's love and the message of salvation throughout the liturgical year. Our annual cycle begins with the great anticipatory period of Advent. The community prepares for the Feast of the Incarnation by reflecting upon the hope of Christ's Second Coming and recalling the historic preparations for the Messiah's coming to our world through the heraldry of John the Baptist. The Christmas season which follows sets our course for the remainder of the year, most of which is celebrated as the season of Pentecost (Ordinary Time in the Roman Catholic tradition). The period of Pentecost is interrupted, however, several weeks after Christmas with two contiguous seasons, Lent and Easter, which prepare the community for and celebrate its salvation through the Paschal Mystery, the passion, death, and resurrection of Jesus Christ. The seasons of Lent and Easter are, therefore a critical period for the Christian to re-think and, as might be necessary, re-construct one's relationship with God. It is a special season of grace given us by God; we must wholly and faithfully participate and give thanks for the opportunities this time affords, personally and for the Christian faithful collectively.

Lent, the first of these two seasons, serves as a significant period of serious preparation for the celebration of Easter. The gospel passages used during Liturgical Cycle A reflect what the church considers most important in this special journey. We must realize that at the outset of our journey a decision must be made — will we choose God or the world? While the latter is certainly the option of contemporary society, the Christian *must* choose God, for it is only through God that we can hope to stay on the road that leads to our immediate goal of Easter and our ultimate dream of salvation and eternal life. Assuming that we do choose God, then we must understand the need to be converted to the Christian message so that we can make a better effort to see things through the eyes of God and not our own, even though we might foolishly think we know best. Lent teaches us that Jesus is the one who will cure our spiritual blindness and release us from the chains, often self-imposed, that hold us prisoner. As our preparation enters Holy Week we learn of our need to walk the road with the Lord and to share his pain, as he bore our infirmities, although he had done nothing wrong. We must recall Saint Peter's words, "By his wounds you have been healed" (1 Peter 2:24). Finally, we must fully understand that there is a price to pay to experience God's glory; we must learn of our need to be cut down in order to discover our true path, the one that leads not to worldly success, but to the eternal life which is God's gift to all who believe.

If the Lenten journey is traversed successfully, then we can fully enter into the celebratory time of Easter. Yet, even as we observe these events, we must acknowledge that the challenges of the Christian life are ever-present. We should never forget British writer G. K. Chesterton's admonition in *What's Wrong with the World* (1910), "The Christian life has not been tried and found wanting; it has been found difficult and left untried." The Easter season reminds us that despite the triumph of Christ there will always be challenges to our belief. We seemingly cannot believe unless we see; yet we know that faith often is beyond proof and, thus, beyond sight as well. We are also challenged to discover ways of transforming problematic situations and what appears to be defeat into triumph through the grace of God. Additionally, this great season of grace teaches us that we must continually evaluate what we do, and keep our eyes fixed on Christ and his mission and message. Finally, as Jesus ascends to the Father, we come to realize that the Lord's work is not complete and, therefore, each day presents us with the opportunity to do something to complete the Master's work.

These homilies represent my understanding of the challenges presented us through this highly significant and very special journey. The church, in its wisdom, gives us this opportunity annually to review where we are and, after ascertaining our present position, the challenge to move to higher realms that are more consistent with our common Christian call to holiness. It is my hope that these reflections will be helpful to you as together we travel the path from Lent to Easter, and eventually to Christ and eternal life.

Richard Gribble, CSC

Building Our Foundation On God

"I'd sell my soul to play for the Washington Senators." Joe Hardy, the protagonist in the popular Broadway musical, *Damn Yankees*, says these words in a fit of frustration. Joe is what we call today an average middle-aged couch potato. He sits in front of his television and watches baseball and most of the time his beloved team, the Senators, are defeated by "those damn New York Yankees." Joe always wanted to play ball but things just did not work out that way. Marriage, children, and work occupied the life of Joe Hardy. Thus, one day in frustration he says he would sell his soul to play for the Senators. It just so happens that the devil is listening to Joe and appears quite suddenly in his living room. Satan will make a deal with the middle-aged man. The devil will transform Joe into a young and strong athlete, as he once was, and he can play for the Senators, but when the season is over Joe's soul belongs to him. After a moment of thought, Joe agrees and he is instantly transformed into a young man again.

Joe manages to get a try-out with the Senators and the manager is quite impressed. Soon Joe is making newspaper headlines as a star and the Senators begin to win games and move up in the standings. As the season begins to draw to a close, the Yankees and Senators are neck and neck for the pennant and a chance to go to the World Series. Joe has made a great contribution, but in most respects his heart misses his old existence, especially his family and friends at work. He begins to think how he might get out of his pact with the devil.

The whole season comes down to one final game; whoever wins goes to the Series. The last game between the Senators and Yankees comes down to the last inning and ultimately the last out. Joe is playing center field for the home team Senators who are ahead by one run. A crack of the bat sends Joe racing toward the fence. As he runs back Joe is transformed into the middle-aged couch potato he really is. The devil is upset that Joe has broken his pact and wants to return to his old existence. Now a middle-aged man again, Joe still manages to run back and make the catch, crashing through the center field fence in the process. He runs for fear that others will discover who he truly is; Joe Hardy was transformed in body but he was not converted in his heart.

Joe Hardy was transformed on the outside but fortunately for him he was never changed on the inside. He was at heart, and always wanted to be, a "couch potato." When he was playing baseball for the Senators the people never saw the real Joe.

Today, the Christian community throughout the world begins the discipline of Lent, and the gospel for today's service, drawn from Saint Matthew's version of Jesus' Sermon on the Mount, tells us of our need to change on the inside, to demonstrate who we are, and not concentrate on what others will see. We must be transformed so that God, the one who looks into the heart and understands our every thought, word, and action, will be pleased.

Jesus is very clear in the gospel that we should not practice piety in any form so as to be noticed by others, for our reward will never be found in what others think. The Lord speaks of the three great works that have, over the Christian era, become the hallmarks of Lenten action — almsgiving, prayer, and fasting. When we give alms, that is share our resources of time, talent, and treasure with others, we must do so in a way so that God and God alone knows what we are doing. To demonstrate in an external way that we are a great philanthropist, that we willing give to others, is not the problem Jesus describes. It is the attitude we possess. Why do we do what we do? When we pray, there is no need to do so in a manner which attracts attention and demonstrates to others how holy we are. On the contrary, Jesus says we should go to our room, close the door, and pray to our Father in private. God will hear our words of praise, thanksgiving, and petition and will reward us for our faithfulness. When we fast, it should not be done in a manner that others might notice. Rather than looking glum and weak, we must groom our person and look strong. God is the one who sees, and is grateful for, our actions. In short, we should not observe the great tenets of Lent so we can be changed on the outside so others will see. Rather, we should seek to be transformed on the inside to a stronger and more permanent relationship of trust in, and faithfulness to, God.

Joe Hardy was only able to obtain fame and notoriety by changing his physical appearance, but his glory was transitory. In the end he had to accept who he truly was. Similarly we must learn from Jesus that the only thing that is truly important is the person we are on the inside. The exterior person changes day-by-day, but the interior is more permanent and true. This is the individual God sees.

We must understand that while Jesus is clearly presenting a strong message in today's gospel that warns against external practice, he is certainly not downplaying the importance of our traditional Lenten practices. It is the attitude that we possess when we participate in these practices that the Lord judges, suggesting that we must look into our hearts and ask the sometimes difficult question, "What is our motivation for the things we do?"

Almsgiving has always been a basic discipline of the Christian life. Most people of good will share the gifts they have been given, realizing that ultimately all is gift from God, and, thus, is not personal, but the right of all. What, however, is our attitude when we share with others? Do we do so in a true spirit of sharing, or more out of guilt for what others might think if we do not contribute? Do we share so others will see how magnanimous we are, or can we truly not let the left hand know what the right hand is doing? Giving freely is, of course, the proper attitude. We all know and have used the expression, "'Tis better to give than receive." God has given freely and abundantly to us. Can we respond to the God who first loved us by demonstrating in action and heart a spirit of giving?

Prayer is another basic practice of our faith, our opportunity at any time to speak with God. Traditionally, we lift our voice in prayers of petition, praise, and thanksgiving. Our prayer is personal, whether we lay in bed, sit in our easy chair, or take a few moments during the madness of the morning or evening commute. It is also communal, as experienced for most through participation with a faith community. We should realize that prayer does not change God who is immutable. But prayer can be highly transformative for us. Most people, I suspect, have the proper motivation in their personal prayer lives. No one forces us to pray; we do so out of our personal need and that of the world. However, if we are honest, our motivation for communal prayer may be less clear and altruistic. We should recall the famous parable of the publican and the sinner (Luke 18:9-14). Jesus was very clear that the rich publican, while he did all for show on the outside, was unacceptable to God, while the sinner, who realized his faults and dared not raise to eyes to God, went home justified. As with almsgiving we need to look into our hearts and ask the difficult question, "Have I changed on the inside, or am I hollow and possess only an external facade?"

Dieting has been a fad for human society, especially first-world nations like the United States, for several generations, but there is a major difference between dieting and fasting. People diet in order to lose weight, to change their physical, external appearance. In our observance of Lent, do we use the season as a pretext to look better, or do we fast in solidarity with the poor and hungry of our world, who have no other choice, on almost a daily basis, than to fast? Can we consider using the money that we save from not eating to assist the poor and marginalized in our society? Can we use the time that would be spent eating in prayer, lifting to God those whose daily lot is hunger and thirst?

In today's gospel, Jesus says we should not store up treasures on earth, for these are transitory; they do not last. They will waste away, be stolen by thieves, or spent over time. But the things of heaven, where neither moth nor rust consume, nor thieves break in, will last forever (Luke 12:3). If we find our value and life in the things of God, there our hearts will be. God looks to the heart, for

116

that is all that counts. Who we appear to be and what others see in us on the outside might prejudice what people say or do, but we need not be concerned about that which does not last.

We must admit that we spend a lot of time concerned with the things of the world, the externals, as did Joe Hardy. But as Joe learned, so we must realize that the basic foundations of our life, that which is on the inside, is what must be fostered, for without the proper foundation the spiritual house of our lives will never be built. The human penchant for the externals of life and the way they impede God's action in our lives is illustrated by a short story.

During the days when God appointed judges to rule over the tribes of Israel, the Ark of the Covenant, the sacred vessel which carried the Law, the Ten Commandments given by God to Moses on Mount Sinai, was lost for a brief period. Without the most important symbol of their religion, the focal point of their worship, the Hebrews began to fall away from their faith. This situation was very distressing to the spiritual leaders of the people. They feared that if the Ark was not soon recovered or a new one built to replace it there would soon be no faith in Israel.

Thus, the high priest commissioned all artisans throughout the land to ply their trade to build a suitable replacement for the lost Ark. God himself would choose the proper vessel for his Law. Thus, every master craftsman in the nation set about the task of building a truly noble and worthy replacement for the Ark. The greatest and most famous to the totally unknown in the art world in Israel applied their talents, using the finest materials they could obtain.

When all the artisans had completed their work, the beautiful arks were placed on display in a large open field. Some of the creations were the greatest works people had ever seen. Arks were constructed of wood, stone, bronze, silver, and even gold. Some featured inlaid ivory while others were ornate with carved figures. Others still were adorned with precious gems. God would have a difficult time choosing one suitable replacement from all these master creations.

The chief priest then began the selection process by standing behind each ark and casting his die to see which one the Lord would choose. One by one these beautiful works of art were rejected. Then the high priest stood behind Joseph's ark. Joseph was a poor carpenter, with limited ability, but he was greatly devoted to God. His ark was quite simple, a box of pine wood with brass hinges attached to a top covering. To the utter amazement of the chief priest and crowd when the die was cast it came up positive. The people asked, "What does this mean? How could God choose such a simple vessel?" Others argued that this ark could not be chosen for other nations would laugh at Israel if people saw the vessel which housed the Hebrew Law. Thus, the people pressured the chief priest to again cast his die. This he did with the same result. But the crowd insisted that he try a third time. As the die again turned positive the voice of a prophet in the crowd spoke God's message: "What a wondrous ark," God said through the prophet. "My people always get lost in what they think is beautiful, right, and important. With a simple and humble ark there will be less to distract them and they will think more about me!"[1]

We must build the foundations of our lives, that is the inside, and not be concerned with the externals, no matter how much the world says such things are important.

As our Lenten journey begins this day, let us build our spiritual house on the rock foundation of Christ. Let us build that foundation deep within us, and ignore the externals so that our Lenten journey will be successful and, more importantly, we will one day find God and eternal life.

---

1. Paraphrased from "Joseph's Ark," in John Aurelio's *Colors! Stories of the Kingdom* (New York: Crossroad, 1993), pp. 68-69.

God, Or The World?

He was a man of mystery and charm; he was a man of broken-ness and faith. He was hunted down like a common criminal; his only crime was seeking God's glory. The "Whiskey Priest" lived in Southern Mexico. The time was the 1920s; the Cristero Rebellion was underway. The Whiskey Priest was not perfect — far from it. He drank too much; he had fathered a child. In those days, the Mexican government said that is was illegal to practice the priesthood, but that did not stop the Whiskey Priest. Everything he did; the Masses, baptisms, funerals, and weddings had to be conducted in secret, staying one step ahead of the authorities.

The Federales and their commanding lieutenant represented the government. This band of soldiers possessed the power. It was their job to find the Whiskey Priest, to stop his activity, and ultimately to eliminate him. The hunt went from town to town, village to village. In one village the lieutenant knew the Whiskey Priest had been present, yet the residents would say nothing. The lieutenant was more persuasive; he selected five villagers at random, lined them up in the town square and shot them in order to loosen the tongues of the others.

The Whiskey Priest was living on borrowed time; he knew this to be true. He continued to move from town to town. The winter rains helped him "disappear" in the mountain highlands for a few precious extra weeks of freedom. The Federales would win, however, it was just a matter of time. In the end he was found, tried, convicted, and executed — a common criminal to the government but a martyr and a hero to the people he served.

British novelist Graham Greene's epic tale, *The Power and the Glory* describes the conflict between broken, sinful, and incomplete humanity, symbolized by the Whiskey Priest, that seeks the glory of God, and the power, wealth, and prestige of the world, characterized by the Federales. On this first Sunday in Lent, our gospel describes a similar struggle — the kingdom of God versus the kingdom of the world.

After his baptism in the River Jordan, Jesus goes to the desert and there experiences his own personal Lent. His forty days in the desert served to prepare him for the most important phase of his life, his public ministry. At the end of this period, the Lord willingly submits to temptation by Satan. This is no accident and Jesus has not fallen victim to demonic powers. Rather, these temptations are part of the divine plan for Jesus. It is an essential element of his obedience to the Father. Thus, Jesus is tempted by the three great sins for all human history — power, wealth, and prestige. Satan is strong and insistent in his words, but Jesus is stronger and wins the confrontation.

The first great temptation is to gain power. After his forty-day fast in the desert, Matthew tells us that Jesus was hungry. Thus, Satan appeals to the physical dimension of Jesus' character to satisfy his hunger: "If you are the Son of God, command these stones to turn into bread." The devil's challenge seems reasonable under the circumstances, but Jesus turns the tables on Satan and responds, citing the scriptures, "One does not live by bread alone, but by every word that comes from the mouth of God." Jesus is able to forego the desire of power and to rise above the temptation. The power suggested by Satan does not attract Jesus.

The second temptation is prestige. Satan takes Jesus to the pinnacle of the temple, the most sacred place in all Judaism, to make his plea. Satan realizes that Jesus is an important person. His prestige is so great that the heavenly host of angels will not allow any harm to come to Jesus. Thus, he chides the Lord, "If you are the Son of God, throw yourself down; for it is written, 'He will command his angels concerning you, and on their hands they will bear you up, so you will not dash your foot against a stone.' " Jesus is above the fray again. He knows who he is and does not

120

need the recognition suggested by Satan. Knowing he is God is sufficient prestige for Jesus. The prestige that the world claims is so important — namely having people see and recognize your importance — is of no significance for the Lord.

The last great temptation is wealth. Satan takes Jesus to a high mountain and displays before him all the kingdoms of the earth and says, "All these I will give you, if you will fall down and worship me." The irony of the temptation is significant since Satan offers Jesus what he already possesses. All things are from God and, thus, all belongs to God; Satan controls nothing. Jesus responds in what must have been an exasperated tone of voice: "Away with you, Satan! for it is written, 'Worship the Lord your God, and serve only him.' " Jesus already possesses all that he needs. Whatever Satan can offer is of no value, for it is already his.

Jesus' temptations in the desert have been understood by scripture scholars in three different ways. Some suggest that the confrontation was Matthew's way of explaining Jesus' inner turmoil after his baptism — his need to sort out his experience and come to grips with his Messianic consciousness and his future public ministry. The most popular scholarly opinion concerning Jesus' temptation is ethical in nature, suggesting that the events recounted are presented as a model for Jesus' disciples, present and future, on how to resist temptation. The third model held by some scholars is more Christological, seeing in the confrontation what the Matthean community might have understood Jesus to be. The events demonstrate the triumph of the Son of God over the forces of evil. The popular ethical understanding shows how Jesus in his encounter with Satan was able to triumph over evil and was, thus, more faithful than Israel, which had fallen victim to temptation and sin throughout its history. Neither the judges, kings, nor prophets of ancient Israel could reign in the rebellious Hebrews who transgressed God's Law through their idolatry and social indifference to the poor and more marginalized peoples of Hebrew society.

Jesus' obedient action in the desert serves as a counter to the disobedience of Adam, as recounted in the book of Genesis. Adam and Eve transgressed God's command. They had everything they could possibly need; God did not leave out one detail. Yet, they still wanted more; they wanted knowledge and to be like God. Their desire for power, wealth, and prestige cost them everything. They lost their innocence and their place in paradise. Temptation triumphed and sin entered the world. Fortunately, however, even though Adam and Eve failed, Jesus of Nazareth, the new Adam, through his obedience to God triumphed for us. Saint Paul, in one of the most theologically significant passages in his entire corpus (Romans 5:18-19) tells us: "Just as one man's trespass led to condemnation for all, so one man's act of righteousness leads to justification and life for all. For just as by the one man's disobedience the many were made sinners, so by the one man's obedience the many will be made righteous." It is through the obedience of Jesus, countering the sin of Adam, that we have the opportunity to live and even flourish in a sometimes difficult and troublesome world.

Saint Matthew's version of the temptation in the desert is his way to show his readers that any route to the kingdom of God cannot bypass Jesus, yet temptation lurks around every corner. As we celebrate this first Sunday in Lent we must ask ourselves the question, where do we stand, with God or the world? Concerning power — does the desire for power consume us? If we have power do we use it for personal gain or for the betterment of all? Is power a thing of value and a necessity, or can we live without it? With regard to prestige, do we do things so others will notice? Do we use our position to dominate others? Or, do we seek the glory of God and not concern ourselves with what society might think? With respect to wealth, are we seeking to outdistance our neighbor by what we have? Is money the item around which our world revolves? Is it the solution to all our problems or is it simply a means to an end in the consumer-driven society of contemporary American life? In short, have power, prestige, and money become the gods to which we pay homage?

We are often tempted by material things, opportunities, and possibilities of contemporary life — items that we generally know will only lead us away from God. The choice to avoid such temptations is ours and, thus, we must be wary of their allure. A Native American folk tale describes this problem: One day an Indian youth, in an effort to prepare for manhood, hiked into a beautiful valley, green with trees and decorated with many lovely flowers. There he fasted and prayed, but on the third day he looked up at the surrounding mountains and noticed one tall and rugged peak capped with snow. He decided that he would test himself by climbing this mountain. Thus, he put on his buckskin shirt, wrapped a blanket around his shoulders, and set out to climb the peak. When he reached the top he looked out from the rim to the world so far below. Then he heard a rustling sound and, looking around, saw a snake slithering about. Before he could move, the snake spoke to him, "I am about to die. It's too cold for me up here; I am freezing. There is little food and I am starving. Please put me under your shirt where I will be warm and take me down the mountain." The young man protested, "No. I have been forewarned about your kind. You are a rattlesnake. If I pick you up you will bite me and I might die." But the snake answered, "Not so. I will treat you differently. If you do this for me, you will be special to me, I will not harm you, and you will receive whatever you want." The young man resisted for some time, but this was a very persuasive snake with beautiful diamond markings. At last the young man tucked the snake under his shirt and carried it down the mountain. Once in the valley he gently placed the snake on the ground. Suddenly the snake coiled, rattled, and then bit the man on the leg. "You promised me!" cried the youth. "You knew what I was when you picked me up," said the snake, which then slithered away.

Sometimes we rationalize our actions as well. A comical, but illustrative, story shows us how adept we are at this practice: A very overweight man decided that it was time to shed a few pounds. He went on a new diet and took it seriously. He even changed his usual driving route to the office in order to avoid his favorite bakery. One morning, however, he arrived at the office carrying a large, sugar-coated coffee cake. His office mates roundly chided him, but he only smiled, shrugged his shoulders and said, "What could I do? This is a very special cake. This morning, out of my forced habit, I accidentally drove by my favorite bakery. There in the window were trays of the most delicious goodies. I felt that it was no accident that I happened to pass by, so I prayed, 'Lord, if you really want me to have one of these delicious coffee cakes, let me

123

find a parking place in front of the bakery.' Sure enough, on the ninth trip around the block, there it was!"

Temptation is strong, but we must be stronger. We should not tempt fate and we should not rationalize our actions. We need to ask ourselves a fundamental question: Will we stand on the side of the broken and sinful human, the Whiskey Priest, who seeks the glory of God or will we seek the allure of power, wealth, and prestige, cave into temptation and rationalize our actions, like the Federales? God, as Saint Paul reminds us, calls us always to seek the higher realms. Now, our response is awaited.

Lent 2
John 3:1-17

Transformed In Christ

"Hoke, you are my best friend." It took Daisy Werthan almost twenty years to make that statement; it wasn't easy. The relationship between Daisy and Hoke was not mutual or cordial at the outset. Daisy had driven her beautiful new 1948 Packard into her neighbor's backyard. Boolie Werthan, Daisy's son, thought that such an incident was sufficient evidence to warrant that his mother stop driving; she needed a driver, a chauffeur. Hoke Coleburn, a middle-aged black man, was Boolie's choice for the job. Daisy, however, would not accept this restriction, this change in her life; she was not open to being transformed.

Boolie may have hired Hoke, but that did not mean that Miss Daisy had to use him. As Hoke stood idle, Miss Daisy took the street car wherever she went, to the hairdresser or the grocery store. Hoke Coleburn was being paid for doing nothing. That is exactly how Miss Daisy wanted things.

As stubborn as she could be, Miss Daisy ultimately did change her attitude. One day she needed a few things from the store. She left the house and began to walk toward the street car. Hoke decided that Miss Daisy's refusal to use his services needed to end. As she walked down the sidewalk, Hoke slowly drove alongside in the new 1948 Hudson Boolie had purchased for his mother. "Where are you going," scowled Daisy. Hoke replied, "I'm fixin' to take you to the store!" Although still not content with the arrangement, Daisy agreed to get into the car; her conversion had begun.

125

Daisy did not approve, but Hoke had become her chauffeur. Whether it was to the temple, you see Miss Daisy was Jewish, the store, or a trip to Mobile to visit relatives, Daisy and Hoke went together. As the years passed, their relationship as driver and passenger grew; they bonded together. Then one day Miss Daisy's conversion became complete. The process had been long and sometimes difficult, but now it was finished. She could finally say, "Hoke, you are my best friend."

Alfred Uhry's 1988 Pulitzer Prize winning play, *Driving Miss Daisy*, tells more than a story of the relationship between a black chauffeur and an elderly, rich, Jewish widow. It is a story of the challenge to be transformed in mind and heart to a sense of acceptance in one's life. Lent is a season when the church calls us to reflect upon our lives and see how we need to be transformed to a stronger relationship with God. Today's popular and familiar passage from John's Gospel challenges us, like Nicodemus, to be transformed to Christ.

Nicodemus represents the quintessence of Judaism in every way. He was a Pharisee, a member of the Sanhedrin (the governing body of the Jews that was recognized by the Romans), and a rabbi. It is this upstanding and completely legitimate member of the Jewish ruling elite who comes to Jesus, under the secrecy and cover of darkness, to speak with him. From the outset it is clear that Nicodemus recognizes that Jesus is not simply one of the prophets of old, for he addresses him as rabbi, a title used by Jesus' disciples only after they recognize him as the Christ — the anointed one. It is certainly not accidental that the Johannine author uses one of the most prominent men in Jewish society as an example of one who seeks to be transformed to Christ. If the Jewish leadership can see the correct path, then others should follow.

In his conversation with Jesus, Nicodemus is confused on what is necessary to be transformed. The symbolism of being born again of water and spirit is certainly an illusion for John's readers to Christian baptism, but for Nicodemus the confusion is purposeful for it allows Jesus to clearly state his teaching. Jesus, quite clearly, is speaking of the need to be transformed not in any physical way, but in heart and mind. For Nicodemus, the transformation is his understanding of the significance and truth of Jesus' message. In one of the most popular verses that many have memorized from scripture, Jesus succinctly states the basic message of the gospels, in truth the basic message of the New Testament: "For God so loved the world that he gave his only Son, so that everyone who believes in him may not perish, but find eternal life" (3:16). For the new kingdom which Jesus inaugurates to be possible, there is a need for one to experience spiritual re-birth. If a person might fear seeking such a change or transformation in one's life, the individual needs only to realize that "God did not send the Son into the world to condemn the world, but in order that the world might be saved through him" (3:17).

Daisy Werthan needed to be converted — to be transformed. Her attitude toward the loss of her independence needed to be changed. But this did not happen overnight; rather the process she experienced was absolutely necessary for her to eventually be able to say, "Hoke, you are my best friend." Daisy's experience is one illustration of a reality for all — transformation takes time and shortcuts to its end product only lead to problems and disappointments.

The need to stay the course in our transformation can be illustrated in the world of science. One day, a student found a cocoon in the wild and brought it to the biology lab at school. The teacher placed the cocoon in an unused aquarium with a lamp shining on it to keep it warm. After one week a small opening was seen on the underside of the cocoon. The students in the class watched as the cocoon shook and suddenly small antennae emerged, followed by a head and some tiny feet. The students were impatient and wanted to see more. As time went by the insect's listless wings were uncovered, revealing beautiful colors that told all that this was a monarch butterfly. The insect wiggled and shook but could not free itself completely from the cocoon; it appeared to be stuck. Finally one rather impulsive student decided to help the butterfly out of its difficulty. He took some scissors and snipped the cocoon's rather restrictive opening, allowing the insect to free itself. The top half looked like a butterfly with droopy wings, but the bottom half which just emerged from the cocoon was malformed. The butterfly could not fly, but only managed to crawl around the bottom of the aquarium, dragging its wings and swollen body. Within a short time the butterfly died. The next day the biology teacher explained that the butterfly's struggle to free itself from the cocoon was absolutely necessary in order to force the fluid from the lower body into the wings. Without the struggle the wings never developed and the insect could not fly. The struggle was necessary to be transformed.

After realizing that transformation is necessary, and takes time, we must have the courage to ask — what needs transformation in our lives? For some the need is to be transformed in the way we view ourselves. One of the great problems of contemporary society is a lack of self-respect, self-love, and self-confidence. Too often today the world pushes us down, making us feel inadequate. We live in a very intolerant and unforgiving society that demands action, performance, and success. Not making the grade is unsatisfactory. We often lose heart and feel defeated. We might not possess the talent, academic potential, or physical stature or appearance of another, causing us to again think less of ourselves. Such a state of personal disrespect requires transformation.

We need to be able to look into a mirror and not only see, but fully believe, that the reflection we view is a child of God. We need to believe in ourselves and we can with the assistance of another. A good example of such transformation is found in the story of Dulcinea, one of the principal characters in the popular Broadway musical, *Man of la Mancha*. The audience learns that Don Quixote, the chief protagonist, lives with many illusions, most especially his idea that he is a knight errant who battles dragons in the form of windmills. At the end of the play as he lays dying, Don Quixote has at his side a prostitute, Aldonza, whom he has called throughout the play Dulcinea — Sweet One — much to the laughter of the local townsfolk. But Don Quixote has loved her in a way unlike she has ever experienced. When Quixote breathes his last Aldonza begins to sing "The Impossible Dream." As the echo of the song dies away, someone shouts to her, "Aldonza!" But she pulls away proudly and responds, "My name is Dulcinea." The crazy's knight's love had transformed her.

Transformation of our attitudes toward others is also needed by many. Sometimes we place people on the margins and fringes of society, as assuredly as others do to us. There are times, as well, that we place ourselves above others. We separate and differentiate between people — those who can help us and those who cannot, those we consider friends and those we do not, those who live on the proper side of the tracks and those who do not, those who have the correct skin color, or religion, and those who do not. We can create a destructive atmosphere in our relationships with others and not lift one finger. Our attitudes, words, and actions can lift people up or tear them down; it is all up to us!

Lent is a time to transform our personal habits. We need to heed the warnings and advice we have received with respect to personal health and have the courage to change to a more sane, healthier, and more productive lifestyle. We know what we need — to lose weight, stop smoking, cease certain activity — but we often balk. At times we are lazy or do not want to pay the price that the removal of a certain habit will cost.

All of us need to transform our faith practice; there is always more that can be done. We need to do a better job of eliminating sin and resisting temptation. We can make great strides toward the achievement of these goals through our daily prayer. Our conversation with God must be central to the life of all people of faith, yet too often the busy contemporary lifestyle we lead causes us to find and make excuses for not taking time to pray. Transformation means we make prayer a priority and make no excuses for our failures. We need to renew our baptismal commitment and take on with a renewed sense of purpose and fervor our relationship with God. The Pauline author reminds us vividly: "If we have died with him, we will also live with him; if we endure, we will also reign with him; if we deny him, he will deny us; if we are faithless, he remains faithful — for he cannot deny himself" (1 Timothy 2:11-13).

Transformation is, in essence, the process of turning the dirty laundry of our lives into something that is clean and useful. This idea is illustrated in an apocryphal but nonetheless instructive story of the famous British monarch Queen Victoria. One day her highness paid a visit to a paper mill on the outskirts of London. Without realizing who his distinguished visitor was, the foreman showed the Queen around the facility. She went into the rag sorting shop of the mill where workers sorted rags that were refuse from the city. Upon inquiring what was done with these seemingly worthless rags, she was informed that they would eventually become the finest white writing paper. After the Queen's departure the foreman was informed who the special visitor was. Some time later, the Queen received a package of the most delicate, pure white stationery, bearing her likeness for a water mark. Enclosed was a note that said the paper came from the dirty rags she had recently inspected.

Transformation takes courage, for if we do it well the personal discoveries may be revelatory: A man, returning from a weekend retreat reported to his neighbor, "I died this weekend." Puzzled the neighbor asked him what he meant. The man responded, "I went on a retreat not knowing what to expect. What I discovered is that I have been spending my whole life hiding from others behind a whole host of different masks. I realized that even my wife had not seen me as I truly am. I had been playing games with her, my children, and many others — never letting anyone know who I truly am. The worse thing I discovered, however, was that I really didn't know myself. I was not in touch with my feelings and who I really am. As this was being discovered this weekend, I died over and over again." He continued, "It was painful as a middle-aged man to discover that I did not know myself. I am convinced that one needs to go through the death experience in order to become the person Gods wishes us to be."

As our Lenten journey continues, let us look into our hearts, as Miss Daisy was forced to do, and ask the difficult question: "What needs to be transformed in my life?" Then, with the information we have secured, let us courageously go forth and seek new beginnings in attitude, personal conduct, and faith. Let us be transformed to Christ, the one who died to set us free and will one day bring us to eternal life.

Through The Lens Of God

One day a man told a story which touched the hearts of all. He began, "I was a timid, frail, lost, and lonely six-year-old child when I first arrived at the farm in Georgia. I would have remained that way had it not been for an extraordinary woman. She lived on the farm in a small two-room cabin where her parents resided when they were slaves. To any outsider she simply appeared as any other African-American on the farm, but to those who knew her, she had a spiritual force whose influence was felt everywhere she went.

"She was the first person called when a person got sick. She made the medicines from roots and herbs that seemed to cure almost anything. She had a family of her own, but all the children in the area felt they belonged to her. Everyone called her 'Maum' Jean, a slurred version of Mama. Maum Jean spoke to the Lord often and we all suspected that when she spoke, the Lord stopped what he was doing, listened, and took the appropriate action. Her heart reached out to the small and the helpless, so she took a particular interest in me from the start.

"Maum Jean's sensitive, emotional antennae instantly picked up the loneliness and withdrawal I felt, after three years of suffering from polio. Moreover, her marvelous diagnostic sense surveyed the polio damage and decided that, regardless of what the doctors might think, something could and should be done to improve my condition. Maum Jean had never heard the word atrophy, but she knew that muscles could waste away unless used. Thus, every night when her tasks were done she would come to my room and kneel down beside my bed and massage my legs. Sometimes when I would cry out in pain, she would sing old songs or tell me stories. When my treatments were over she would always speak earnestly to the Lord, explaining that she was doing what she could, but that she would need help. She asked the Lord for a sign when he was ready.

"A creek ran through the farm and Maum Jean, who had never heard of hydrotherapy, said there was strength in running water. She made her grandsons carry me down to a sandy bank where I could splash around quite well. I used crutches and often buckled on the clumsy braces I wore. Still, night after night, Maum Jean continued the massaging and prayers.

"Then one morning when I was twelve she told me she had a surprise for me. She led me out into the yard and placed me with my back against a mighty oak. She took away the crutches and braces. She moved back a dozen paces and told me that the Lord had spoken to her in a dream. He had said that it had come time for me to walk. Thus, Maum Jean said, 'I want you to walk toward me.' My instant reaction was fear. I knew I could not walk un-aided. I had tried. I leaned back on the solid support of the tree, but Maum Jean continued to urge me forward. I begged her to stop and I burst into tears. Her voice rose suddenly, no longer gentle and coaxing, but full of power and command. 'You can walk, boy! The Lord has spoken! Now walk over here!' She knelt down and held out her arms. Somehow, impelled by something greater than fear, I took a faltering first step, and another and another, until I reached Maum Jean and fell into her arms, both of us weeping. It was two more years before I was able to walk normally, but I never used crutches again.

"For a while longer I lived in the town, but then one day the circus came to the locale and when it left I went with it. Over the next few years I worked one circus and then another. Then one night Maum Jean's grandsons found me and knocked on my door. She was dying and wanted to see me. I left immediately and fol-lowed the young men back to the town. The area had not changed much, nor had the Maum Jean's cabin. She lay in the bed, sur-rounded by well-wishers. Although her face was in the shadow I heard her whisper my name. I went to her side and she spoke, 'Oh, it's so beautiful.' She then gave a contented sigh and died. Then something remarkable happened. In the semidarkness her face glowed. No one had touched the lamp; there was no other source of light. Her face was plainly visible and she was smiling. It was strange, but not frightening. I could not account for it then, and I can't now.

"This all happened a long time ago, but I still often think of Maum Jean and I remember what she taught me: that nothing is a barrier when love is strong enough — not age, not race, not death, not anything!"[1]

Maum Jean was a woman who broke through barriers in order to bring the love of God to others. She would not take "No" for an answer, but rather pressed forward challenging people to do their best, with the certain knowledge that there was nothing a person could not do, if provided the right tools and environment. In a similar way Jesus, as demonstrated in today's gospel, broke through barriers, refusing to accept the norms of exclusivity common in his day that kept certain people on the fringes. He reached out to all, made bridges of love and friendship, as he brought the message of God to our world.

Reading the gospels shows us that Jesus was constantly in conflict with the religious authorities of his day. He associated with the wrong people, broke the Sabbath, challenged the Hebrew Law, and spoke out against the practices of the temple priests, Pharisees, Scribes, and other Jewish leaders. Today's gospel is a perfect example of how Jesus transforms conventional expectations and challenged the status quo of his world. The Lord broke the strict conventions of his day in two fundamental and important ways. First, he reached out to a Samaritan. The Jews of Jesus' day hated Samaritans. They were the descendants of the ten lost tribes of the Northern Kingdom of Israel, overrun and conquered by the Assyrians 700 years before Christ. It was unthinkable for a self-respecting Jew to have anything to do with a Samaritan, yet Jesus intentionally journeys to this region. Moreover, it was against all accepted practice for a Jewish man to engage a woman in conversation. Yet, Jesus talks with a woman. First-century Jews would have been appalled at such behavior, at the audacity of one who claimed to be a rabbi to engage in such practices. The outrage people felt would have been the same as those who heard Jesus' proclaim his parable of the Good Samaritan (Luke 10:25-37), when the upstanding of Hebrew society, the priest and Levite, pass by the wounded traveler, seemingly unconcerned, while the hated Samaritan treats the man with compassion.

Why did Jesus engage the Samaritan woman in conversation? On the surface it seems that Jesus is thirsty and is asking for assistance to obtain the water of nature. But we need to read more closely and listen more attentively. The waters of nature are of little significance to Jesus at this point. He engages the woman to teach her, the Samaritans, his disciples, and you and me as well, of the need to seek and find the life-giving water which only the Lord can provide. What is this life-giving water? Some might say it is God's wisdom; others may believe it to be God's grace. Still others might see it as faith. I would like to suggest that the living water that Christ gives is his love, which like water overflowing from a full glass pours out in all directions. Jesus' love goes to all people for all time. Jesus wants us to be open to the fresh and new reality of what he is offering, the life-giving water, instead of continuing to view everything from the lens of old realities. The possibilities that Jesus provides are truly remarkable, but we must be sufficiently open in order to recognize them.

For Christians today, this gospel passage must have great significance. As members of Christ's Body (1 Corinthians 12), the church, we are called to stop shaping life according to societal definitions of what is acceptable and comfortable, and to demonstrate our openness to those who are different, as Jesus did in his encounter with the Samaritan woman. The living water of God's love which Jesus invites us to share goes out indiscriminately to all people at all times. Jesus was never exclusive. His inclusive compassion, assistance, and care for others led him to the cross. If we are true to our common vocation to holiness and follow in the footsteps of our Lord, our fate will be the same. But just as Jesus' suffering and cross led to his glory, so if we persevere will we see our own resurrection.

As Jesus came to break down barriers and reach out to all, so must we be willing to do the same. First, we must recognize the reality that we do create barriers. Barriers exist in our lives in many ways that often we don't even realize. We set up boundaries in our relationships with others. There are certain people who we find acceptable and others who are not. If people possess the right credentials, whether that be intelligence, appearance, power, wealth, or influence, then they are on the inside. Those without these credentials are left out. We set up barriers against ourselves. We perceive that we do not possess the requisite credentials, that we don't measure up to the task and we short change ourselves or give up. We set up barriers between ourselves and God. Sometimes the barrier takes the form of lack of attention. We ignore God, placing him in a bottle on the shelf that becomes as dusty as the family Bible. When we need the Lord, only then do we pull the cork and ask for his assistance. Other times the barrier takes the form of ignorance. We seem content in our own world and refuse to look around and acknowledge the pain of our world which cries out for our assistance. We possess certain expectations of others, ourselves, and God and when they are not fulfilled, the disappointment is sometimes severe.

Jesus broke through all convention and he disappointed many whose expectations of the Messiah were not fulfilled, yet the lessons he taught must never be ignored. Jesus taught the Samaritan woman that the love of God is poured out at all times for all people, those we accept and those we do not, including ourselves. Maum Jean became the Christ to that little boy, pouring out her love to him in abundance. Lent is a time when we seek to be transformed and to be renewed. Jesus provides the perfect example and today's celebration is the ideal environment to enter fully into this process. Let us, therefore, be renewed by breaking down the barriers of hostility, hatred, prejudice, and exclusivity. Let us build bridges of friendship, love, peace, and justice. Let us do what we can to build God's kingdom in our world this day. If we can, our reward in heaven will be great.

1. Paraphrased from "Maum Jean," in William J. Bausch's *A World of Stories for Preachers and Teachers* (Mystic, Connecticut: Twenty-Third Publications, 1998), pp. 104-106.

Jesus Cures Our Spiritual Blindness

Anne Mansfield Sullivan was a miracle worker who overcame obstacles in seeking to assist others. Partially blind from birth, she managed to overcome this handicap and graduated from the prestigious Perkins School for the Blind in Boston. The miracle of Anne Sullivan's life, however, had very little to do with her own handicap, but it had everything to do with the multiple handicaps of a young girl. The miracle began to be manifest on March 2, 1887, when twenty-year-old Anne Mansfield Sullivan met six-year-old Helen Keller.

Helen was born in 1880, a healthy and strong child. At nineteen months of age, however, she contracted a disease which left her blind, deaf, and ultimately mute; Helen Keller lived in a world of total darkness and silence. When she was six, Helen's parents, frustrated in their inability to aid their daughter, sought the counsel and advice of the famous inventor of the telephone, Alexander Graham Bell, a man who knew adversity from his own problem with hearing loss. Bell knew Anne Sullivan and arranged for the first meeting between student and teacher.

Anne Sullivan's task was monumental — how could she enter into the world of darkness and silence which was the reality of Helen Keller's existence? The first thing that was necessary was for Anne to gain Helen's confidence, which was accomplished with relative ease. The next step, however, would be much more difficult. Anne needed to teach Helen that her multiple handicaps, her inability to see, hear, and speak like most people, were not impediments at all. Rather, her condition afforded her the opportunity to

137

see, hear, and speak in new and different ways, to communicate on another level. Helen Keller could not see images and she could not read the words on the printed page, but she could feel and, thus, learned to read through the use of braille. Helen could not hear or speak, but she did learn to finger spell and sign in order to communicate with others. Helen Keller learned her lessons well. In fact, she learned so well that in 1904 she graduated *cum laude* from Radcliffe College, one of the most prestigious institutions of higher education for women. She went on to be a successful author and an internationally known celebrity who aided the cause of handicapped people throughout the world. It was the life of Anne Mansfield Sullivan, however, which in many ways was the true miracle. She opened the mind of Helen Keller to a world of possibilities. Maybe it is odd to say, but it seems that normal sight, hearing, and speech were impediments to Helen Keller. Without them she reached her full potential and greatness.

Anne Sullivan was a woman who brought the light to a young woman shrouded in darkness, silence, and fear. She was not able to cure any of the many physical maladies that plagued Helen Keller, but she brought her what may have been more important — that is the light and hope of faith. Jesus, as we hear in today's famous passage from John's Gospel, physically healed the man born blind, but Jesus gave him much more; Jesus secured for him the vision of faith. We, in a similar way, are called to seek the light, cast out the blindness that exists in our lives and do what we can to assist others to do the same.

The story of the man born blind is an excellent example of how John is able to weave narrative and theology in a highly significant way. The evangelist presents a story that demonstrates an important message of how he sees the life and ministry of Jesus. In the blind man's journey from physical blindness to physical and spiritual sight, we are able to watch as one person receives the light and new life in Christ. In contrast, in the Jewish authorities' journey from physical sight to spiritual blindness, one is able to watch as the authorities close off the light, placing themselves at the judgment of God. The message is clear, not only to the people of Jesus' day, but ourselves as well — we must seek the spiritual sight which only Christ can give. But often we refuse to allow the light to penetrate us. We wall ourselves in and hide behind the facade of our own arrogance and ignorance. Jesus' message and the possibility of discovering the light is offered to all. It is through our own free will that we choose to ignore the light and the freedom that it brings. We choose to live in ignorance and darkness. We choose sin over God.

Our world is daily bathed in the light of the sun that brings warmth, direction, and a sense of hope to our world. In the light we can see where we want to go; we have no difficulty choosing the correct path, or so it should be. The reality of our world, however, is that despite the light, we often are shrouded in the darkness of ignorance, unbelief, and silence. The darkness of ignorance is manifest in various ways. We often choose what to believe and refuse to listen to other opinions. Our attitudes toward certain people who may be different from us do not allow us to accept the good they bring. We take one side on issues, especially those that are especially controversial, and will not open our minds and hearts to other viewpoints. We believe that we have the right answers and refuse to read or learn more. Our refusal to change creates a certain ignorance that casts us into darkness and blindness.

The darkness of unbelief and idolatry are rampant in today's world, although, because we fail to recognize it, we believe that such practice is rare and that we normally stand in the light. We may not profess outwardly with our words that we do not believe, or that we worship other gods, but we often bow down to the gods of power, wealth, and prestige. We become blinded to the needs of others through the power that we seek or possess. Power brings possibilities for great progress, but it possesses the potential for great corruption. In seeking to exercise power, we are blinded to the way our actions ill-effect others. Prestige as well can blind us, especially when we feel that all the good we do must become public knowledge so all can recognize our efforts. We live in the false hope and security that our self-importance must be known. The false god of wealth may be the biggest obstacle that blurs our vision of the truth and makes us spiritually blind. We sometimes think that money has all the answers to our problems. Do we see money and the material world in general as a solution or simply as tools in the consumer-driven society in which we live?

Silence can have a deafening effect on our spiritual lives as well. When we see problems and refuse to say anything we are, in essence, living the lie of silence. Sometimes we are not courageous enough to act; other times we feel inadequate to rectify the situation. Silence and inaction, however, allow the darkness to continue and even advance. The light can only dispel the darkness when we make overt efforts to effect change or suggest other avenues of approach.

Lent is a season when we are asked to undergo many trials, as did Jesus in the desert. We are tempted by the things of the world; we are asked to transform our lives; we are told to seek the living water of God's love found in Jesus. Today we are asked to shake off the darkness that shrouds us in blindness. We are asked to seek the light and avoid the darkness.

As Christians we are called as well to share the light with others. A couple of short stories help us to see our role in God's plan. One day the eighteenth-century British writer John Ruskin was looking out his living room window onto the street. It was dusk and the lamplighter was engaged in his nightly routine of lighting the street lamps. From the window he could only see the lamps that were lit and the light the lamplighter was carrying. The lamplighter himself could not be seen. Ruskin wrote that the lamplighter was a good example of the genuine Christian. His way was clearly marked by the lights he lit and the lights he kept burning — even though he may not be seen or known.

A woman involved in a weekly Bible study made a significant discovery quite accidentally in her basement. One day she noticed that some potatoes had sprouted in the darkest corner of the room. At first she could not figure out how they had received any light to grow. Then she noticed that she had hung a copper kettle from a rafter near the cellar window. She kept the kettle so brightly polished that it reflected the rays of the sun onto the potatoes. She exclaimed privately, "When I saw that reflection, I thought, 'I may not be a preacher or a teacher with the ability to expound upon the scriptures, but at least I can be a copper-kettle Christian. I can catch the rays of the Son of God and reflect his light to someone in a dark corner of life.' "

Helen Keller was physically deaf, mute, and blind, but through the efforts of Anne Mansfield Sullivan, a true miracle worker, she was able to see the light. In many ways she could see better than those physically more able. In a similar vein, Jesus not only cured the blind man, he enlightened him and showed him the direction to new life. We are called to cast off darkness and live in the light. We are to be the lamplighter and the copper-kettle Christian. As our Lenten journey continues, let us seek the light and be spiritually enlightened. It is the perfect opportunity to find Christ, and that means eternal life.

Jesus Breaks Our Chains

He was chained, held bound in a life of torment and blasphemy. In the end, however, God would set him free. John Newton, a name probably not familiar to many of us, was born in July, 1725, to a pious English woman and her seafaring husband. From his earliest days, young Newton was attracted to his father's side of the family and to the life at sea. Thus, when he was only eleven years old he became an apprentice aboard his father's vessel, a cargo ship which ferried products throughout the major ports of the Mediterranean region. To say the least at this time in his life John Newton did not know God. Those with whom he associated for the most part on his father's ship were criminals, rogues, and other "undesirables" of society, many of whom were sent to Captain Newton's ship as punishment for some offense in England.

When Newton was nineteen he became a midshipman on another vessel. After only one year, however, he was publicly flogged for insubordination. Despite this event, and most probably with the help of his father, John was able to secure a commission and a few years later his own vessel, a slave trading ship. John Newton commanded a vessel which ferried Africans from their native land to the American colonies. He was good at what he did. He carried out his duties fully and with precision. Still, he felt chained, trapped; he was unable to release himself.

This all changed one night in 1748. That evening, while at sea, Newton's slave ship was caught in a vicious storm. Waves crashed over the bow and the ship was tossed about like a toy. Through the skill of the captain and his crew, the ship and all personnel were saved. The experience, however, changed Newton forever. He felt the chains that held him bound begin to weaken. It took seven more years, but finally, in 1755, John Newton gave up the slave trade and his life at sea. That same year he met John Wesley and George Whitefield, two Episcopal clergymen who at that time were the leaders in the Evangelical revival which would lead to foundation of Methodism in the United States. In 1764, Newton himself was ordained an Episcopal priest. He became a well-known preacher and was the one of the first members of what later became known as the Abolitionist Movement, with such leaders as Daniel O'Connell in Ireland and William Lloyd Garrison in the United States. It was in 1779, however, that Newton wrote some famous words, autobiographical in nature, that are familiar to us all. "Amazing grace, how sweet the sound that saved a wretch like me. I once was lost, but now I'm found, was blind but now I see." Yes, John Newton wrote the words to "Amazing Grace." He was held bound in a life he did not want. In the end, God was the one who set him free.

The life of John Newton serves as a good example to illustrate one central and important idea in today's gospel. Lazarus, representative in John's Gospel for all men and women, was held in the bonds of death, chains from which he could not be released. But Jesus, in an action which led to his own death, breaks the chains of Lazarus' confinement and sets him free. We will one day find ourselves in the chains of death and it is highly unlikely that Jesus will raise us like Lazarus, but our day-to-day journey in life finds us numerous times in various forms of chains from which we need to find release. Jesus is the one who can release us and set us free.

Today's gospel poses an interesting question that might have come to you as it has to me on several occasions: Why were Jesus, Martha, Mary, and Lazarus such good friends? What was the nature of their relationship? We do not know the answers, but we do know that they were very close. Why then does Jesus linger for three days when he learns that one of his best friends is sick, possibly to the point of death? Would any of us so linger if we could go to the aid of one of our friends who needed us? Hopefully not. Jesus answers this question, saying that Lazarus' illness is to show

God's glory. We might take that one step further and say that Jesus lingered so that the Spirit could set Lazarus and all people free from death, not just physical death, but more importantly the deadness that exists inside each one of us in different ways. Jesus says "I am the resurrection and the life." If anyone believes in Jesus, that one will never be without hope. If anyone believes in the Lord that one will never die without the Spirit. Jesus wants Martha, Mary, and all those present, and you and I as well, to know that his presence is not so much to raise us from physical death but to restore hope to all and unchain us from all that holds us back from being the fullness of who we want to be. The words of Jesus at the end of the gospel are powerful indeed, "Unbind him and let him go." Jesus has removed the shackles and chains, the cloth of death from Lazarus. It can be that way for all of us as well.

We know well that God has always been active on behalf of God's people in releasing us from the bonds of this earth's existence. We remember that God broke the shackles of the Israelites in bondage in Egypt through the work of God's servant Moses. Later, God sent the judges and the prophets, the Deborahs and the Esthers, the Isaiahs as well, to guide the people to a better life and understanding of God's way. Ezekiel, one of the major prophets of the Hebrew Scriptures, wrote to the Hebrews while they were in exile in Babylon. Yes, the people were suffering from the physical confinement and isolation from their homeland, but the psychological bonds were probably greater. The people were without hope, they were living in despair. The people most assuredly felt that God had abandoned them, that their fate might be like that of their northern neighbors, the land of Israel, which has been overrun by the Assyrians and lost to history 150 years earlier. But Ezekiel, among others, tells the people that God will breathe life into the community once more. In a famous passage in chapter 37:1-14, the prophet speaks of God bringing life again to the Hebrews who are seen metaphorically as a field of dry bones. As the dry bones come together, with sinews and flesh, and the breath of life is given them, so God will bring life once more to the Hebrews and return them to their land. God will break through the chains that hold the people bound in exile and return them to their land. A new day will dawn and a new spring will blossom.

Yes, God's rescue of the Hebrew people from the land of Babylon and Jesus' raising Lazarus from the dead demonstrate the faithfulness of God in unleashing us from all that binds us. All of us are bound, dead in some way or another. Maybe some of us are held bound by the cares of this world, which have such a strong and popular attraction these days. People seemingly cannot break from the materialism that constantly vies for our attention and calls us to seek to be rich in the eyes of the world. We spend a lot of time "keeping up with the Joneses" and in the process we become trapped in the rat race of contemporary society. For others, a burden in our family, at work, or in the community where we live, might have hold of us and will not let go. Many people must carry heavy crosses in walking the journey of ill health or addiction suffered by a member of their family. Sometimes relationships at work or with our neighbors are tenuous and we feel there is no way to adequately respond or mend the situation. Thus, we choose the easy way out and do nothing. Yet, the problem is not solved and, thus, we are held as a prisoner in a relationship that needs healing. Others are chained by some situation which will not give release. Some may be prisoners of the past, of sin, and falsely believe that no one cares. Many people carry heavy burdens of guilt which are often self-imposed. We cannot forgive ourselves even though others let go many years ago. There are times, as well, that we make ourselves prisoners by our refusal to forgive others. We feel that our anger will somehow make the other person feel badly, but the reality is that such an attitude only hurts ourselves and keeps us as prisoners.

Through our chains, our bonds, there will be a certain sense of dying. Lazarus was caught in the trap of physical death and maybe other forms of death of which we are not aware. The Hebrews were victims of the death of despair, hopelessness, and isolation. Through the action of Christ, the one who brings the light as he reminds his apostles in today's gospel, we are released from all that chains us. All we need is to be open to the action of God in our lives. We can be certain that God is active, for the Spirit sent into the world to guide and direct our every action, is ever-present and faithful. The Spirit can release us from all that binds us. The walking dead, those who are held bound are all around us. They are here today; we are they. There is an answer; there is a release. Jesus says, "Unbind him and let him go." Jesus is the one who can untie us from all that chains us in this life. Let us give our lives over to the Lord so that he can break the bonds that hold us in this life, and, in the end, tie us to God forever in the eternal life that we all hope to share!

Sharing The Pain Of Others

"Rags, rags! Give me your tired, dirty, and old rag and I will give you a fresh, clean, and new one. Rags, rags." That was the cry to which I awoke one bright sunny Friday morning. I sprang from my bed and peered out my second-story apartment window. There he was: the Ragman of our town. He was 6'4" if he was an inch, youthful in appearance and strong of build. I had heard so much about him but never actually seen him. I threw on some clothes, bounded down the stairs, and ran out the front door of my apartment building. I thought, this is my opportunity to see where he goes and what he does. I decided to watch at a distance.

The Ragman pushed his basket of rags ahead of him. He continued his cry, "Rags, rags. Give me your old, tired, and dirty rag and I will give a fresh, clean, and new one. Rags, rags." As the Ragman pushed his basket of rags he came across a young woman who sat on the front porch to her home. Even from a distance I could see that she held a handkerchief to her face which was swollen and her eyes were red. She had been crying. "Please," said the Ragman to the young woman, "give me your old and soiled handkerchief and I will give you a clean and fresh one." The woman looked at the Ragman with a puzzled stare, yet she agreed to his request. The Ragman pulled out a clean and fresh linen handkerchief. When the woman put the cloth to her face, something wonderful happened. Her face was no longer swollen; her eyes were no longer red. She appeared happy and gay. But when the Ragman put the woman's handkerchief to his face, he began to cry, his eyes

149

turned red, and his face began to swell. My amazement at what I was witnessing knew no bounds. And the Ragman continued on.

He pushed his basket of rags ahead of him as he walked through the city streets. He came to the main square and there on a park bench he encountered another woman. She was older and her clothes were dirty and torn. Around her head was a bandage from which blood oozed from a fresh wound. The Ragman said to her, "Please give that old and dirty bandage and I will give you a new and clean one." The woman looked at the Ragman with disdain, yet there was something in what he said, or how he said it, that attracted her. She took the bandage from her head and replaced it with the fresh one given her. As she placed the bandage on her head, the blood flow stopped. No longer was her face tortured with pain. When the Ragman placed the old bandage on his head, he began to bleed in the same place the woman had been injured. His face took on the look of one in pain. I continued to wonder at what I saw, and the Ragman continued on.

Bleeding and crying, the Ragman continued to push his basket of rags. He came upon the local town drunk who was sleeping off his night of frivolity between two buildings in the center of town. The Ragman approached, quietly, so as to not disturb the man. He pulled the old blanket from the man and covered him with a new and clean one. He also left a set of new clothes. As the Ragman wrapped the old blanket around him, he began to stagger and stumble as if he was the one who had been drinking. And the Ragman continued on.

The Ragman continued to push his cart, stumbling as he went, leaving a trail of blood and tears. He came to the edge of town. There he encountered someone whom I did not know. He must have been a new person in town. He was an older man with only one arm who wore a tattered jacket. "Give me that old coat," said the Ragman, "and I will give you a new and clean one." The man readily agreed, after all he was to get a new coat out of the deal. As the old man put on the new jacket not one but two arms came through, arms that were strong and youthful. But when the Ragman put on the coat of the old man, only one arm came through. As I watched I could not believe what I saw. The Ragman continued on.

The Ragman, bleeding, crying, stumbling, and with one arm continued to push his basketful of rags. At the outskirts of town he found the local dump. With the remaining strength he possessed he pushed his basket through the gate and up the hill. There in the middle of the garbage dump he lay down to sleep and as he slept he died. From a distance I found safe haven in the front seat of an old abandoned vehicle in the dump. I began to cry, so powerful were the events that I had witnessed. My tears put me to sleep — a deep and restful slumber. Friday was lost and Saturday passed without my knowing it. But the next day, Sunday morning I awoke to the most brilliant light. There before me stood the Ragman. He had a small scar on his head, but both his arms were restored. He was dressed in the most glorious white clothes I had ever seen. Yes, he was the Ragman of our town; he was the Christ.[1]

Today, my friends, the Christian community throughout the world begins its most sacred and special time, Holy Week. The church provides this very special week so that we can journey with Jesus and remember the great events that led to our salvation. Our journey begins today and ends on Easter morning, but there are several important and intermediate steps. Through this week we will learn as the story tells us that there is a price to pay to find God's glory and that cost is the need to suffer, to pass through the difficulties in life in order to find the eternal reward of everlasting life which is God's promise to all who believe. If we are to find the great gift which we all seek, namely eternal life, there is a price to pay. We must follow the Lord and suffer as he did. If we bear the name Christian we can expect no better lot than the one whom we follow.

Today, Jesus enters in triumph into the holy city of Jerusalem, but as we know and our gospel indicates, it is, unfortunately a false greeting. The people sing "Hosanna" and lay palms in Jesus' path, but in five days the reality of Jesus' mission will become very clear. Jesus will be executed as a common criminal. We might ask, what was it that irritated the Jewish officials so much that their only recourse was capital punishment? In our society people

151

are sentenced to death for the most heinous crimes, but Jesus did nothing of that nature. Jesus was certainly a man who challenged the sensibilities of the ruling Jewish ecclesiastical elite. The gospels provide numerous examples of how Jesus broke the law, which was so sacred and inviolate to the Jews. He ruffled more feathers when he continually associated with outcasts of various natures — sinners, the diseased, women, and foreigners. He ridiculed the religious leaders of his day in many ways, but none more pointed than through parables, such as the Good Samaritan. Maybe most problematic for the Jews was that the Jesus demonstrated through signs, and even stated that he was God. This outrage against the unanimity of God, might have been the straw that broke the camel's back. He forgave sins and claimed to be God's Son. The Jewish religious leaders found Jesus highly dangerous and, thus, they resorted to extreme means to solve their problem.

The passion narratives are presented by all four evangelists. The cruel and outrageous punishment to which Jesus of Nazareth was subjected is beyond comprehension in modern society. While people debate both sides of the issue of capital punishment, we as a society have chosen in recent years to exercise a method (lethal injection) which could be seen as less violent. Jesus' death, however, was horribly violent. Yet, strange as it seems to us today, Jesus did not go to the cross in handcuffs, nor did he go kicking and screaming. No, he went to the cross willingly. He chose to die to set us free. Such love Jesus showed to lay down his life for us. Now we, the contemporary disciples of Jesus, must follow his lead.

Holy Week is a rare and blessed time, a special opportunity to walk in the footsteps of the Lord. Since Jesus did not shy away from the fate that he knew was his, we, if we truly seek to be disciples, must not shy away from the opportunities that come our way to be the Christ to others and share their burdens. The Ragman willingly took on the pain and suffering of those he encountered. He shouldered their crosses and lifted their burdens. Jesus similarly took on the pain and suffering of all people for all time. As Saint Paul says in his letter to the Romans (5:18-19), "Therefore just as one man's trespass led to condemnation for all, so one man's act of righteousness leads to justification and life for all. For just as by the one man's disobedience the many were made sinners, so by the one man's obedience the many will be made righteous." We must do likewise and share the burdens of those we encounter. Holy Week is the perfect opportunity for us to reflect upon how we can better assist others in walking the road that is often littered with hurdles, potholes, and other obstacles. Some people are in pain — sometimes physical but more often psychological. Others are alienated from family, friends, church, or society. Many live on the fringes of society, not because of their own desires, but through the attitude and conduct of others. We are called to be the Ragman, the Christ, and shoulder their burdens and share their pain.

Let us, therefore, during this sacred and blessed Holy Week take some extra time in our very busy lives to consider what we can do willingly, as did Jesus, to share the burdens of others. We begin today on Palm Sunday and we will continue throughout the week. Our journey may take us to the streets or to the interior of the heart, but let us take up the challenge. This journey, if traversed well will bring us suffering, pain, and death, but in the end we will find with Jesus, resurrection and eternal life.

---

1. Walter Wangerin, Jr., *Ragman And Other Cries Of Faith* (San Francisco: Harper and Row, 1984), pp. 3-6.

The Price Of God's Glory

Long ago, on a high mountaintop, three trees were speaking about their future dreams. The first tree said, "I would really like to be made into a cradle so that a newborn baby might rest comfortably and I could support that new life." The second tree looked down at a small stream that was flowing into a big river and said, "I want to be made into a great ship so I can carry useful cargo to all corners of the world." The third tree viewed the valley from its mountaintop and said, "I don't want to be made into anything. I just want to remain here and grow tall so I can remind people to raise their eyes and think of God in heaven who loves them so much."

Years passed and the trees grew tall and mighty. Then one day three woodcutters climbed the mountain in order to harvest some trees. As they cut down the first tree one of the men said, "We will make this one into a manger." The tree shook its branches in protest; it did not want to become a feed box for animals. It had grander ideas for its beauty. But the woodcutters made it into a manger and sold it to an innkeeper in a small town called Bethlehem. When the Lord Jesus was born, he was placed in that manger. Suddenly the first tree realized it was cradling the greatest treasure the world had ever seen. As the woodcutters cut down the second tree they said, "We will make this into a fishing boat." The tree shook its branches in protest; it did not want to become a simple fishing boat. The woodcutters did as they planned and a man named Simon Peter bought it. When the Lord Jesus needed a place from which to address the crowds that were pressing upon him, he got into the little fishing boat and proclaimed the good news. The second tree suddenly realized it was carrying the most precious cargo, the King of heaven and earth.

The woodcutters then came to the third tree and said, "The Romans are paying good money these days for wooden beams for their crosses. We will cut this tree into beams for a cross." The tree protested so hard that its leaves began to shake and then fall onto the ground, but it was cut down, nonetheless, and made into beams. One Friday morning, the third tree was startled when its beams were taken from a woodpile and shoved onto the shoulders of a man. The tree flinched when soldiers nailed the man's hands to the wood; the tree felt shamed and humiliated. But early on Sunday morning, as the dawn appeared, the earth trembled with joy beneath the tree. The tree knew that the Lord of all the earth had been crucified on its cross, but now God's love had changed everything. The cross from that third tree stands tall to remind people to raise their eyes and think of the God in heaven who loves them. Did you notice, how in each case, being cut down was the price that was paid for entering into God's glory?

Our journey of Holy Week has reached a critical point. Today we commemorate an event, which on the surface is filled with remorse and sadness, as the Savior of the world, Jesus Christ, is put to death by angry men. What had Jesus done that was so onerous that it led to his crucifixion? The answer is that Jesus had done nothing that would merit such punishment, yet in obedience to the Father's will, he was cut down in the prime of life, as the one acceptable sacrifice for the salvation of all humankind. We must understand that if we truly wish to follow in the footsteps of the Master there will be a measure of dying along the way. Jesus says it so plainly: "Very truly, I tell you, unless a grain of wheat falls in the earth and dies, it remains just a single grain; but if it dies, it bears much fruit. Those who love their life lose it, and those who hate their life in the world will keep it for eternal life" (John 12:24-25).

The price that must be paid to find the glory of God is to a large extent not what we want or are often willing to pay; we must be open to what is not expected and what we would rather avoid.

We must be willing to suffer. But people today ask why should one suffer? Why would anyone willingly pay the price of the trees so as to enter into God's glory? We hear an answer in the gospel we have heard proclaimed. In Saint John's portrayal of the crucifixion, the high point and greatest achievement of Christ's life, is his death on the cross. Contrary to what most might see, namely the resurrection as Jesus' greatest triumph, Saint John sees the suffering Christ as the epitome of the Christian call. Jesus not only goes to the cross willingly, as depicted by the synoptic evangelists, he finds his greatest exaltation in his willingness to sacrifice his own desires and needs for the betterment of all. Jesus finds his glory in being cut down for all. If we wish to be true disciples, then we must follow, fully. If we believe that Jesus' death is salvific, then to follow his lead will assist us along our journey home. Yet, many are unwilling to suffer. Obviously, no one seeks to bring pain upon oneself, but the question remains — do we avoid such pain at all costs; do we run and hide from its manifestations? Or, can we realize that the road may be difficult, but for those who hold out, the greatest of all treasures, eternal life with God will be the reward? G. K. Chesterton summarized the dilemma in 1910 when he wrote, "The Christian ideal has not been tried and found wanting. It has been found difficult and left untried."

Jesus used his gift of free will to carry the cross of others and in the process set them free from all their burdens. We must be willing to do the same. Almost every day God provides opportunities for us to assist others to carry their burdens. In our lives we encounter people who are terribly burdened. It may be a youth who needs more than our assistance in the academic realm, but wants a person to listen and possibly offer a word of advice about the many things young people deal with these days. The cross we lighten might be showing others the need to release the baggage that they carry from past hurts, and telling them that holding onto grudges and bad memories does nothing to punish those who caused the problem, but only hurts those who carry the burden today. We may even be able to assist a member of our family, a close friend, or a colleague at work, to shoulder the burden of ill health, to meet the challenges associated with various problematic neighborhood situations, or even reconciling differences between ourselves and others.

The price to pay as a disciple of Christ is high — in fact, if we follow well, it will cost us our whole lives. Dietrich Bonhoeffer, the famous Lutheran pastor and theologian, wrote in *The Cost of Discipleship*, a book that has been influential to many, "When Christ calls a man, he bids that man to come and die." Bonhoeffer lived his Christian call to holiness without counting the cost, and he did what God asked of him without qualification, reservation, or question. He did not look over his shoulder and wonder why, but rather, he lived what he wrote, for his call to discipleship cost him his life. Staying one step ahead of the Nazis, Bonhoeffer courageously maintained an underground seminary and wrote in opposition to Hitler's regime and his ideology of anti-Semitism. In the end, he was incarcerated and executed on April 9, 1945, only days before the allied liberation of his concentration camp.

God will always be with us to assist and encourage, especially when things get rough and the path is often obscured and even invisible. Today, a day of remembrance for how our inattention and sinfulness has been hurtful to the Lord, is also a day when we see that it is only through the suffering of life that we will find the eternal reward we seek. However, we must have complete trust and confidence in the Lord. We can trust the Lord, and willingly use our free will to accept Jesus' invitation and to suffer for the good of the world. If we have any doubt that this is true, picture this image: It is a hot, beautiful summer day, and a little girl stands on the edge of a large swimming pool. She looks out at the shimmering water and her eyes well up with tears. She is afraid because she does not know how to swim. Then, she raises her eyes, looks out and sees her mom, with her arms outstretched. Mom says, "Go ahead, jump in, there is nothing to fear; I will hold you up." In a similar way, my friends, Jesus has his arms outstretched on the cross and he says to all of us, "Go ahead, take a chance, shoulder the burden of others. I will hold you up; I will bring you to eternal life."

Jesus Transforms The
Darkness Into Light

Pastor David Johnson was all ready, he thought, for his Easter sermon. Having only graduated from the seminary three months prior to taking his present position at the Maple Street Community Church, he possessed all the latest and most interesting theology. He made the final touches to his sermon on Holy Saturday morning and outlined its content to his wife. He told her that his sermon was based on theology of Paul Tillich and spoke of the resurrection as a symbol that the estrangement from our authentic self was over. His wife shook her head, but David didn't seem to notice.

Early that evening, David drove to the church for the rehearsal of the sunrise service the next morning. When the practice ended, a youth, lovingly called "Tiny" because of his six-foot five-inch frame, asked, "Pastor, can you give me a ride home?" David said he would be glad to do so, but that the young man would have to give him directions. With Tiny pointing the way, David delivered the youth home without incident. When he left, however, he could not remember if he was to turn right at the end of the cement and left at the crossroads or the other way around. It had only taken ten minutes to reach Tiny's home, but now after twenty minutes of driving he found himself on a deserted dirt road, totally lost. When the car sputtered he realized he was out of gas.

David was overcome with anxiety. It was 10 p.m. on Holy Saturday evening, he was lost, out of gas, and needed to be at the church by 6 a.m. to set up for the sunrise service. He got out of the car and began to walk. Ten minutes later he saw some bright lights up ahead on the right. As he drew closer he could see that the lights came from a bar, the neon sign reading "The Boondocks." Everyone, including those new to the community like David, knew that this was one of the seediest taverns in town. As he walked to the front door he saw a group of motorcycles which made him nervous. When he entered, he smelled rancid beer and the stench of tobacco. He did not see anyone he recognized, a fact that was both good and bad. He wondered what church members might think if they knew their pastor was at "The Boondocks" on Holy Saturday night.

David approached the bar intending to ask for a ride to town but found himself ordering a coke and, noticing a billiard table behind him, soon engaged in a game. David had played pool since he was six and was very good. This night, however, he was fantastic; he twice ran the table after the break. This action was noticed by Turk, a short but powerful "biker" who, taking off his leather jacket, challenged David to a game. Turk was good, but that evening David was better. After three consecutive wins, Turk conceded defeat. He bought David another coke and announced that henceforth David would be called "Shark." He then asked the inevitable question, "What do you do?" David was uncertain to tell the truth or lie, but he summoned his courage and said, "I'm a minister in town at the Maple Street Community Church." The crowd was shocked and began to mumble, but from the background Turk bellowed, "Quiet!"

Immediately the mood in the bar changed and the patrons, one-by-one began to tell their stories. When Turk's turn came, he began, "I've never been to church. My mother was never married so people told her she was not good enough for any church. I've never been to Sunday school, either. What I know about the Bible comes from television. I don't even know what we celebrate at Easter." All the eyes of the patrons trained on David, who realized that Turk had given him an invitation and he needed to respond. Thus, David began to tell all assembled about Jesus. David told about Jesus' birth and how when Jesus was old enough, he began a public ministry. David told them that those who were rich and powerful had little time or energy for Jesus, who reached out in a special way to those who were despised by society at large. Jesus did many wonderful things, cured many of diseases, forgave sins, and demonstrated love in every word and action of his life.

After three years of active work, Jesus, who mostly stayed in the northern section of his nation ventured south to the capital city of Jerusalem. Although he had done many wonderful things and taught people about the love of God, he was, nonetheless, hated by many of the very people whom he came to save. Thus, on Friday, after a kangaroo court had agreed he was guilty of high crimes, he was led to crucifixion, wearing a crown of thorns. All his best friends abandoned him, save a couple who watched all these horrible events. Because he was tortured so severely, Jesus died on the cross after about three hours. His loyal friends took him down and laid him in a tomb. Hearing the story, several of those in the bar began to cry openly.

David then told the men that on Sunday morning Jesus' friends went to the tomb to visit, but they met two angels who told them that Jesus was no longer there; he had risen and was alive. Later that day Jesus appeared to his friends, the same ones who had abandoned him just a few days before.

Turk and the others were impressed but they said, "That is a crazy story." David responded, "It is a crazy world. But our God can turn losers into winners; he has shown many times that what most believe is weakness in a person is truly strength. He demonstrated that God will always be there for us. By raising his Son from death, God has destroyed death forever."

When all was said David then told Turk about his car problem. Quickly the rugged "biker" siphoned some gas from another vehicle, gave David directions, and sent him on his way. When he arrived home, his wife, who was obviously concerned about her husband's late return, told him that he needed to get to bed and rest, but he told her, "I need to rewrite my sermon." The next day, David did not talk about "New Being" or estrangement from authentic selfhood; he simply told the story of how God raised Jesus from the dead and in the process gave him and all people new life and hope. People in the congregation thought the sermon was good, but what really got them talking was the strange group of visitors who parked their shiny motorcycles in front of the church and sat

161

in one of the front pews. When one of the ushers inquired about the visitors, one burly man, obviously uncomfortable in a suit and tie, growled, "We are friends of Shark."

Pastor Johnson's encounter with Turk and his friends at The Boondocks is a story of transformation and conversion, the movement from death to life. A chance and unintended meeting between a young and inexperienced minister and a hard-bitten "biker" allowed both to cast off blindness, the veil that kept them in darkness, and to discover new vistas never before explored. Today as we celebrate this festival day of Easter, we are challenged to see Jesus' conquering of sin and death, his movement from death to life, as the opportunity and experience we need to transform our own lives and conform them to that of the risen Lord.

The Lenten journey just ended provided many opportunities for us to evaluate our lives of faith and make adjustments. Initially we were challenged to go to the desert with Jesus and be tempted with the three great sins of contemporary society — power, wealth, and prestige. Today's world is filled with examples of overindulgence in these areas. We find ourselves bowing down and giving homage to these contemporary "gods." Jesus was strong enough to say no to such temptation; we must do the same. Then we went up to the top of the high mountain and witnessed, along with Peter, James, and John, Jesus' transfiguration. What we experienced in Jesus' physical nature was the goal we set for our spiritual selves. We sought to be converted on the inside to a new and stronger relationship with Christ. We then journeyed to Samaria and overheard Jesus' conversation with the woman at Jacob's well. We sought, as did she, the living water which Jesus offered. We were told of our need to break down barriers that keep us from one another and from God. Then we encountered Lazarus and realized that as Jesus set him free from the chains of death, we are often bound by other forms of chain that hold us hostage and do not allow us the freedom to pursue the life God asks of us. Jesus is the one who can unbind us from these restraints and set us free.

In today's gospel, we hear how Jesus conquers death and encourages us to be transformed. What needs transformation? The answer can be found through a question posed in today's gospel.

John reports of the "Beloved Disciple," "He saw and believed." What did John see and thus believe that day? He saw that the tomb was empty and realized that his life was full, cluttered with many things. The question for him was — could he empty himself enough to receive God, the risen Lord?

We need to ask ourselves the same question. Can we see and believe or are our lives too cluttered to receive God? We are all busy people; we are addicted to many things. Some of us are addicted to work; some are addicted to school. Some people are addicted to pleasure. Some, unfortunately, are addicted to themselves. At times we are so busy that our priorities get messed up. Sometimes our addictions come ahead of our God. It cannot be this way, if we are to see and believe!

We might not feel comfortable doing nothing, just being. It is difficult to accept the moment. However, if we empty ourselves somewhat, then we can make room for God and God's works. In order to make room we must have the hope that God can fill our needs and desires. I have often questioned why the apostles were running to the tomb. After all, Jesus had died, was there any need to run? They must have had the hope that Jesus' promise, namely that he would rise, was true, and, thus, they ran to find the resurrected Christ. The reality of Jesus' resurrection is a message of hope for our own resurrection. But our resurrection need not wait until our union with God in eternity. We can begin now by emptying ourselves. If we are empty enough, if we are open, then we have chosen, as Saint Paul suggests in his writings (Colossians 3:1), the higher realm which comes from God. We will then be able to find God and in the process perform the works of the Lord, preaching, teaching, good works, and healing.

Jesus' resurrection asks us to revive the human spirit deep down inside each one of us and be transformed like Pastor Johnson and the others in The Boondocks. The empty tomb encourages us to be empty enough to be filled with God. Let us today be resurrected; let us empty ourselves and let us be transformed so that we too can see and believe!

163

Enduring The Trials Of Faith

"In the seventh year of his reign, two days before his sixty-fifth birthday, in the presence of a full consistory of cardinals, Jean Marie Barette, Pope Gregory XVII, signed an instrument of abdication, took off the Fisherman's ring, handed his seal to the Cardinal Camerlengo and made a curt speech of farewell." So begins the power novel *The Clowns of God*, the second volume of a trilogy of tales about popes and faith written by Morris West, the Australian-born author. In the story, the pope has seen a vision of the Second Coming. He feels that the message of Christ's return must be promulgated throughout the world. Therefore, he gathers his closest advisors, the curia and college of cardinals, and asks their advice. They tell him that such a message cannot be published. "It will throw the world into a panic," they claim. The pope is confused but feels that he has only one alternative. He must be true to himself and, thus, he abdicates his position and places himself under the obedience of an abbot in a monastery outside of Rome.

After one week at the monastery, Jean Marie receives his first visitor, Carl Mendelius, a long-time friend and former Jesuit priest, who now, as a married man, is teaching theology in a prestigious German university. The two friends speak and begin to map out a strategy whereby the message of Jean Marie's vision can be promulgated to the world. The plan is foiled, however, before it can be enacted. Mendelius, working in Germany, is felled by a letter bomb sent by a would-be assassin just as he is ready to present the text of the message to a group of scholars. Jean Marie, in England to give a speech where the message will be revealed, suffers a severe heart attack. As he clings to life in a London hospital, Jean Marie receives a strange visitor. The man is young, about thirty years old, tall, strong, and speaks with a Middle East accent, although his origin seems a mystery. He wears a beautiful and ancient ring which has inscribed on it the Christian symbol of a fish. This man calls himself Mr. Atha. The stranger tells Jean Marie that he must persevere but that the message which he feels must be told has already been proclaimed if people will only recognize it.

Several weeks later Jean Marie returns to his native France to recuperate fully. One day he goes for a walk in Parisian park, sits down, and observes a group of children playing nearby who are mentally handicapped. These children accept their fate without a word of objection. Through this experience Jean Marie begins to realize that the essential message of his vision is to accept God and to endure the trials of faith. The unpretentious lives of these children, whom he calls the "Clowns of God," have made the message crystal clear.

Months later, in a remote mountain villa, Jean Marie joins his new-found friends, the Clowns of God, to celebrate the Christmas feast. To this isolated place, Mr. Atha comes quite unexpectedly. Jean Marie has endured the great trial of faith and discovered Jesus, who has returned to claim the world.

Morris West's epic tale describes how one man was challenged to look beyond the obvious in order to find the presence of God. The former pope was forced to endure a great trial of faith, not because he chose, but only out of necessity. Trials of faith are an everyday part of life, although some may not be as obvious as others. We must learn, as did Jean Marie Barette, to persevere and continue along the road, despite the pain and setbacks that may come our way. We will find, as did Jean Marie, that through the trials and tribulations of life, we will gain strength and be that much better prepared to follow in the footsteps of the Lord.

The trials of faith that come our way are part and parcel of the mission to which all God's children, the baptized, are called. In his gospel, Saint John presents a rather unique connection between the Easter event and the concept of service which must be integral to our lives. Through the reading we just heard, John demonstrates the connection between Christ's resurrection and the mission of the church. Jesus appears to his disciples, despite the locked doors, and tells his best friends, those who have walked the journey with him, "As the Father has sent me, so I send you" (20:21b). He then breathed on them as a sign of the presence of the Spirit that was now upon them. In his first meeting with the disciples after the resurrection, Jesus commissions his best friends to go forward and continue his work. The ministry would not be easy and the methods of approach not always effective or clear, but the call was made. The response of the apostles was to be awaited.

We, the contemporary disciples of Jesus, have been challenged to answer Jesus' call to labor in the vineyard. As Jesus says, "The harvest is plentiful, but the laborers are few; therefore ask the Lord of the harvest to send laborers to his harvest" (Matthew 9:37-38). Our response will vary but in essence we are all called to be servants, but most especially to those who are least brothers and sisters (Matthew 25:40). We may assist in direct service to God and God's people in some ministry that is allied with the specific works of the church. Most of us, however, will serve the collective whole though our day-to-day jobs. To some, our eight-to-five job might not seem to be God's work, but all that we do has the possibility of giving praise and glory to God. The attitude we take and exercise in the routine of our day dictates whether our labors are directed toward the betterment of God and God's people or simply to assist ourselves and a few select others. All that we say and do must in some way be the work of God. This is a great challenge in a world that centers on self-achievement and satisfaction.

The work we do, and the lives we lead, are part of God's master plan that necessitates, at times, that we negotiate hurdles that are trials of faith. The familiar story of Thomas' encounter with the resurrected Lord is, like the events in the life of Jean Marie Barette, a classic tale of a significant trial of faith. Thomas is not present when Jesus appears, breathing the Holy Spirit upon the apostles and commissioning them to go forward to complete his work in this world. Thomas seems to be a realist; if he doesn't see, he will not believe. Even after having walked with the Lord in his public ministry for three years, if Saint John's chronology is correct, and seeing all the miraculous cures and inexplicable events in Jesus' life, Thomas is unable to negotiate the hurdle of faith that requires him to believe without seeing. When the Lord again appears and shows himself before Thomas, the apostle is apologetic, but Jesus is not pleased: "Put you finger here and see my hands. Reach out your hand and put it in my side. Do not doubt but believe." Even after Thomas' mournful cry, "My Lord and my God," Jesus continues, "Have you believed because you have seen me? Blessed are those who have not seen and yet have come to believe" (John 20:27-29).

The work that we do, the ministry in which we participate, is a significant part of the life that God gives us, a life that is often dotted with bumps, obstacles, road blocks, and detours. At times it seems that nothing goes right, that the challenges of faith are too great. We must remember the positive story of Jean Marie Barette and his encounter with the Clowns of God and contrast it with the failure of Thomas to know that there is an absolute need to persevere and maintain faith so as to get through the dark tunnels of life to find the light on the other side.

All of us experience trials of faith — how do we fare? Our faith is tried through sickness or death. Do we continually ask why — why my relative or friend is sick, why God chose to claim a member of my family? Or, do we seek ways from which we can draw renewed and strengthened faith from the trial we must endure. Faith can be tried through the pain of unemployment. If we lose our job or cannot find work does it destroy our faith? Do we become angry; do we cry out and ask where is God? Or, does such a trial of faith allow us greater communion and better understanding of the chronically unemployed, those who cannot work because of a mental or physical handicap? Faith can be tested through problem and broken relationships. Does the separation of friends, the pain of divorce or rejection in love make us "throw in the towel"; do we say, "I can't go on"? Or, does our trial of faith lead us to greater independence; does it allow us to feel better about ourselves? Can we say, "God loves me"?

We have all had trials of faith and we know others who have had similar experiences. Can we accept the trial and learn, as did Jean Marie Barette, that the Clowns of God, those more vulnerable people in our world, can show us the way that leads to life? Or, are we like Thomas and refuse to believe? When trials come, do we say, "I want no part of this; it isn't fair"?

Should we need more encouragement to keep moving through the trials of faith in our lives? The true story of Bill Mitchell will inspire even the least confident of heart: On the morning of June 19, 1971, Bill Mitchell was on top of the world. Riding his brand new motorcycle to a job he loved, gripman on a San Francisco cable car, Bill seemed on cloud nine. Earlier that day he had soloed in an airplane for the first time, the fulfillment of one his fondest dreams. Twenty-eight — handsome, healthy, and popular — Bill was in his element. In the flash of an eye, however, Bill's whole world changed. Rounding a corner as he neared the cable car barn, Bill collided with a laundry truck. Gas from the motorcycle poured out and ignited through the heat of the engine. Bill emerged from the accident with a broken pelvis and elbow and burns over 65 percent of his body.

The next six months were a period of great trial for Bill. After several blood transfusions, numerous operations, and many skin grafts, Bill was released from the hospital. Walking down the street, he passed a school playground where the children stared at his face. "Look at the monster," they exclaimed. Although he was deeply hurt by the thoughtlessness of the children, he still had the love and compassion of friends and family, and the grace of a good personal philosophy on life. Bill realized that he did not have to be handsome to make a contribution to society. Success was in his hands if he chose to begin again.

Within a year of the accident, Bill was moving again toward the success he enjoyed earlier. He began to fly planes. He moved to Colorado and founded a company that built wood stoves. Within no time, Bill was a millionaire with a Victorian home, his own plane, and significant real estate holdings.

In November 1975, however, the bottom again fell out of Bill Mitchell's world. Piloting a turbo-charged Cessna with four passengers onboard Bill was forced to abort a take-off, causing the plane to drop about 75 feet like a rock back to the runway. Smoke filled the plane and fearing that he would again be burned Bill attempted to escape. Pain in his back and his inability to move his legs thwarted his efforts.

In the hospital again, Bill was informed that his thoracic vertebrae were crushed and the spinal cord was damaged beyond repair. He would spend the rest of his life as a paraplegic. Although doubt began to invade his generally optimistic mind, Bill began to focus on the cans and not the cannots of his life. He decided to follow the advice of the German philosopher Goethe: "Whatever you can do, or dream you can do, begin it. Boldness has genius, power, and magic in it." Before his accidents, there were many things Bill could do. He could spend his time dwelling on what was lost or focus on what was left.

Since that 1975 plane accident, Bill Mitchell has twice been elected mayor of his town, earned recognition as an environmental activist, and has run for Congress. He has hosted his own television show and travels the nation speaking to groups about his message of proper attitude, service, and transformation. Bill's message is to show people that it isn't what happens to you that is important, but how you handle the trials of faith in your life. Let us have the courage that he exhibited. Let us triumph over the trials of our lives. Let us be strengthened by our faith. Let us believe that the trials of faith we weather can bring us closer to God and to eternal life.

Defeat Transformed Into Victory

Two men, both seriously ill, shared the same room in a hospital. One of the men was allowed each day to sit up for an hour to clear the fluid from his lungs. His bed was next to the only window in the room. The other man was forced to lie on his back at all times. The two men would talk for hours each day, discussing their families, the jobs they hoped to return to, their common service in the military, and even vacations they had taken. Each afternoon, the man by the window would describe to his roommate what he saw. The other man lived for those special times each afternoon. He would lay back, close his eyes, and imagine all that was being described.

The man by the window told his roommate that he could see a beautiful park with a lake. Ducks and swans played on the water while children floated their plastic boats. Young lovers walked arm-in-arm through beautiful flowers that adorned the periphery of the lake. He could even see the beautiful skyline of the city in the distance. One exceptionally warm afternoon the man by the window described a parade that was passing by on the street below. The other man could not hear the bands, but he could certainly imagine the scene. This situation went on for days and then weeks.

One day, the day nurse came in to give the two men their medicines. At that time she noticed the lifeless body of the man by the window who had died peacefully in his sleep. She was sad, but called the hospital orderlies who removed his body. When he thought it was appropriate, the other man asked if he could be moved next to the window. The nurse arranged the transfer and when the man was settled she left the room. After an hour or so the man struggled but managed to raise himself on one elbow so he could look out the window, but to his great surprise he saw only a blank wall. The man called in the nurse and asked, "Why would my now deceased roommate describe such beautiful scenes when he saw a blank wall?" The nurse replied, "Didn't you know; your roommate was blind. I guess he wanted to cheer you up. Maybe he wanted to bring light to the darkness of your life, some victory to what seemed to be defeat."

The story of the two men in the hospital presents us with a challenge — how can we transform what seems to be so bleak into what is good and life giving? The blind man gave himself and his roommate much joy and hope. In a similar way, today's familiar gospel passage of Jesus' encounter with the disciples along the road to Emmaus presents us with the challenge to transform events in our lives which appear to be problematic, painful, and defeatist, into opportunities for growth and even victory. The road we take is largely determined by the attitude we possess and the process we use.

Luke's account of the walk along the road to Emmaus, in essence, is a story of how Jesus was able to bring victory and joy to the pain and defeat that his disciples felt. He opened not only their eyes but their hearts to what was possible for those who believe in and witness to the power of the risen Christ in their lives. Cleopas, and the other unnamed disciple of the Lord, are walking along the road. They encounter Jesus although they do not recognize him. In their lively conversation, the disciples tell their unknown companion about Jesus. They were hoping that he would be the Messiah, the one who would overturn the rule of the Romans and once again make Israel respected amongst all nations. The Messiah would restore the kingship of David. With such expectations, the Jews were highly disappointed when Jesus died on the cross. Their dreams for the restoration of Israel died along with him; their spirits were crushed and their hopes for the future were now dashed. Jesus listens to the disciples as they walk and realizes that now, as in his public ministry, his plan and mission have been misunderstood. Thus, the Lord explains to his companions all of what scripture

-Dc
HOW LONG HAVE WE WALKED
W/OUR LORD + NOT RECOGNIZED
HIM? HOW LONG HAVE WE NOT
SEEN WHERE HE WANTS US TO
GO, WHAT HE WANTS US TO BE?

172

HOW LONG HAVE WE
HELD ONTO OUR VISIONS,
OUR DREAMS OUR IMAD,
ALL THAT KEEPS US FROM
SEEING HIM?

said about him. It was necessary for Jesus to die. The Jews saw the
passages in scripture which spoke of the greatness of the Messiah,
but they missed or chose to forget the "Suffering Servant" passages in Isaiah, the one who offered himself to others, who gave
no resistance to injury.

Why, one might ask, were the disciples' going to Emmaus?
There are many possibilities — business, to visit others, or possibly to just "get away." This latter idea has been suggested as the
best possibility. These disciples' journey to Emmaus was symbolic
of their need to hide from their perceived reality that all hope was
lost; without Jesus there was nothing else to do but run away from
the situation. Thus, they went to Emmaus to escape from the sadness of their lives and their great disappointment. Yet, in the end,
the disciples learned that if they possessed the correct attitude and
were willing to persevere under a "cloud of unknowing," confident that the Lord would present the light at the end of the tunnel,
defeat would be transformed into victory.

We are very much like Cleopas and the other disciple in that
we often walk or even run to our own Emmaus; we do whatever is
necessary to escape from the disappointments and hurts of life.
We cannot see, but we must believe, that despite the pain we share
and even carry for others, the triumph of resurrection will be ours
if we persevere. The methods of escape that we design are generally very subtle but sometimes more overt. For many, the place
and method of escape is to crawl inside ourselves and keep the
rest of the world that threatens us at bay. We fend off others who
reach out, ignore possibilities and opportunities that come our way,
and reject the affections of others, perceiving that these will only
deepen our pain and alienation. We live in our own little world
and convince ourselves that everything is fine. The reality, however, is that we are deeply wounded and feel defeated. We must
break out, and recognize, as did Cleopas and his partner on the
road, that Christ is present and will relieve the pain, heal the wound,
and transform our sadness to joy, defeat into victory.

Besides the simple inward escape, there are some we know,
ourselves and too often people we know and love, who escape in
more overt and highly dangerous ways. This reality is manifest

most horribly in forms of abberative and/or addictive behavior that, if people are not careful, can transform the pain and defeat we feel into permanent damage or even death. Alcohol has claimed the hopes, fortunes, and lives of countless people. It is so easy and socially acceptable to drown all our fears and problems in the false calm of another reality. Similarly, the period since the 1960s has seen an explosion in the use of drugs as a method of escape. Most people think of the illegal drug traffic, which is certainly a frightful scourge on society, but it is far easier and more prevalent for people to elude their pain, problems, and defeats in medications that are prescribed for one purpose but are readily used simply as a means to escape.

The various Emmauses of our lives, the places to which we escape, are many and varied, and, thus, we must consciously be aware and on guard that we do not fall, as is so easily the case, into the "quick fix" mode for solutions to the problems of our lives. One of the great challenges of Christianity is finding ways to transform pain, difficulty, and even defeat into positive, and hopefully, faith-building experiences that will assist us in our own walk toward the Lord and the responsibility we have as Christians to lead others along this same path toward eternal life. This task will seldom be easy. On the contrary, for those who follow in the footsteps of the Master, we can expect nothing more than he experienced. The words of G. K. Chesterton, the famous early twentieth-century British essayist, are always appropriate: "Christianity has not been tried and found wanting. It has been found difficult and left untried." The road will often be unclear and unfortunately is too often strewn with various obstacles, hurdles, and potholes, but with faith we must look to the future, down the road, and remember the promise of Christ as Saint Paul articulated it so beautifully: "What no eye has seen, nor ear heard, nor the human heart conceived, what God has prepared for those who love him" (1 Corinthians 2:9).

The man who could physically see and the disciples who conversed with Jesus along the road to Emmaus were devastated by the events that transpired, the revelation of his roommate's blindness and Jesus' crucifixion, but through the power of Christ, their

174

defeat was transformed into victory. They wanted to escape, but God brought them back. In a similar way, contemporary life often throws us many curves that lead us to seek a method of escape ourselves. This road is a dead-end, however, and will only exacerbate the problematic situation which we face. We need to truly believe that Christ's resurrection, the greatest event in all human history, has set us free and placed us, if we have faith and perseverance, on the proper road to victory and life. Escape is not the answer to life's challenges and problems. Rather, we need to honestly evaluate our lives, seek positive solutions to the questions that we hold and the problems that plague us, and never forget our need to follow in the footsteps of Christ. He is the one who died to set us free; he is the one whose resurrection will bring us to eternal life.

Easter 4
John 10:1-10

The Choice For God Or The World

Once upon a time, a great and loving king ruled over a vast territory. There was something very strange about this kingdom, however. Everything was the same. The people ate the same food, drank the same drink, wore the same clothes, and lived in the same type of homes. The people even did all the same work. There was another oddity about this place. Everything was gray — the food, the drink, the clothes, the houses; there were no other colors.

One day, a majestic and very beautiful bird flew from the west into a small village that lay a great distance from the capital city. The bird deposited a yellow egg and flew off. The people were fascinated with their new possession since they had never seen anything but gray. They played with the egg and poked it. In the process the egg broke. Inside was a yellow powder. Anything that came in contact with the powder instantly turned yellow. At the outset, a few peoples' clothes and some other objects turned yellow, but the people were soon so struck with their new discovery that the whole village was "painted" yellow. The next day, the same bird flew from the west and deposited a blue egg in another small village. It did not take long before everything in this village was blue. This same scenario repeated itself on seven consecutive days, as the majestic bird deposited seven different colored eggs in seven villages.

The great king in the capital city, where all was still gray, heard about these strange events and wondered what the sign might mean. He called in his royal councilors and advisors and asked them if anything like this had happened in the past. They checked

177

the ancient manuscripts and discovered that many generations ago the kingdom was ruled by a philosopher king. At the time there was much dissension, strife, and conflict in the kingdom. It was further discovered that the source of this dissension came about from the differences that existed among the people. The king, who wanted peace, believed that the only way to restore harmony was to eliminate all differences among the people. This is why all the people did the same things and all was gray.

The present king was worried that the various colors in the villages would again lead to dissension and strife. Thus, he ordered the royal archers to locate the majestic bird and slay it. The archers found the bird and their arrows were sent straight and true, but they had no effect on the bird which simply flew away. If the bird could not be stopped then the people must be, thought the king. Thus, he ordered the people to remove all the colors and return to gray. But the people, who were enamored with the new colors in their lives, refused to obey the king's order. Dissension, strife, and conflict ensued — the very things the king was trying to prevent.

The king was unsure as to what to do, until one day the beautiful majestic bird flew into the royal palace and deposited seven different colored eggs. The king was frustrated and angry and in a fit of rage he hurled the eggs in all different directions. They burst into an array of color. The beauty was so great that the king, in a moment of inspiration, knew precisely what he needed to do. He now realized that the bird was a sign that change was needed, but he had ignored the sign. Thus, the king ordered that all the people must have all the colors. Again there were no differences and dissension, strife, and conflict ceased. All the people lived happily ever after.[1]

John Aurelio's story "Colors" speaks of how a king was given a choice — follow the sign of God or ignore the sign and go your own way. His failure to heed the sign almost brought disaster for him and his kingdom. Jesus, in today's gospel, presents us with a choice — will we enter life through him, the gatekeeper, or seek another road. The choice is ours!

John's Gospel, which we know is filled with powerful images, presents us with one of the most significant in our reading today. Jesus describes himself as the gate through which all must pass who seek God and eternal life. The Lord is very clear, "I am the gate. Whoever enters by me will be saved, and will come in and go out and find pasture" (10:9). Jesus tells his disciples that there are many ways to enter, that is to live one's life, but only those who hear the voice of the gatekeeper will discover, follow, and hold to the correct path. All who seek to find another route are described as "thieves and bandits" who have come to steal and kill. Jesus, however, has come to give abundant life to those who follow him.

The imagery of this passage provides two important and distinct messages. First, we hear a polemical warning by Jesus against all who seek to call the sheep, that is God's people, away from the only true road, namely through the sheepgate. In branding such people as criminals, Jesus is clearly suggesting that the teachings and the path that he offers must be followed if one desires to find God's presence at the end of life. So many false prophets are present in society and they come in various forms. Some of these "teachers" are prognosticators of doom, those who forecast only the worst and seemingly can never find anything in their lives or that of society to celebrate. These people have given up hope, have "thrown in the towel" and surrendered to the difficulties and obstacles of life. Other false prophets take the opposite road and declare that there are no problems and that we must maintain the status quo at all costs. Like the proverbial ostrich that hides its head in the sand, these "prophets" choose to look the other way and ignore the plight of those less fortunate, including the poor, the sick, and those who live on the margins of our society. There are those teachers, as well, who suggest that all the answers to life's questions and problems can be found in the world and all that it has to offer. The allure of power, wealth, and prestige, the three great sins of human nature, is strong and many preach this as the message of salvation. Such prophets are the thieves and bandits to whom Jesus refers in his metaphor. In many ways all are prophets of doom who insist that God should play no role in our world or our lives.

179

In striking contrast to this first message, is Jesus' insistence that there must be a strong bond between the sheep, God's people, and the gatekeeper, Jesus. This missive of hope is integral to the whole mission of Christ, and states that all who follow him faithfully will never see death, but rather will enjoy the eternal life which is God's gift to all who believe. We must listen to the voice of the true shepherd, the gatekeeper, amidst the noise of many false prophets. This is often a difficult task, but if we keep our attention fixed on Christ, then we will not be swayed by the errant messages that seem to surround us. Christ is the light at the end of the dark tunnel; we must persevere and diligently hold fast to the road and not seek detours or shortcuts. There is one, and only one, way to find life and that is through Jesus, the gatekeeper.

Today's society presents us with many choices and possibilities that only seem to grow more numerous with time and the "advance" of culture. They say that "variety is the spice of life" and I suspect it is true. Yet, the many choices that stand before us can be confusing. We need to learn how to wisely use the gift of free will, our ability to choose. This gift, if used constructively, can provide much good for our world, but if abused it can create untold grief.

Wisdom dictates that in order to use our gift of free will wisely, we must ask ourselves some important questions concerning how well we follow Jesus, the shepherd and gatekeeper, in the decisions we make. What are the criteria that we use to make the important decisions of our lives? Do we seek out family and friends, colleagues and associates? What place does God have in our decision making process? What responsibility do we feel for those God has entrusted to us? Young people, students, or subordinates at work all look to elders and superiors to lead them. By following our lead will people find the pasture of life or are we leading people astray by the conduct of our lives? What choices have we made lately? Were they helpful and did they aid us along the path of life or were they destructive? If they were harmful, did we have the courage to change and make a better choice? When we make decisions are they based solely on our needs and wants or do we consider the desires of others? If we find ourselves in positions of authority, do we make choices that are beneficial to all or are we

180

selfish in our choices? Jesus' life demonstrates that suffering is part of the Christian life. Are we willing to make the decision that may cause suffering because it is the right choice, or do we shy away because we are afraid to endure a crisis for the sake of Christ's name?

All of these ideas concerning decisions beg one more important and pertinent question — why does the world suffer? Why do pain, problems, and suffering exist in such abundance? We all believe that God is all good, all love, full of compassion, and all powerful. This is how we define God and we believe this is true. Thus, the question bears repeating, why does our world suffer? Why do wars exist and people die in innocence? Why do people in positions of public trust commit acts that cause others not only to lose faith in the individual, but in the system as well? Why do people fight one another when the only difference between them is the color of their skin, their political preference, or religious belief?

The basic answer to these challenging questions is personal choice, our free will to say, "Yes" or "No," to God at any time in any way. Soren Kierkegaard, the famous nineteenth-century existentialist philosopher and theologian, once wrote, "Faith is a matter of choice, our personal decision in finding God." This personal decision, our free will, is why the world suffers. It is free will that allows the drunk to drive and kill others. It is free will that allows people in public service to break the law and, thus, lower the integrity of the system. It is free will that places certain members and groups in society on the fringe and does not allow them to participate. Free will moves us closer to or further from God. As Kierkegaard wrote, it is our decision; faith is our choice.

Jesus, the gate that leads to life, invites us to follow him to his pasture. Our great gift of free will allows us to say, "Yes" or "No," to God. God loves us so much, that we were given the option whether or not we wish to follow the Lord. In some ways it might be easier if we were animals that relied totally on instinct. We would then be programmed to follow the Lord and find eternal life. God, however, believes that the choice must be ours. God wants us to give our daily ascent to his invitation. Many will present themselves along the way as the gate we should employ. We must find our way through the maze of false teachers, hopeless situations, and problematic circumstances to find Jesus and the true path to God which he provides. The choice is ours! Jesus put it well in Matthew's Gospel (7:13-14): "Enter through the narrow gate; for the gate is wide and the road is easy that leads to destruction, and there are many who take it. For the gate is narrow and the road is hard that leads to life, and there are few who find it."

---

1. "Colors," paraphrased from John Aurelio. *Colors! Stories of the Kingdom* (New York: Crossroad, 1993), pp. 134-136.

Jesus, Our Rock Foundation

When Charlie Atlas was a teenager his parents bought him a dresser mirror that he placed in his bedroom. Before this time, whenever Charlie needed to use a mirror he went to the bathroom, but there he was only able to see his head and possibly his shoulders. When he got dressed up he used his parents' full length mirror in their bedroom. Charlie was happy with his new mirror; he spent many hours in front of it.

One day when he was standing in front of the mirror, Charlie decided to take off his shirt. He was very disappointed. His chest was scrawny and his biceps were so thin that he could place his hand completely around one. This was an intolerable situation; he did not want to be known as a scrawny weakling. Thus, on that very day, Charlie Atlas made a pact with himself; he would work as hard as necessary in order to build up his upper body, so that he would not be embarrassed in the mirror ever again. Charlie began a rugged daily regimen of exercise. For several hours each and every day he did exercises — push-ups, pull-ups, and sit-ups. Later he began to lift weights — barbells and dumbbells. He bought a special machine with weights, pulleys, and springs which allowed him to exercise even more.

After several months, Charlie again looked in the mirror. There was definite improvement. His chest had grown and his arms were more muscular. The positive results encouraged him and thus he doubled his efforts. He did more difficult exercises, lifted more weights, and now even began to eat only certain foods. He took lots of vitamins as well. After a couple of years of this strenuous exercise program, Charlie again looked in the mirror. He was quite satisfied, even elated. His chest was huge and taut and his biceps were so large that two hands could not encircle one. His stomach rippled like waves on the ocean. As he stood in personal admiration, all of a sudden Charlie collapsed. His parents were quite concerned and rushed him to the doctor. They thought for certain that it was a case of overexertion, but the doctor, after examining Charlie, said it was much more simple. Charlie's ankles and legs were too weak, they could not support his massive bulk, thus he collapsed. You see Charlie could only see his upper body in the mirror and that was all he developed.[1]

The story of Charlie Atlas is a good illustration of a problem most of us have — we build up the externals of our life, but we forget about the rock foundation upon which our life must be based. We are like the house of which Jesus speaks that is built on sand and is washed away in a storm (Matthew 7:26-27). We need to fully recognize that we must build our house on the rock foundation which is Christ, the Way, the Truth, and the Life. As we learned last week, there are many roads that can be followed but we must pass through Jesus the gate that leads to the Father and eternal life. Today we are challenged to build our life in every aspect on Christ. We seem to be concerned with many things and work feverishly to accomplish many goals and achieve many accolades, but if we are not firmly grounded in Christ, we will fall as rapidly and unexpectedly as did Charlie Atlas.

The eschatological discourse of Jesus in Saint John's Gospel (chapters 13-17) presents some of the most profound theology of the fourth evangelist. In today's gospel, we hear in very clear and certain terms that there is a specific relationship between the Lord and God's people. Jesus is the rock foundation from which all that we have ever been, are now, and hope to be springs. In an analogous way to Jesus' description last week that he is the gate through which we must pass, so today we hear as clearly, "No one comes to the Father except through me" (14:6b). Jesus is the source of our sustenance; he is the path and guide to the Father and salvation. We must heed the call of Christ and make certain that it is his lead we follow, his word we hear, and his message we proclaim —

184

a task made that much more difficult in a world that does not appreciate nor greatly value the message of fidelity and fealty that the Lord proclaims.

Jesus' response to Thomas' question, "Lord, we do not know where we are going. How can we know the way?" (14:5), demonstrates the centrality of Christ's role in all that we do and say. "I am the Way, and the Truth, and the Life, " says Jesus, "No one comes to the Father except through me." Yes, Jesus is the way, but it seems that we willingly choose other routes that are only detours, or paths which seem clear but are laden with obstacles, hurdles, and potholes. Other routes seems so easy and, thus, we take the path of least resistance. We must not forget, however, how clear Jesus was in the Sermon on the Mount, as reported by Saint Matthew, "Enter through the narrow gate. For the gate is wide and the road is easy that leads to destruction, and there are many who take it. For the gate is narrow and the road is hard that leads to life, and there are few who find it" (Matthew 7:13-14).

In our hearts we know that Jesus is the only way, the true gate that leads to life, but often there is a disconnect between our hearts and heads, for too often we "think" there is a better, faster, or more profitable way and make the mistake of taking these roads. On the surface, the alternative paths that we take may seem the best option at the time, but we suffer from tunnel vision or we possess blinders that do not allow us to see the bigger picture. We live in and concentrate on the here and now; we seldom look down the road or see what the long-term effects of our actions may bring. The common contemporary desire for instant results and satisfaction tempts us to take shortcuts and other paths that, in the end, are really detours and dead ends; they lead us in all sorts of directions, but not along the path of life. We must truly take to heart Jesus' words, that he is the one and only way that leads to salvation.

Jesus tells Thomas that he is the truth, but this reality also seems to allude our consciousness. We become very adept at convincing ourselves that there are numerous truths, and varied understandings of the Christian message. But there is only one truth and that is the message which Jesus clearly articulates in the gospels. Some may center in on the "Golden Rule," love of God and

185

love of neighbor as oneself. Others may gravitate toward the challenge of Matthew 25 where in his apocalyptic discourse Jesus tells his disciples that we will be judged on how we have treated our least brothers and sisters, for by our actions toward them we demonstrate our actions toward Christ. Still others may say that Jesus' central message is, "Owe no one anything, except to love one another, for the one who loves another has fulfilled the law" (Romans 13:8). All of these ideas, however, find their roots in the message to love. Jesus is complete love and, therefore, this is the truth that he brings. It is not easy and probably is impossible to like all people. We have so many varied ideas, personalities, and backgrounds, that such a utopian idea can never be reached. But, we are called to love all people, giving them the common Christian dignity that is their due as members of God's family, regardless of creed, national origin, ethnicity, or religious understanding. Jesus is the truth which is love and, thus, if we desire to follow, we must exercise the love which he exemplified.

Lastly, Jesus calls himself the life, the only life that truly should have meaning for us. Fads, gurus, easy-fix solutions, self-help ideas, and a host of other ways of life challenge the polity of Jesus' reign, but there is only one life that we should follow. Too often we get off track and follow people, ideas, ideologies, and even institutions that we perceive will bring us life. But, like the false roads that we sometimes traverse, so, too, those who preach a way of life that seems easy, less burdened, and apparently attractive only lead us away from the one and true life that we must always seek. Jesus is the one whose salvific death and resurrection has true meaning for us. There is no other life that can offer us salvation, the free gift to those who believe, yet the prize which we seemingly do not value more than the things of the earth, if we consider how easily we are swayed away from this one and only life of truth.

Jesus is the Way, the Truth, and the Life; he is the font for the Father. The Lord goes further and tells his apostles that if they have seen him they have seen the Father. The truth of this statement forces us in our contemporary context to go one step further and declare that if we, the presence of Christ in our world, are true

186

disciples, then we must take up the cross and follow Jesus' lead, as did those first disciples. We must do our part, day-by-day to bring Christ's message to the world. We must not shy away from this basic call of discipleship with the excuse that we are too busy, not qualified, or worse yet, we don't have the time. How will the world know the correct path to follow, that Jesus truly is the Way, the Truth, and the Life, that he is the one who brings us to God and eternal life, if we, his contemporary disciples do not show the proper way and lead by example? The Christian life brings us many privileges, but with these wonderful benefits comes a myriad of responsibilities that we cannot shirk if we are to find life with God. We cannot bury our heads in the sand with the hopes that God will not see and we cannot claim incompetence with the hope that others will take up the slack and carry our share of the burden. The absolute need to carry our share of the burden as we follow Jesus, the Way, the Truth and Life is dramatically portrayed in a little story: Once in a far-off land there was a great king whose dominion extended far and wide. His power and authority were absolute. One day, as events would happen, a young man, a commoner, committed a grave offense against the king. In response the king and his counselors gathered together to determine what should be done. They decided that since the offense was so grave and had been committed by a commoner against someone so august as the king, the only punishment that would satisfy justice was death. The king's son, the crown prince, however, interceded on the young offender's behalf — you see, they were best friends. The prince spoke with his father and the counselors; the debate grew rather heated. In the end the king declared, "The offender must pay a price for his offense. I decree that he must carry a heavy burden up Temple Mountain. If he survives the ordeal he shall live!"

The prince again interceded for his friend. He knew the burden of which his father spoke was the weight of death and he knew his friend would not be able to carry it. Thus the prince declared, "Royal blood has been offended, therefore only royal blood can pay the price." So the prince shouldered the heavy burden himself, and with his friend trailing behind him, he began the ascent of the mountain. The task was very difficult. The higher the prince climbed the heavier the burden became. The prince slipped and stumbled several times, but he always managed to right himself and keep going. When the two friends first saw the summit, their goal, the prince collapsed from sheer exhaustion. He said to his friend, "In order for justice to be served, the price must be paid." The young man understood the prince and, thus, he shouldered the burden himself and, now with the prince following, managed to climb the rest of the way to the summit. When the two friends reached their goal, the prince, with his last ounces of strength, lifted the burden high over his head and then he died.

The king, observing all these events from below, declared, "Justice has been completed." Then with his great power he returned his son to life. The prince, now returned to life, said, "Not so, not yet. Justice has not been served. Royal blood received help along the way!" The king had to agree. He pardoned the young offender and the two best friends lived happily ever after.[2]

Like the commoner in the story who followed the prince, we are called to follow Christ, who will shoulder our burdens, but we must do our share. He will bring direction, light, and sustenance to our life, if we follow and are willing to lead others along a similar path. Do we firmly believe that Jesus is the Way, the Truth, and the Life and are we willing to lead others to the Lord? Only you can answer!

---

1. Paraphrased from "Charlie Atlas and the Dresser Mirror," in John Aurelio, *Colors! Stories of the Kingdom* (New York: Crossroad, 1993), pp. 26-27.

2. *Ibid.*, paraphrased from "The Burden: A Tale of Christ," pp. 130-132.

God Never Gives Up On Anyone

The name Robert Stroud is not one commonly heard in ordinary conversation, but this man's contribution to humanity will live on in the minds of many under a different title, "The Birdman of Alcatraz." By nature, Robert Stroud was not a congenial man. As a youth he was always getting into fights, disagreements, and various altercations. When he was only nineteen he killed a man in a barroom brawl, was convicted of second-degree murder, and was sentenced to the Federal penitentiary at Leavenworth, Kansas, since the crime was committed on Federal land.

One might think that incarceration in a federal prison would lead Robert Stroud to reform and get his life in order, but he continued his former ways, being even more disruptive and troublesome. One day, a fight broke out in the prison, among the inmates, which brought guards from throughout the compound to the site in an attempt to restore order. In the melee, Stroud killed one of the guards using a little wooden knife he had crafted in his cell. The warden at Leavenworth thought the attack so onerous that he recommended Stroud be executed for his offense; the jury at his trial agreed. Robert Stroud was scheduled to be executed in the electric chair.

Although it seemed Stroud's fate was sealed, God had a plan for this man which necessitated that he be alive and, thus, an intercessor arose in the form of Stroud's mother. Like any loving parent, Mrs. Stroud did not want to see her son die, especially such an ignoble death as execution in the electric chair. Since the only person who could commute Stroud's sentence was the president of the United States, she journeyed to Washington, D.C., to see President Woodrow Wilson. She was not able to see the president, but she did have an interview with the First Lady who, in turn, spoke to her husband on Stroud's behalf. Woodrow Wilson commuted Stroud's sentence to life in prison in solitary confinement. Robert Stroud was, thus, sentenced to spend the rest of this life without seeing any human beings, except the guard once per week when he was allowed the privilege of a shower. Even his meals were slipped through a special opening in his cell door.

God had a plan for Robert Stroud; God have not given up on him. The manifestation of God's plan began quite innocently one day when a small bird came and perched on the windowsill of Stroud's cell which looked out onto the Kansas countryside. Over time, the bird came back, and with more time still, one bird turned into many birds. Stroud received permission to house these birds in his small cell. He read voraciously all the material he could obtain on birds and their care, especially diseases to which these animals were susceptible and he conducted numerous experiments over several years. His study, research, and findings were collected into a book published in 1939 as *Stroud's Digest on the Diseases of Birds*. At the time it was the most comprehensive and authoritative study ever done on bird diseases and their cures.

Robert Stroud was a troublemaker who was twice convicted of murder, yet God never gave up on him. God was calling with a plan and a mission for Robert Stroud. In the end, the call was heeded, the plan was revealed, and the mission was successfully completed.

Scripture speaks over and over about how God rejoices over one who hears the call and returns to him, for God never gives up on anyone. Today's gospel from John, part of what is known as Jesus' "Farewell Discourse," is an excellent illustration of the way God consistently pursues everyone of us, never wasting a moment and always doing whatever is necessary to assist us. God is with us every step of the journey. In the gospel, Jesus realizes that he will soon leave this world and return to the Father. Thus, he gathers his best friends, the apostles, together and gives them some important instructions before he leaves. Listening to their Master

190

speak about his impending departure, the apostles most probably were fearful and worried. How would they be able to continue in the world without the assistance of their leader and guide? Jesus, realizing their apprehension, responds by telling them that they will never be far from God; God will never abandon them. First, Jesus promises that he will send the Paraclete, the Holy Spirit, who will serve as their guide in every word and action. It would only be through Jesus' departure that the power of the Spirit would be released upon the world. Next, Jesus assures his friends that they will not be left orphans. We recall how the Lord made this promise to his apostles, as reported by Saint Matthew, when he prepared to return to the Father: "Go therefore and make disciples of all nations, baptizing them in the name of the Father and of the Son and of the Holy Spirit, and teaching them to obey everything that I have commanded you. And remember, I am with you always, to the end of the age" (Matthew 28:19-20). Lastly, Jesus promises the apostles that he will one day return to bring them home to be with him, the Father, and the Spirit.

Jesus' message in this farewell discourse, that he will be ever-present and never abandon his followers, is totally consistent with his entire ministry on earth and challenges us to do as he has demonstrated. Jesus first came to our world to teach. The gospels are filled with examples that describe times when Jesus instructed his apostles or the crowds in general about the reality of God's abiding, unchanging, and totally faithful love. We recall his words, "As the Father has loved me, so I have loved you, abide in my love" (John 15:9). Then Jesus instructs his friends, "I give you a new commandment, that you love one another. Just as I have loved you, you also should love one another. By this everyone will know that you are my disciples, if you have love for one another" (John 13:34-35). Jesus also came to support his fledgling community. Remember when Peter was challenged with the question, "Does your teacher not pay the temple tax?" The Lord responded with a teaching but then told his chosen leader, "So that you do not give offense to them, go to the sea and cast a hook; then take the first fish that comes up; and when you open its mouth, you will find a coin; take that and give it to them for you and me" (Matthew 17:24b, 27).

191

Lastly, Jesus came to lead and show direction to his followers. Just last week we heard the Lord proclaim, "I am the way, and the truth, and the life. No one comes to the Father except through me" (John 14:6). Jesus will never abandon us nor will his Father. All will be provided if we will only follow faithfully.

The reality of God's abiding presence in our world is seen in many examples of famous people upon whom God never gave up, but rather doggedly pursued so they could make the contribution to society planned for them. When he was a youth, Saint Augustine, certainly one of the foremost minds and influences in western civilization, was rebellious and spent much time searching for his place in the world. It took thirty years, but after trying several different religions and searching for happiness and security through human relationships, Augustine, through the prayers of his saintly mother, Monica, was converted to Christianity. In his powerful autobiography, *The Confessions*, his description of the culmination of God's search for him is known by many:

> *Late have I loved you, O Beauty ever ancient, ever new, late have I loved you! You were within me, but I was outside, and it was there that I searched for you. In my unloveliness I plunged into the lovely things which you created. You were with me, but I was not with you. Created things kept me from you; yet if they had not been in you they would not have been at all. You called, you shouted and you broke through my deafness. You flashed, you shone, and you dispelled my blindness. You breathed your fragrance on me; I drew in breath and now I pant for you. I have tasted you, now I hunger and thirst for more. You touched me and I burned for your peace.*

A more contemporary example of God's pursuit of our soul's is found in the life of the famous British poet Francis Thompson. Thompson was a drug addict on the streets of London, but a man with great talent as a poet. Who would ever discover the skill he possessed? It was only through the pursuit of God that he was able to have his ability discovered by the proper people, leading him to clean up his life and make his significant contribution to the world of literature. Francis Thompson wrote from his own experience in his famous work *The Hound of Heaven*: "I fled Him, down the nights and down the days; I fled Him, down the arches of the years; I fled Him, down the labyrinthine ways of my mind; and in the midst of tears I hid from Him." God, the "Hound of Heaven," pursued him without rest; he is doing the same thing for us!

We might ask a proper question as we observe the world around us. If God so diligently seeks after us, why is the world in the horrible state we see? Why is war such a common occurrence among nations and peoples? Why is there so much corruption in the varied institutions of government, business, and even the churches that causes us to lose hope? Why is there so much poverty, pain, distress, and unhappiness in our world? The answer is obvious. God is ever faithful, but what about all of us? God allows the dynamism of our world, whether that be the dynamic forces of the created earth or the precious gift of free will to operate as they were created. Thus, the reason the world suffers, the reason that the world is so difficult is because we have not been faithful.

As God pursues us so we must pursue God. We need to turn to God as the source of our strength. But in order to do this we must first allow God to come to us. God does not place us in handcuffs and order our obedience. God does not place us in straitjackets and demand compliance. God does not come where God is not invited. Thus, we must first bid welcome to God. Then we can begin to pursue God as God pursues us. We must pursue God in prayer each day and stop making excuses for our failures. We must respond to God in service with the understanding that a life of service is required of all the baptized.

The Spirit of God gives us life; the Spirit will never abandon us. As God pursues us and never relents in his search, so must we too pursue others, especially those whom God has given to us in special roles of responsibility. It is, for most, relatively easy to pursue those we like, those who do something for us, those who make us laugh and feel joyful. How hard it can be to pursue those we find problematic or troublesome. God is not exclusive in his pursuit of us; the Hound of Heaven searches for all without reservation. We must pursue members of our family, not only those we like, but maybe most especially those with whom we are estranged or find difficult. We must pursue our neighbor, whether that be the person down the street in our neighborhood or the person who occupies the office next to ours at our place of work. We must especially pursue those society has cast off and placed on the margins — the aged, the infirmed, the stranger, alien, or immigrant, the handicapped — all those who for whatever reason have been placed on the margins and have little, if any, chance to find the center and quality of our society. God never gives a litmus test to anyone; rather, he relentlessly pursues our souls. We must do the same, if we truly are the hands, the feet, and the senses of God, as Saint Teresa of Avila reminds us.

Yes, the Hound of Heaven doggedly pursues our souls, as he did Robert Stroud, and never gives up. We must pursue God and one another. In order to do this, we must first be totally confident of God's call and answer. There is a famous painting and a popular verse of scripture that provides both the challenge and the answer for us. In the National Gallery of London, there is a painting by Holbein with which many are familiar. Jesus stands in a garden and he is knocking on the front door of a little cottage. Everything is normal in the scene, except one small, but important, detail. There is no knob on the door, for Jesus is knocking on the door of our hearts. The painting depicts what Revelation 3:20 describes: "Here I stand, knocking at the door. If anyone hears me calling and opens the door, I will enter his house and have supper with him, and he with me." Yes the Hound of Heaven, our God, is knocking on the door of our hearts. Let us today respond to the knock of the Lord; let us open the door to our hearts. Let us have dinner with Jesus and he with us, today and to life everlasting.

Ascension Of The Lord
Luke 24:44-53

Completing The Master's Work

Classical music provides some significant examples of great musical compositions that were never finished by their creators. A perennial favorite with many, Wolfgang Amadeus Mozart, never completed his magnificent *Requiem Mass*. Franz Schubert, who like Mozart, lived only a short life but produced over 600 works of music, wrote only two movements of his *Eighth Symphony*. Orchestras today still play this great composition, known appropriately as the *Unfinished Symphony*. Living in the latter nineteenth and early twentieth century, the Italian opera composer Giacomo Puccini also left a master creation unfinished, but thanks to his students, Puccini's last and greatest composition, *Turandot*, is performed many times each year throughout the world, because his disciples completed their master's work.

Giacomo Puccini was one of the greatest composers of opera who ever lived. His great and glorious music, written for and performed in the great opera houses of the world has delighted people for more than a century. It was quite common to hear people along the streets of any great city whistling or humming one of the many popular melodies from such great works as *Tosca*, *La Boheme*, *Madama Butterfly*, *Manon Lescaut*, and *Gianni Schicchi*. Toward the end of his life, Puccini took on a significant challenge, the composition of another great opera. Using a libretto written by fellow Italian Renato Simoni, who adapted a work of the eighteenth-century Venetian playwright Carlo Gozzi, Puccini tackled the composition of an opera that related the efforts of a gallant young man, Calaf, to win the hand in marriage of the stern, mysterious, and

195

seemingly cold Chinese Princess Turandot. Puccini was in his sixties when he began the opera's composition. For four years he labored long and hard, but Puccini was a very sick man and he knew he was running out of time. God would soon call him home.

Puccini returned home to God before his master work was completed. Because he was a famous man, Puccini had many friends, including a cadre of loyal students who were known as his disciples. These young men and women would not allow their master's great work, his *magnum opus* to lie unfinished. Thus, they gathered together, studied the text of the opera, and then, when ready, began the difficult task of finishing their master's work. In 1926, two years after his death, Puccini's greatest work, *Turandot*, was performed for the first time, appropriately enough, at Milan's La Scala Opera House with Arturo Toscanni, the most famous conductor of the day, at the podium. When the opera reached the middle of the third and final act, the music abruptly stopped. Toscanni paused, set down his baton, and said, "Thus far the master wrote, but he died." After a moment of silence, the great conductor again picked up his baton, turned to the audience, and with tears in his eyes said, "But his disciples finished his work." Thunderous applause was heard as the opera continued; the work of the master had been completed.

Giacomo Puccini was a master composer who created many delightful and significant operas and, in the process, gained many disciples and thrilled millions of music patrons. He, like several other significant composers, left his master creation unfinished, but fortunately for the world, his disciples completed their master's work.

Today we celebrate the Ascension of Jesus to heaven; we celebrate his return home to God. Jesus was sent by God to be with us for a certain amount of time; he was sent on a mission. Like Puccini, who was sent by God to delight our ears with beautiful music, so Jesus was sent to show us how to lead good and holy lives, to show us that God is present today. As we heard in last Sunday's Gospel from John, Jesus was given authority over all people to bring them to salvation. Jesus used his many and significant gifts to do his best to complete the work he was given. Jesus did what the Father asked of him, and he did it well. Still, Jesus knew that there would be much more work to do and that is why he established a group of loyal followers, his apostles and other disciples, who were given the commission to go forward and bring Christ's message to the nations. Jesus' words in Matthew's Gospel are very significant for the mission of the apostles: "All authority in heaven and on earth has been given to me. Go therefore and make disciples of all nations, baptizing them in the name of the Father and of the Son and of the Holy Spirit, and teaching them to obey everything that I have commanded you. And remember, I am with you always, to the end of the age" (Matthew 28:19-20).

Jesus certainly commissioned the apostles to go forward but he did not send them out without the requisite tools for the job. Today's gospel, which ends Saint Luke's narrative of Jesus' life, describes the Lord's promise to the apostles: "I am sending upon you what my Father promised; so stay here in the city until you have been clothed with power from on high" (Luke 24:49). Jesus will provide the Holy Spirit, whose arrival we will celebrate next week at Pentecost. The Spirit not only guides and directs our ways, but will provide inspiration and any and all things that might be needed for the commission the apostles have received. Thus, as Jesus ascends to the heavens and a reunion with the Father, the apostles need not be fearful. They can be confident that God will be with them every step of the way as they initiated the construction of God's kingdom in a formal way.

Jesus came to our world with a special mission. He wanted to show by what he did and said that God is not far away, but rather, God is close, imminent; God is present within ourselves and our society. Jesus came to establish the kingdom of God on earth, but he returned to home before the mission was completed. We who gather in Christ's name are his friends, disciples, and students. When Puccini died without his master work completed, his disciples gathered together and finished the work. In a similar way, we who bear the name Christian must do our share to bring Jesus' work to completion in our world.

God has given all of us many talents and we must use them to bring the kingdom to come. Some, like Puccini are gifted musically, others are writers, still others are gifted speakers. Some of

197

us excel in science and others are wonderful teachers. Some people have been given great athletic ability and some of God's people are very fortunate — they have been blessed with multiple talents. Whatever gifts received from God must be returned in our effort to make known to others the imminence of God in our world. We must show others that love conquers hate, faith dispels fear, that community can take us further than personal initiative alone. We must do our share to build the kingdom now.

Jesus ascends to heaven, but we his disciples are still here. As missionaries on the road, God has granted us limited time. For some, the time is 25 years; for others, sixty; and, for a select few, 100. Each and every day of our journey presents the opportunity to show the face of God to others, to complete Jesus' work in building the kingdom of God. The road will seldom if ever be completely free and clear. In fact, there are many days when the road is so cluttered with obstacles and various detours that we might think it is not worth the effort. But, then we can be reminded of the powerful words of Saint Paul: "What no eye has seen, nor ear heard, nor the human heart conceived, what God has prepared for those who love him" (1 Corinthians 2:9). Let us, despite the pain and possible problems, do our share as we walk in the footsteps of the master, Jesus, who is our brother, friend, and Lord. Let us do our best to complete the Master's work — the reward will be eternal life.

Reevaluating Our Mission For Christ

Once there was a village with a chief who had three sons, each of which possessed a special talent. The oldest was skilled in his ability to raise and care for olive trees. The second was a shepherd, but when the sheep got sick, he possessed special abilities to make them well. The third son was a great dancer. When there was a string of bad luck in his family or in the village or if anyone needed some cheer added to their lives, he would dance and bring them joy.

One day the father told his sons that he had to go on a long journey. He instructed them, "My sons, the people of the village will be depending on you to help them. Each of you has a special talent, so while I am gone, I expect you to use your gift wisely and well, so that upon my return I will find our village more happy and prosperous than it is today." He embraced his sons and then left on his journey.

For a few months, things went quite well in the village, but then came the cold winter with its snow, winds, and assorted problems. First, the buds on the olive trees shrank and cracked and it would, therefore, be a long time before the trees would recover. The village, because of the extremely long winter, ran out of firewood, so the people began to cut down the trees and in the process stripped the village bare. Even though the first son did not want to see the trees cut down, he knew that the villagers needed heat to survive, and so he began to help them make firewood from the olive trees. Then the snow and ice made it impossible for traders to

199

come up the river and negotiate the mountain passes. So the villagers said, "Let us kill the sheep and eat them so we will not starve to death." The village chief's second son refused for a time, but eventually gave in to the villagers demands. He said, "What good will it do to spare the sheep, only to have the villagers perish?"

In this way, the villagers had just enough firewood for their fires and food for their tables. But the horrible winter had broken the peoples' spirit. They began to think that things were really much worse than they were and many began to lose hope. This belief was so strong that, family by family, they began to desert the village in search for a more hospitable environment.

As spring came, the icy grip of winter began to loosen and at the same time the chief of the village returned, to find smoke rising only from his own chimney. "What have you done?" he asked when he reached his village. "What has happened to the villagers?" "Oh, father, forgive me," said the eldest son. "The people were freezing and begged me to cut down the olive trees, and so I did. I gave away my talent. I am no longer fit to be an orchard keeper." "Don't be angry, father," said the second son. "The sheep would have frozen anyway, and the people were starving and thus I sent the herd to slaughter." The father understood and said, "Don't be ashamed my sons. You did the best you could, and acted rightly and humanely. You used your talents wisely in trying to save the people. But, tell me, what has become of them? Where are they?" The two brothers fixed their eyes on their younger brother who said, "Welcome home, father. Yes, it has been a hard winter. There was little to eat and little firewood for heat. I thought it would be insensitive and improper to dance during such suffering. Besides, I needed to conserve my strength so that I could dance for you when you came home."

"Then dance, my son," said the father, "for the village is empty and so, too, my heart. Fill us with joy and courage once again. Yes, please dance!" But when the third son made ready to dance, he grimaced and fell down. His legs were so stiff and sore from sitting that they could no longer be used for dancing. The father was so sad that he could not even be angry. He simply said to his youngest son, "Ours was a strong village that could have survived the want of fuel and food, but it could never survive without hope. And because you failed to use your talent wisely and well, our people gave up what little hope they had. So now what? The village is deserted and you are crippled. Your punishment has already fallen upon you." With that he embraced his two elder sons and wept.

This powerful little story demonstrates what happens when we fail to use wisely the gifts and talents God gives us. In today's gospel, Jesus proclaims a beautiful prayer to his Father and reviews, one might say, the mission he engaged at the Father's request. Christ knows that his time on this earth is very short and that he will soon return to the Father. Thus, he prays to God and expresses how he has done his best to complete the work he was sent to accomplish. Jesus acknowledges that the Father gave him authority over all people in order to bring them the message of salvation by knowing the only true God. He says, "I have made your name known to those whom you gave me from the world. They were yours, and you gave them to me, and they have kept your word" (17:6). Because he knows his time is short, Jesus asks the Father to protect them so that they be one with Christ as Jesus is with the Father. From his personal experience, Jesus knew the world could be a very tough place and that is why he asks the Father to protect those for whom he knows he will die. We all know that Jesus' prayer was answered. Soon we will celebrate the great feast of Pentecost.

There is no doubt that Jesus did his work very well. The Son possessed many great talents to conduct his ministry. He was the greatest of teachers, as seen so often in the scriptures. Every work and action of Jesus was an opportunity to teach and he never once shied away from this call. He taught his disciples privately on many occasions. We recall how Jesus taught them that it is better to serve than be served, that humility was more important than power, and that there was an absolute need to sacrifice, even to die to self and live for others in order to find life eternal. Jesus taught publicly through the veiled message of the parables and more directly through the famous Sermon on the Mount (Matthew 5:1—7:29). He used his ability to effect miraculous cures, of mind, spirit, and body to show God's love for the people. He never missed an opportunity to assist another, especially those who demonstrated faith. The woman with the hemorrhage (Matthew 9:18-22) believed that all she needed to do was touch Jesus' clothing and she would be healed. Her confidence was rewarded with Jesus' words, "Take heart, daughter; your faith has made you well." In another instance Jesus cured the Roman centurion's servant because of his trust: "Truly I tell you, in no one in Israel have I found such faith." Jesus cured paralytics, opened the eyes of the blind, and cast out evil spirits from the possessed. He demonstrated compassion in raising to life the son of the widow of Nain, as well as his friend Lazarus. Jesus demonstrated the great quality of forgiveness, dismissing the sin of the adulterous woman (John 8:1-11) and even forgiving Peter (John 21:15-19) after he had denied the Lord three times on the night before he suffered and died. Jesus, like the two elder sons in the story, used his talents well and wisely.

We, the contemporary disciples of Jesus, have been given many talents and gifts to be used for the construction of God's kingdom. We have been sent to this world, individually and uniquely, to wisely and fully use the many and wonderful gifts we have been given. We have been given the gifts of teaching, speaking, and writing. Words are very important and possess great power. We were told as children, "Sticks and stones can break my bones, but words can never hurt us." This sounded good at the time, but the adage, while helpful to children, is not true for adults. Words are very important, orally and in writing and must be used with judicious care to build God's kingdom. Some of us have great athletic prowess and others are great musicians and singers. Some of us are very good with numbers and ply our skill as engineers, scientists, and researchers. There are a few who possess multiple talents. If we were to review our lives, as Jesus does in this prayer, would we be able to honestly say that we have used God's gifts wisely and well for the benefit of all? Or have we been more like the younger son who squandered his gift of bringing hope and in the process lost his talent and devastated his village?

It is not always easy to use our gifts well, wisely, and for the betterment of all, and, thus, we often need the assistance of others.

This we have, however, in the community faith. We can and must rely on the Christian community to assist, lead, and, if necessary, challenge us to use our gifts well and wisely as we daily, stone by stone, build the kingdom of God in our world. Many of us know from personal experience that sometimes utilizing our gifts for the building of God's kingdom will bring ridicule and rejection. But, this should not be a surprise, for any of us. Jesus told us that we would be hated by the world, but he reminded us as well that we must take courage for he has overcome the world. We can also take solace in the words of the Pauline author of the Pastoral Epistles: "If we have died with him, we will also live with him; if we endure, we will also reign with him; if we deny him, he will deny us; if we are faithless, he remains faithful — for he cannot deny himself" (2 Timothy 2:11-13).

Our journey of Lent and now Easter is rapidly drawing to a close. Next week's celebration of Pentecost beckons us today to take stock of our lives and ask the difficult question — have I done my best to complete the work God has given me, or is there much more that needs to be done? Let us have the courage to ask the question. Let us discover what needs to be done as we day-by-day prepare for God's coming and the eternal life which is God's promise for all who believe.

Sermons On The Gospel Readings

For Sundays
After Pentecost
(First Third)

Hidden In Plain View

Stephen M. Crotts
and
Stan Purdum

Pentecost! Slow ... And Sure!

Have you ever noticed how we preachers often promote the early church as if it were the ideal? "Why, they did a miracle a day in the early church." "When they had a prayer meeting, *everyone* came!" " They spoke in Greek then!" (As if it were some sort of superior language!) On and on we can go browbeating ourselves by comparison.

Yet, when one really studies the Bible, he discovers that early believers weren't perfect either. Moses had his temper. Noah got drunk. David fell into adultery. Peter couldn't keep his vows and Paul and Barnabas split up over a disagreement.

With all of this in mind, I'd like us to turn to the text for today and see how the first disciples celebrated Pentecost. To approach this text I'd like to do it twofold.

Journey Inward

The first part of the text is the journey inward. It represents the disciples' personal need to comprehend the resurrection, the Holy Spirit, and its application in their own lives.

The text tells us that the events in this first portion of narrative take place "on the evening of that day, the first day of the week." This means the early church was having a Sunday evening fellowship meeting. And what would you find should you enter that church? Let's suppose you're searching for a church home and you go visit the early first church. What sort of group would you find?

The text tells us there was a pervasive atmosphere of fear in the meeting. Not joy, not love, not teaching — but fear. You see,

Jesus had been crucified within the past week, and the disciples did not know but what they would be next. So, they were afraid. The text also tells us that it was particularly hard to even get into the fellowship. That's because the doors were locked. This was no bold, open, evangelizing body of believers reaching out. It was, rather, a cowering, closed little band of disciples who'd forgotten everything Jesus ever said to them.

A further feature of this first resurrection and Pentecost Sunday celebration is the conspicuous absence of so many of their members. "Thomas, one of the twelve, was not with them." And neither were dozens of others! Why, Judas had even killed himself.

Then, too, there is no mention of singing, no Lord's Supper observed, no preaching, no passing of the peace — why, the disciples seem to be doing little more than wallowing in their fears. The fact was, they'd denied Christ, abandoned him to the cross, and all run away. Now they felt guilty. They missed him. And they sure didn't feel like singing.

And one final note: There seems to be precious little faith, if any, in the room. Why, when Jesus came he had to show them "his hands and his side" to convince them he was really the risen Christ.

So, these are the disciples we like to brag about. This was church on that first night.

But that's not all! This may be the picture of the disciples we get in the text. But just look at the picture of God we get!

First off, Jesus Christ is alive. After man has done his worst, God has done his best. After scourging, mockery, crucifixion, and a hasty burial, Jesus is risen from the dead. No power of man can kill the life of God! He is risen forever to be the vanquisher of both sin and of death.

The text says, "Jesus came and stood among them and said, 'Peace be with you.' " When he had said this he showed them his hands and his feet. See the grace of God here? Into this imperfect fellowship he came. The risen Lord was to be found right in the middle of this fearful, doubting, half-attended church meeting behind locked doors. He doesn't wait till they've gotten their act together. He comes to them just as they are.

And note, too, how Jesus does not come angrily upbraiding them for their weaknesses. He stands right in the middle of them and says, "Peace be with you." Then he shows them his hands and his feet. he provides the credible evidence that he is who he says he is — the risen Christ, their Savior!

One of the often-overlooked portions of this Easter story is the humor of Christ. I personally think this is one of the funniest episodes in the Bible, yet the fact that you're not laughing is proof you don't get it. So, let me explain ...

In the South, the typical greeting is "Hey!" In south Texas, it's "Howdy partner!" In Ireland, people say, "Top o' the morning to you!" In Australia, "Good day mate!" In New York City, "Stick 'em up!" No, seriously, we say, "Hello." But in Israel, the typical greeting is the Hebrew word, "Shalom!" which translates as, "Peace be with you!"

So, Jesus is arrested, tried, crucified, dead, and buried away for three whole days. The frightened band of disciples is meeting upstairs behind locked doors, and Jesus strides in alive and well, grins, and says, "Hey!" "Yo!" "Hello!" Isn't that hysterical!?

Now, notice, if you will, the disciples' response to God's ministry to their misery that day. The text says, "Then the disciples were glad when they saw the Lord." Their doubts, their fears, their guilt, began to melt away, replaced by peace and gladness. Easter came slowly to them. But it did come.

Often we limp into a service the same way today, do we not? We come with great gaping wounds of guilt, our fears, our doubts, are here with us even today. And still, in every church, there are the conspicuously absent, those for whom Jesus didn't live up to their expectations, those for whom crucifixion is too high a price to pay for any religion.

And still, as of old, the risen Lord comes to us. Right in the midst of all of our fallen humanity he takes his stand and ministers his peace and gladness, his proof, and his own brand of humor.

Journey Outward

That's the first part of the text, the journey inward *to Easter.* Now this, the second part of the text, the journey outward *with Pentecost.*

In the text for the second time Jesus ministers, saying, "Peace be with you." Why did he do this twice? Wasn't once enough? Is he trying to use the same joke twice? Of a truth, we can be so ill, that the medicine we require must be taken in repeated doses. And the same with our trust in God. Once is not enough. Our ministry from God is a daily necessity. It can even be such that we require His continued ministry to us throughout the day ... even to the point of two *Peace-be-with-you*'s in the same hour!

It's interesting to note that the Hebrew concept which the word "peace" points to is the word "Shalom." Christ could have said "Love be with you!" or "Faith" or "Prosperity" or "The Holy Spirit" be with you. But, of all things, Jesus says, "Peace be with you ... Shalom be with you."

Now, "Shalom" means more than a cessation of hostilities. It also means the presence of everything required for your full development as a human being. For example, take a greenhouse. Inside a hothouse is the absence of all things which might harm a plant. There is no frost, no drought, no disease, no busy feet to step on them. But there is one thing more. There is the presence of all things vital to a plant's development. Water, sunshine, a gardener's careful pruning, fertilizer, and warmth.

This is what Jesus is saying is with the disciples. "Peace! Shalom!" "The absence of everything harmful, the presence of everything helpful *be with you*." And not once but twice does he tell us this!

Now he goes on to say, "As the Father has sent me, even so I send you." This is his commission to the church. He wants those he has ministered to go out and minister.

All too often we limp into church, limp into God's presence, with some gaping need in our lives, and God and his people are there to listen, to care, to heal, to counsel, teach, and train. But so often once our needs are met and the hurt is gone we are gone, too! We came to get help but we don't want to become a helper. We came to take, but don't ask me to give. We came to be served, but we won't serve. We came to know God, but don't ask me to make him known.

And the text tells us that Jesus would have none of this with his disciples that first Easter. And I can assure you he'll have none of it here this most recent Easter! "As the Father has sent me, so send I you!" "I've come, now you go! I've ministered to you, now go and I shall minister through you!"

Bible translator J. B. Phillips said that the early church could be symbolized by a group of Christians holding hands in a circle all facing outward. However, today's church, he pointed out, is best symbolized by a group of Christians all holding hands and facing inward. And the text here proves the remedy for this backwardness.

In Christ we must make a journey inward and journey outward. We must maintain contact with God and one another so as to be fed and cared for. But we must also look outward to the world, be eager to provide ministry for others. This is what Jesus commissioned his disciples to do in the text.

Now go on with the text. It says that Jesus, after commissioning the church to go out to the world with the gospel, "He breathed on them and said 'Receive the Holy Spirit.' "

"He breathed on them." Why? What is the meaning of this? A key to interpreting the scriptures is to come upon a word or a situation and, to discover its meaning, go back to the first place in the Bible where such is mentioned. So, when did God first breathe in scripture? You'll find it in early Genesis where God breathed into clay and man became a living soul. There it was the breath of God that invigorated. And here Jesus is saying as he breathes again that it is the Holy Spirit who makes us new creations, who causes us to come alive and go forth to minister.

See the grace of God here? He not only tells us what to do, he gives us the power to do it!

Such was the first Pentecost service in church. It started off slowly, but ended fast. It began with the heaviness of guilt, fear, and doubt, but ended with assurance, gladness, and peace.

Now the lectionary reading stops there, but it's worth reading on a bit, for a sad note follows. Jesus has come and ministered. Now he is gone. And who should walk in the door next but Thomas, one of the twelve!

211

"Where have you been, Thomas?" the disciples ask in frustration. "We have seen the Lord! He has come. He is risen! He has ministered to us his peace and gladness and commissioned us to go in his name!"

And Thomas would have none of it. Grouchily he says, "Unless I see, unless I touch him, I won't believe!"

It's still that way today, isn't it? There are those who continually absent themselves from the gatherings of the body here who later pay us a visit and then wonder what on earth is going on. "Why are you so glad when I'm so glum?" "Why are you so bent on world missions when I can't even get over my guilt?" "Why do you seem to have in your life the absence of those things harmful and the presence of those things helpful?"

And the answer is forever that the risen Lord Jesus has come and stopped in our midst and ministered his peace, his presence, his proof, and we are full of gladness. And you missed it!

Where do you think Thomas was? Visiting on Sunday? Traveling? Pouting? Shopping at some flea market? Or, perhaps it was raining and it wasn't worth getting wet for him to be in church. Or, maybe he was just too tired to come and was home sleeping.

Never mind. The text says the church met on the next Sunday and this time Thomas was with them. He'd missed once. But now he had learned his lesson. He wouldn't miss again. And Oh! The grace of God! Jesus came and stood among them again, and for the third time he said "Peace be with you!" And Thomas, the doubting straggler, was ushered into the circle of believers.

Yes, this is how Easter and Pentecost came to the early church that first Sunday so long ago. It came slowly. But it came sure.

It came to the fearful, the doubtful, songless saints hiding behind locked doors. It came not with one, or two, but three "peace-be-with-yous."

And what of us this day? What of your life and mine?

Are you here today having denied Christ and run away? Is your life made complicated by guilt and fear and doubts?

Have you been away pouting, having had some bad experience with church? Has a cross proven too high a price to pay for your religion? Has God, too, not lived up to your expectations?

Have you missed church so much that you've missed Christ as he's given others the peace that passes all understanding?

Whatever, you are here this Easter, this Pentecost. And so is the risen Lord.

"Peace be with you!"

"Put your finger here, and see my hands; and put out your hand, and place it in my side; do not be faithless, but believing."

"Receive the Holy Spirit!"

"As the Father has sent me, so send I you!"

Suggested Prayer

O God, Thou who make all things new again, make me new. Cause me to know your presence, your peace, and proof, and gladness and ministry. For Christ's sake. Amen.

Stephen M. Crotts

His Last Command
... Our First Concern!

In the fall of 1971, I visited Leo Tolstoy's home in Moscow. There, tied in bundles and stacked against the wall, were his handwritten manuscripts for all of his great novels — *War and Peace*, *Anna Karenina*, and *Resurrection*. For an hour I leafed through the mountain of paper, observing the man's handwriting, his strikeovers, and even the doodles he made in the margins.

An elderly Russian woman, the curator of the museum, noticed my deep interest in Tolstoy and began to talk to me. "He was a friend of the people, Leo Tolstoy was," she said. "Would you like to see his desk where he wrote?"

She didn't have to ask me twice! And the next thing I knew she had me seated in Tolstoy's chair leaning over his desk and holding his writing pen in my hand! I tell you, it was an awesome moment for me!

Often during the rest of my college days, my mind would wander back to that study in Moscow. I'd see myself sitting at that same desk, holding that same pen as the bearded Tolstoy himself opened the door and strode in. "Stephen," he'd say, "I'm working on a new novel and I need your help! Let's get down to work!" And I'd sit up straight, look him in the eye, and say, "Yes, Leo, I'll work with you."

That'd be a great commission, wouldn't it?

Actually there have been many persons given exciting commissions in their lifetimes. There was Michelangelo's commission to paint the ceiling of the Sistine Chapel, Sir Christopher Wren's commission to build St. Paul's Cathedral in London, Walter

Reed's assignment to stop yellow fever at the "Big Ditch" in Panama, and Chamberlain's orders to stop the Confederates at Little Roundtop in Gettysburg.

But I tell you, in my life and yours, there is an even greater commission. It is found here in Matthew 28:18-20 where Jesus Christ turns to his disciples and says, "Go! Go therefore and make disciples of all nations...." Think of it! Almighty God, not Tolstoy or the Pope or the Queen, but God himself, turns and looks you and me full in the face and commissions us to work with him on his latest creative project. I tell you, when the most important thing some of us have been asked to do all week is to wash the dishes or take out the trash, this comes as quite a jolt! I know of no other statement in the Bible that can give a man more of a sense of esteem, joy, and purpose than Christ's great commission to his disciples. It turns the farm, the assembly line, the office, the kitchen, the mill, the classroom, the truck, and the retail store into an artist's studio where we may fairly affirm, "I'm here on temporary assignment with God. My talent and time and money are needed. God has personally called me here to be his representative."

It's interesting that the great commission, written originally in the Greek, actually says, "As you go into all the world, make disciples." It has almost a casual or spontaneous air about it. And sure enough, search the scriptures as you might, you'll find the disciples nowhere starting "How to Witness" schools or planning a missions conference where they look at each other and say, "We've got to make some plans. Strategy! That's what we need! The missions committee meets this Wednesday night at eight!"

Mostly the disciples went about their great commission with spontaneous and breathless excitement. And considering the dimensions of the great commission, we can discover more of this breathless excitement in our own lives as well.

The Height

First of all, consider the height of our commission. In the text Jesus said, "All authority in heaven and on earth has been given to me. Go therefore and make disciples." *All authority.* That doesn't leave much out, does it? "All authority in heaven and on earth has

216

been given to me." That is, Jesus. Not the committee or the mayor or pastor or elders or some court. It's all centered in one person — Jesus Christ. What does this authority say? He says, "Go and make disciples." He says it to a group of fisherman, merchants, and government officials. You see, this commission is so vast it'll take more than a bunch of individuals to get it done. It'll take a worldwide body of encouraging, working, loving, committed, cooperative people to accomplish this task. Never forget, the great commission was given to a group, not an individual. It was given to the church!

When Jesus set about his ministry of teaching and healing there were those who asked, "By what authority do you do this? Is it your own ego or Satan or some man who compels you to do these things?" And Jesus consistently pointed to God as the basis of his authority. It is the same today. You just get busy going and discipling and teaching, and real soon, somebody's going to want to know why.

Out on the college campus a few years back, a young man named Gary broke up with his girlfriend, his grades were poor, and a fraternity had not asked him to join. So Gary slit both wrists in a suicide attempt. He was found, hospitalized, and recovered. The dean of students, a very efficient administrator, got involved and found that I'd spent some time with Gary in Bible study trying to help get his life straightened out. So he called me in for a talk. What was I sharing with Gary? Who hired me to do it? What gave me the right to say what was truth? He even suggested that I stop visiting the campus and mind my own business. When I told him that was impossible, he threatened me with a lawsuit. Sad, but he never really understood it all. You see, he worked for a college president, but I worked for God under the correction and accountability of a group of mature elders.

"Go," Jesus said. And his marching orders still stand. "Go! Disciple! Teach!" No human being has the authority to countermand the order.

I love the story of the raw army recruit standing at attention on the drill field. The drill instructor yells, "Forward, march!" And the entire ranks begin to move, all except this one raw recruit.

217

He's still standing there at attention. So the drill instructor strolls over to him and yells in his right ear, "Is this thing working?"

"Sir, yes, sir!" The recruit yells.

Then the drill instructor walks around to the other ear and yells, "Is this thing working?"

"Sir, yes, sir!" The soldier says.

"Then why didn't you march when I gave the order?"

"Sir, I didn't hear you call my name."

Some of us are like that soldier standing around waiting for God to call our names. But the great commission is a blanket order. It has everyone's name on it. And you can be sure that the man in charge says, "Go! Disciple! Teach!"

Width

That was something of the height of our commission. Now this: something of the width of our commission. The text describes the proportions as including "all nations."

Funny how we like to narrow our ministry to Presbyterians or upper middle class or the educated or youth or the elderly. "I minister to whites only." Or, "I have a black ministry." "My ministry is in prisons...."

Jonah had to get all of this straight in his own commission. God said to him, "Go to Nineveh!" But Jonah hated Gentiles. He only wanted a ministry to his own Hebrew people. It took a storm, a fish, a hot sun, and God's rebuke to straighten him out.

Hunters are aware that there are different seasons and strict bag limits for various game. Let's see, there are dove season, deer season, turkey, quail, and bear season. And it's frustrating to see game that you can't hunt. Imagine the joy when the state declares "open season" on all game. And that's exactly what this great commission declares. "Go and make disciples of all nations" makes every person fair game for evangelism, discipleship, and the church covenant.

Let me encourage you to take what I call a "John 3:16 walk" this week. Take an hour and go for a stroll being careful to notice every person you see. The newsboy is someone God created and loves. Does he know it? Can you find a way to share with him?

The same with that Pakistani student, the lawyer, the janitor, that clerk, and the policeman.

As John Wesley said, "The world is my parish!" Paul wrote in 2 Corinthians 5:16, "From now on, therefore, we regard no one from a human point of view...." Instead, everyone we see is a potential brother or sister in Jesus.

Dr. Mordecai Johnson, the African-American educator, once told of a colleague of his. He tried to interest his friend in Christ, but he was always met with polite refusals. Finally Johnson got the man to talk. It seems that when he was growing up in a small southern town, an evangelist visited for a week of meetings in a tent. The little boy had gone, drawn by the excitement of it all, and sat in the back of the tent reserved for Negroes. At the end of the week it was announced that Sunday morning would climax the week when all those who were ready to receive Christ would be baptized in the river. Those wanting baptism were to appear on the bank dressed in white. So the little boy had hurried home to tell his mother what he wanted. His poor, old mother had to take a sheet off one of the beds to make him a little robe. Proudly, yet somewhat frightened, the child made his way to the river on Sunday morning. Oh, it was quite a meeting with singing masses of folk. Scripture reading, testifying, and preaching. One by one, many were baptized into Jesus Christ, the king of lovers. When finally the service was over and the crowd dispersed a little black boy stood alone on the riverbank in a little white robe that was all dry. He was waiting for someone to notice him, to talk to him, to baptize him.

He's still standing there, that little child. His face is many colors. He lives on every continent. His eyes still plead. "Come, love me, and share with me. Teach me faith in Jesus. Baptize me. Disciple me. Fulfill the commission of Christ!"

Depth

Passing on, let's consider not only the height and width of our Christ commission, but also its depth. The text says we are to baptize people, make them disciples, and teach them to observe all that Christ commanded us.

Notice he didn't call on us to make converts or church members, but baptized, obedient disciples!

Nietchze, the German philosopher, said, "God is dead and the stench of his corpse is all across Europe." He advocated humanism and proposed the development of a "superman" of Aryan heritage protected by selective breeding and superior education. The Nazi Party picked up his idea, and men like Hitler, Goering, Goebbels, Mengle, Himmler, and Rommel set about building such a society in Germany's Third Reich. But it all ended with bullets and bombs, chaos and suffering such as the world has seldom seen.

The Christian faith has no less a plan. But it involves a higher order. Hitler would have renewed man by his own efforts. We seek to renew the human race by the effort of God.

For us, man-made-new begins with hearing of God's holiness and man's sin and our most certain judgment. It continues with the good news of God's love and provision in Christ and a clear call to repentance, faith, the fullness of the Holy Spirit, and obedience. Those who respond are then led to the water to be baptized.

In one of the great cathedrals of Europe there is a baptistry that tells the story. The water flows through it reminding us that Jesus says he is *the living water*. To be baptized, a person walks down three steps, each one marked by a word: the world, the flesh, and the devil. Descending the steps the convert is plunged beneath the water to die to sin and then raised from the depths to newness of life in Christ. To leave the baptistry now he must climb three steps, each one marked by a word: the Father, the Son, and the Holy Spirit. So it is that a new creature is born, a new breed of man, a citizen of a new kingdom, a breed apart. Dead to sin, he is alive to God and sent forth to grow and love and give light to a lost and dying world. He doesn't do it alone. He does it in little communities called the church in which people demonstrate, in their way of being together, God's eternal kingdom come upon them.

Politics can't make a man like this. Nor can education or medicine or finances. Only the love of God can work such a change in human souls.

Such is the depth of our commission.

Length

A final dimension of our challenge! It's length.

It took Michelangelo over ten years to paint the Sistine Chapel. So it's fair to ask how long it'll take us to fulfill the commission Jesus has given us. "What'll it take, Lord? Five minutes? A year? Two years? Five? Ten?"

And *Christ* says, "Go ... to all nations ... teach all I have commanded you ... *to the close of the age.*" In other words, each of our commissions lasts until the job gets done, until life is over, "until the close of the age."

I can't imagine a football player coming off the field in the third quarter, walking up to his coach, and saying, "Coach, I've been thinking. I've played enough. Let some other guys finish the contest. I'm going over there for a box of popcorn and relax with my girlfriend." It'd never happen! Yet it does happen in the church. "For ten years I've labored for you, *Jesus.* Sunday school, group prayer, worship, small groups. I've done it all. So now I'm going to buy me a sailboat and head for the beach every weekend I can. Let somebody else do your work for a while."

And *Jesus* says, "Until the close of the age." You see, the Christian life is not a 100-yard dash. It's a lifelong marathon.

When Susan Harris was leaving this church to go to Papua-New Guinea as a missionary, one of the people in our Wednesday group prayer meeting hugged her neck and said, "Susan, you take the rope and go down into the darkness and I'll stay home and hold the other end of the rope." And how long do we hold it? Two months or two years or ten? As long as necessary! "... Until the close of the age."

Conclusion

So, here we sit — fishermen, government officials, leading women, teachers. Today, as of old, *Christ* comes and speaks his great commission. "All authority in heaven and on earth has been given to me. Go therefore and make disciples of all nations, baptizing them in the name of the Father, and of the Son, and of the Holy Spirit, teaching them to observe all that I have commanded you: And lo, I am with you always, to the close of the age."

221

In the front of the Peachtree Church in Atlanta there is a stained glass window of the disciples gathered on the mountaintop around the ascending *Christ*. The *Lord* has just commissioned them. Filled with wonder, awe, and a deep sense of responsibility, the disciples' faces reflect the gravity of the moment. One may count them — Peter, John, James, Matthew, Thomas.... But there are only eleven in all. Judas is missing. Judas, the impatient one — the man who sought the kingdom but not by the gospel ... Judas ... the betrayer ... the one who ultimately hung himself.

It's easy to put this great commission aside for something else, isn't it? And I wonder. When our story is told some day, will we be in the picture?

Some of us will have to take hold of the rope and go down in the darkness to bring the light. Some of us will have to let go as our sons and daughters are called out from among us.

Others of us will have to help go by staying home to hold the rope in fund raising, prayer, administration, and so on.

But for all of us it's time to get going!

Suggested Prayer
Lord, I'll obey. For Christ's sake. Amen.

Stephen M. Crotts

What Is Success?

Erma Bombeck wrote, "I can't remember the name of the man who spoke at my high school commencement, but I remember what he said. He told us the future of the world rested on our shoulders and he charged us with finding our destiny and fulfilling it. He went on to say we alone must cure disease, hunger and poverty throughout the world, and above all, we must find success.

"I glanced over at Jack, the class deficient who couldn't even find his parents after they parked the car, and I got an uneasy feeling. Not only that, but for those of us who planned to sleep in for a week, the speech was very depressing, as it seemed to call for a lot of work from such a small class.

"After the speech, the entire group scrambled out of the auditorium in search of success as if it were the first item on a scavenger hunt. We had no idea what it was, where to look for it, how much it cost, whether it was in season or what it looked like, but from that day on we got up early in the morning and pursued it until late at night. Sometimes we heard that another classmate had found it, but when we confronted him, he assured us that if he had, he would be happier.

"By our tenth reunion, no one had found it yet. The men struggled in their jobs and fertilized their lawns on weekends, and the women raised babies and polished the bottoms of their Revere Ware. It seemed we were never rich enough, thin enough or important enough to qualify for success.

"I've spent a lifetime trying to figure out who has success."

223

Don't we know how it is? So, today I want us to look to Christ and his words in the Bible and see if we can learn what success is. In Matthew 7:24-27 Jesus told the parable of the wise and foolish builders. In this story both men decided to build a house, both men worked at it, both desired to succeed. Furthermore, both of them heard the word of God, finished their work, moved into their buildings and both suffered through a severe storm. The trouble is, while one heard the word and was careful to do it, the other only heard the word but did not do it. The result was, one man's house collapsed while the other's stood. So in a sense, one man was successful while the other failed.

With this in mind, let's ask some serious questions about success.

Length

First of all, is success found in length of life? Do we measure it like a string? The longer the string, the better? The longer a person lives, the better his life?

Methuselah lived to be 969 years old, according to Genesis 5:27. No one has ever lived longer! Yes, that's all we know of Methuselah. There is no record of his accomplishing much of anything else except 969 birthdays.

Our society today is really into longevity. What with our facelifts, Oil of Olay, vitamins, organ transplants, and regimen of exercise, we try to look and act young. Actually, this is nothing new. In the 1500s, Spanish explorer Ponce de Leon explored Florida searching for the fountain of youth. Today, in our fervent belief that it is better to be young than old, we turn to doctors, the new high priest in our cult of long life, health, and youth. To them go our faith, money, and frequent pilgrimages in hopes that one more test, one more treatment, can add length to our lives.

An elderly gentleman wasn't feeling well, and became irritated with his doctor because he wasn't getting any better after five visits. "Look," said the doctor, "I'm doing all I can to help you. I can't make you younger!" The old man said, "I wasn't particularly interested in getting younger. I just want to continue growing older!"

224

The American Medical Association recently finished a ten-year study on aging. They concluded that a 150-year life span might soon be realistic. But, will living longer make us more successful or only give us more time to fail?

From Adam to the flood, a person averaged 846 years in a life span. From the flood to Moses people lived around 333 years. From Moses to Solomon, the average was about 95 years. In the Middle Ages, the average was down to an all-time low of 35 years. Today the average life span for an American citizen is 72 years. Yet, in all of this history of longevity, one finds that length of years has very little to do with a person's success.

Indeed, some of the most successful persons died quite young! Shubert, Mozart, Shelley, John the Baptizer, and Jesus Christ all died in their thirties. Peter Marshall put it well when he wrote, "The measure of a life is not its duration, but its donation."

Width

If success isn't to be found in length of life, then maybe it is in width.

In the Middle Ages, Genghis Khan developed the military strategy of firepower and mobility, and utilizing the pincher movement he invaded the western world. At one time, he ruled from China to Eastern Europe. And still today, he holds the distinction of having made the largest land conquest in military history. In the twentieth century Adolf Hitler ruled more of the modern world than any other person.

Both men had great width. But who would want to be like Khan or Hitler? Yet, we are so convinced that width is a measure of success today. We crave power, influence, control as if to have these proves we are somebody.

Why do you think a small college professor pushes himself to write a book, interview for employment with a bigger university, and eventually control a large research budget, all the while abusing his spouse, ignoring his children, and neglecting his students? He's selling his soul for width!

About a year before his death, George Bernard Shaw, largely considered to be the twentieth century's most educated person, granted one of his rare interviews to a journalist. The reporter questioned the aged playwright at length. Finally he asked, "Mr. Shaw, you have known some of the greatest men of our time: statesmen, artists, philosophers, writers, and musicians. You've now outlived most of them. Suppose it were possible for you to call back one of those great minds — which one would it be? What person do you most miss?" Without hesitation, the old man answered, "The man I miss the most is the man I used to be!"

What is success? What does it look like? How much does it cost? Where do I find it? If it is not in length or width, perhaps it is in ...

Height

Height says that success is in fame, popularity, wealth, the size of your house, the sort of car you drive, and in your wardrobe. Yet there are those who hustle to get all of those things only to find themselves strangely empty.

Poet Robert W. Service in his poem, "The Spell of the Yukon," admits,

> *I wanted the gold, and I sought it; I scrabbled and
> mucked like a slave.*
> *Was it famine or scurvy — I fought it; I hurled my youth
> into a grave.*
> *I wanted the gold, and I got it — Came out with a for-
> tune last fall.*
> *Yet somehow life's not what I thought it, and somehow
> the gold isn't all.*

Tucked away in the Old Testament is an obscure book called Ecclesiastes. Basically it is a journal King Solomon kept. In it he confesses that he's reached the height and width and length of life. Was it money? He had it. Was it sexual pleasure? He had hundreds of beautiful wives. Was it military power, architectural splendor, fame — he'd known it all. "All this is vanity," he complained. Nothing satisfied.

Again and again the poets, playwrights, rock stars, athletes, presidents, and playboys of history have told us that worldly riches are like nuts — many a clothes torn in trying to climb high to get

226

them, many a tooth chipped in trying to crack them, but never a belly full in eating them.

I once visited a man who had just suffered a drastic financial setback. Crushed from the economic loss the man cried, "Everything is gone! Gone! It's all lost!" Without hesitation, I said, "Oh, I'm so sorry to hear that your wife is dead." The man looked up at me in alarm. "My wife?" I continued, "And I'm doubly sad to hear that you have lost your children!" "My children?" the man whispered. "And, oh, how it pains me to learn you've lost your character, your church, your friends, and your God, Christ!" The man protested, saying he'd lost none of those things I'd mentioned. "But I thought you said you'd lost everything!" The man sobered, and it wasn't long before he realized that he'd actually lost none of the things that matter most in life.

After all, money can buy a bed, but not sleep; books, but not wisdom; a harlot, but not love; food, but not appetite; sin's pleasures, but not salvation's peace. It can buy a house, but not a home; medicine, but not health; notoriety, but not character.

Depth

So, what's left? If success is not in height or width or length of life, is it then in depth?

Jesus' parable of the wise and foolish, or successful and failed builders tells us that depth or foundations are the most important element in building successfully.

One man built high and wide and long on a shallow, sandy foundation. The other built up and out and long on a deep foundation of stone. The shallow one caved in while the deep one stood.

Foundations are everything, Jesus said.

Botanists tell me that there is more unseen to a tree than is seen. Roots are everything. Branches, leaves, and fruit are only secondary. Jesus is saying that just as a tree's measure is in its roots, just as the measure of a building is in its foundation, so the measure of a person's life is depth.

Shallow people are like rootless trees or houses with poor foundations; they cannot take pressure very well. In storms they collapse. Their lives are only good in easy, fair-weather times.

227

Deep people, however, are good for real emergencies. They can think and act, endure and provide. The more difficult the time, the better their leadership.

Oceanographers tell me that there are depths of the sea never disturbed by the hurricanes that often buffet the surface of the sea with terrible waves, winds, and rain. Just beneath the surface is a depth of unruffled quiet. A person of depth is like that. All around him may be a world of confusion, a storm of controversy, yet inside is a deep pool of serenity.

Someone asked John Quincy Adams, at age eighty, how he was doing. "John Quincy Adams is very well, thank you," he replied, "but the house he lives in is sadly dilapidated." As the Bible says in 2 Corinthians 4:16, "Our outer nature is wasting away, but our inner nature is being renewed." We lose our width and height, even length. But the depth inside grows!

Roy Burhart has a novel about Purdy, an old family retainer of a Scottish castle. His fortune is gone, his land devastated by years, his wife long dead, yet Purdy lives on. "How do you do it?" he is asked. "You see the outworks," Purdy explained. "For years they have lain in ruins, but the castle has always stood. So with me. When I lost my savings, when my wife died, when my son didn't come back from the war — well as you might say, the outworks were stormed, but, sir, I have kept the castle! I haven't surrendered my faith in Jesus, and hardness and bitterness haven't gotten inside. And if they do, sir, it will be my fault!"

Yes, a person can lose his height, his width, even his length of life, but if he still has his depth, if his life is still founded on the rock, why, measure him or her a success!

Abe Lincoln is a study in depth. Because he was tall and gawky-looking, "polite" Washington society called him a "gorilla." Because he was born in a log cabin, self-taught, and from rural America, he was considered a country bumpkin. His own presidential cabinet was disloyal to him. Congress did not respect him. Some even accused his wife of being a Southern spy. George McClellan, his primary general, even ran against him in the next election. President Lincoln had no width or height. Even the length of his life was cut short by an assassin's bullet. But he had depth.

228

Foundation. Roots. Because of that, he has endured to become the greatest president the United States has ever had.

Such depth is no accident. It is, as Jesus said in the parable, built in intentionally as one hears the word of Jesus and is careful to obey. Depth is the product of the time and relationship with Christ over many years. In Ephesians 3:16-20, Paul writes that we may be "strengthened with might through his spirit in the inner man, and that Christ may dwell in your hearts through faith; that you being rooted and grounded in love, may have power to comprehend with all the saints what is the breadth and length and height and depth, and to know the love of Christ which surpasses all knowledge."

Foundation. Roots. Depth. It comes in the love of God, in Christ, in knowing his word, walking obediently in his Spirit, in realizing his sovereignty, in prayer, in trust, in building the church, in living out his calling in relationship to his people. Such things, Jesus taught, are foundational. They make life sturdy.

Conclusion

Carol, a friend of mine, was a reporter with a Florida television station. She once confided in me, "Stephen, I've interviewed them all. Ford, Carter, Mondale, Reagan. I've talked to judges, athletes, beauty queens, and millionaires. But these aren't the most interesting people. The ones I enjoy most, the most real people, are the store clerks at the little hardware store by the crossroads, the woman who is single and has taught school in the same inner-city neighborhood for 21 years. Possessing very little width or length or even height, they have one thing — depth. In a shallow world, that made them stick out."

I know in my own life I struggle with success. I, too, can easily give myself to the pursuit of making more money, publishing, making a name for myself, looking younger, gaining power ... maybe it's in the next job or the church in the next city. But I have learned a thing or two in my 54 years.

It is not what I do, but in who I am.

It doesn't matter what I look like, where I live or how I dress.

I am basically responsible for the depth of my life — hearing and doing Christ's Word. And God is responsible for how long I live, how much width and height I attain.

William H. Channing had it right when he wrote his creed —

> *To live content with small means.*
> *To seek elegance rather than luxury,*
> *And refinement rather than fashion.*
> *To be worthy, not respectable.*
> *And wealthy, not rich.*
> *To study hard, think quietly,*
> *Talk gently, act frankly.*
> *To listen to stars and birds,*
> *To babes and sages with open heart.*
> *To bear all cheerfully, do all bravely,*
> *Await occasion, hurry never.*
> *In a word, to let the spiritual,*
> *Unbidden and unconscious grow up*
> *Through the common.*
> *This is my symphony.*

Stephen M. Crotts

How To Motivate People

A few years ago a fellow took me on a tour of his sock manufacturing plant. He showed me the loading dock where raw materials were unloaded, the washing machines, fluffers, twisters, looms, finishers, and packagers. In all, I found out there were over 150 different steps taken to manufacture one pair of socks! Well, that set me to thinking about the church and the making of disciples. How many steps are there from conversion to discipleship? Let's look and see.

The text reports an incident near the beginning of Christ's ministry. It happened at Matthew's place of business. Jesus called him to follow. The text says that Matthew got up and followed him and that Jesus then had dinner at Matthew's house. The Pharisees chastised Jesus because he was eating "with tax collectors and sinners." Clearly, Jesus was setting his agenda of calling *all* people, not just a select few. Jesus showed Matthew and those gathered with him how important they were to God.

He Chose

Now here is a key principle to establish in discipling. Christ wouldn't allow people to choose him. Instead he chose them. He selected those "whom he desired." The question is, why?

Think for a moment. Aren't there a lot of people who want to be with you, people who constantly make demands on your time, but who aren't really all that interested in your gospel? Oh, they like you because you are a good listener, or because you have a

Gameboy or because you're a fine softball player. But what they don't want from you is discipleship.

Jesus had people pulling on him all the time. "Bid my brother divide the inheritance with me." "My son is ill. Come and heal him." But he spent most of his time with the twelve he selected to be with him. They were the ones who wanted his gospel. They were the ones who asked, "Lord, teach us to pray." "Lord, explain again to us the parable."

Why Just Twelve?

Now the question might arise, why did Christ select only twelve men? Why didn't he select 24 or 100 or, better still, 1,000? Some say he selected twelve to symbolize the twelve tribes of Israel and to point to Christianity as being the new Israel. There is merit in such a notion.

Then, too, maybe Jesus couldn't find any more than twelve people who were interested in his gospel. Even today if you start a small group Bible study in your home, you're lucky to find twelve men who will come.

But I think there is a deeper reason here, and that is human limitations. Answer me this: which of you has more than twelve people in whose lives you are intimately involved, with whom you are directly available? Why, the most of us would be hard-pressed to point to six much less twelve. The fact is, life being what it is, and people being who they are, one man cannot disciple more than a dozen people at a time.

The principle here is this: We must narrow our focus to a dozen or less people or our energies will be dissipated to nothingness.

Why These Dozen Men?

Christ did the choosing. He narrowed it down to twelve men. But why these twelve? And in the case of our text, why Matthew as one of them?

James and John, so hot-tempered they were called the sons of thunder. Really! And Peter, that blustering big-mouthed backslider. Why him? Thomas, the doubter? Judas, a zealot terrorist who was to betray him? Why these twelve? They weren't rich. They weren't

232

of high social standing. They weren't so well educated. Why, even their commitments varied! Matthew was a hated tax collector, one who, because he worked for the Roman overlords, was an outcast to his own people.

What were they then? Why were they acceptable to Jesus as disciples?

They were teachable. They could learn. They were willing to rethink Judaism.

Are you teachable? Can you learn? Or have you already made up your mind what you believe about God?

They were also available. Matthew left his tax office, James and John their fishing nets, and together they spent time with Jesus. The text says, "And he rose and followed."

Are you available? Will you leave your fun, your boat, your computer, your television set to follow him?

And another thing they were. These twelve were willing to assume responsibility for ministry. They were willing to get involved and stay involved with people. Matthew actually wrote a gospel book.

To Be With Him

So what have we seen so far?

Jesus did the choosing. He narrowed it to twelve. He chose the ones who were teachable, available, and willing to assume responsibility.

Okay, so what's the next step in the process of discipleship? What did Jesus do with them now? They spent time together. They lived together. They observed people. They weathered conflict. They ate and slept together. They succeeded some, failed some, asked questions, and heard sermon after parable after teaching! In the text they ministered in a sick room.

Here's the principle! Christianity is caught and not taught. A magnet cannot teach magnetism to a lump of iron. But if the two spend time together, if the magnet rubs up against the iron, very soon you will have two magnets. It's the same with disciple making. Choose a teachable, available, responsible person and spend

233

time with him in Christ for three years, and you've got yourself a disciple.

This is where the church is failing today. Many church leaders aren't discipled themselves. If they are, the people won't allow them to do their jobs as disciple makers. All their time is spent doing chaplaincy ministry to the unteachable, unavailable, and irresponsible members who somehow got on the church roll.

Dear people, I'm here to make disciples. I'm not here to coddle you. If you will be teachable, responsible, available, then rise, take up your cross and follow Jesus.

He chose twelve to be with him. That means they experienced life together. Their lives were prioritized around Jesus.

Is yours? Socially? Mentally? Spiritually? Physically? Too many prioritize their lives around making money and having a fine time. But these twelve spent time with Jesus. They were "with him."

It's interesting. In Matthew 10:11 following, Jesus told his disciples, "And whatever town or village you enter, find out who is worthy in it and stay with him until you depart." We don't do this today. Instead, we buy our own home, or rent one, and live to ourselves and get together with people on Sundays at 11 a.m. The result is that we don't spend enough time together for thorough discipling to take place.

One place we do live together with teachable, available people who are willing to assume responsibility is in our families. Your most disciple-able people will forever be your children and your mate!

Another insight into this portion of the text is the fact that the gospel is a person, not a theology. Christ didn't just give Matthew and the others the facts. He also gave them a living experience of himself morning, noon, and night. It's the same here in this church. For instance, prayer is more than a theology, a sermon, a book. It is getting down on our knees together regularly and experiencing life together in Christ. Do that for three years and you'll learn how to live in prayer!

234

Responsibility

Be careful to notice the next step in the process. After Christ gave himself to Matthew. He began to see to it that Matthew gave himself to others. Those who were ministered to became ministers. Takers became givers. Verse 19 in our text says that Jesus went to touch a child who had just died, and the disciples went with him, Matthew included. They went to share in the ministry.

Here again is where we run afoul of the discipleship process in today's Christianity. People don't want to assume responsibility today. We'd rather pass it off on someone else. We are afraid to get involved in ministry like evangelism or preaching or comfort calls. So we set up barriers like "Ministry is not authentic unless a Reverend does it" or "I can't! I haven't been to seminary." Listen, Jesus was the only seminary these twelve ever attended. And Jesus can be your seminary, too. And it is Christ's Holy Spirit who makes one a minister — not an educational degree or position or clerical collar.

Are you willing to assume responsibility for the love of people? Are you willing to get involved in ministry? Are you willing to receive from Jesus and pass ministry on to another twelve or so people? If you are, you can become both a disciple of Jesus and a disciple maker. If not, well frankly, you just washed out of Christendom's boot camp! So why pretend?

Accountability

There is one final step in the process of disciple making. Those whom Christ sent out to minister, he held accountable for their duties. You can see this in Luke 10:17 following. The disciples "returned with joy, saying, 'Lord, even the demons are subject to us in your name!' " There you have the exciting results of ministry. "They returned with joy!" It wasn't boring or fearful, but joyful. Was their ministry authentic? "Even the demons" were subject to them. But notice the further accountability and evaluation Christ offered. "I saw Satan fall!" Christ said in triumph. Satan still falls when people assume responsibility to go out and minister! But then Jesus sobers his disciples. "Do not rejoice in this, that the spirits are subject to you, but rejoice that your names are

235

written in heaven." You see, there would come a time, and there still comes a time, in the lives of disciples when ministry wasn't always successful or easy or necessarily triumphant. Christ was pointing them to heaven where it will all come right in God's plan.

It is amazing how many of Christ's parables deal with responsibility and accountability. A steward given a sum of money to work with while the master is away and a master who returns to say, "Okay, now what have you been doing?" Or a servant put in charge of a household who gets drunk and squanders his time while the boss is away, but who gets fired when he returns. Accountability. We are held accountable to God for what we do with what we have.

Conclusion

Are you a disciple? If not, do you want to be? Are you available? Teachable? Are you willing to abandon preconceived notions and learn from Christ's own words? Are you willing to spend time with other Christians who can disciple you? Are you willing to accept responsibility, to minister, and to be held accountable?

Beyond the question of your personal discipleship is the question, "Are you making any disciples of other people?" How about your mate? What about your children? What about others around you in the Body of Christ? Maybe you're not up to discipling twelve people like the Master did, but what about starting with yourself and one other person? Love demands as much!

Suggested Prayer

Lord, I would follow thee. Help me, Lord, help me! For Christ's sake. Amen.

Stephen M. Crotts

236

Proper 6
Pentecost 4
Ordinary Time 11
Matthew 9:35—10:8

Sick And Tired Of
Being Sick And Tired?

"Heal the sick," Jesus commanded (Matthew 10:8). His orders leave our knees knocking and us feeling inadequate.

In Edward Albee's play, *The Death of Bessie Smith*, a character rages, "I'm sick! Sick of everything in this fly-ridden world! I am sick of waking up, I am tired of the truth, I am tired of lying about the truth, tired of my skin! I want out, I want off this world!" Now, that, my friend, is desperate sickness! And perhaps today, as you read this, you find yourself ill. My question is, "Would you like to be well?"

Have you ever wondered about sickness? Wondered what the Bible says about healing? In the text, Christ heals the infirm. And he commissions his disciples to do the same. Let's take a look at scripture and see what can be learned about healing.

In Genesis 2:7, we are told what there is about us to be sick or well. We are told God made Adam's physical body out of the clay of the ground. Then God blew his Divine Spirit into the man, and Adam became a living soul. That means he had an emotion, a will, and an intellect. In 1 Thessalonians 5:23, the Apostle Paul writes to the Greek church, and he prays for their health saying, "May the God of peace himself sanctify you wholly; and may your *spirit* and *soul* and *body* be kept sound and blameless at the coming of our Lord Jesus Christ." So, you see, good health is not just physical. It is also spiritual, emotional, intellectual, willful, and even relational. Such is the health the Lord wants us to enjoy.

In our text today, Jesus gives instruction to the disciples as he sends them out to do the works of compassion and the kingdom

237

work that all believers need to do. Jesus reminds them there is always more work than there are people to do it, but that they should go out anyway.

Then Jesus instructs the twelve. Listen to the things Jesus tells them to do:

- Preach the message that the kingdom of heaven is near
- Heal the sick
- Raise the dead
- Drive out demons
- Freely you have received, freely give

That's quite a list! We could spend a long time dealing with each of these, but today we're going to focus on the command to heal the sick.

Jesus was not alone in the New Testament in calling for believers to heal the sick. James especially gives some detailed instruction for believers as they seek to bring healing through the power of God.

James asks the question, "Is any among you sick?" Scripture points out that there are several types of illnesses. There is a sickness unto sin. Psalm 107:17 says, "Some were sick through their sinful ways, and because of their iniquities suffered affliction." An illness due to sin could be something like worry and a nervous breakdown, overeating and a bad heart, sexual immorality and venereal disease, cigarette smoking and cancer, and more. You don't need me to tell you that sicknesses due to sin are epidemic today!

A doctor recently expressed. "My patients abuse themselves with food, overwork, smoking, lack of exercise, and too much booze. Then they come to me for a pill to make it all better. Their illnesses are self-inflicted. Their cure must be self-administered by right choices."

The Bible also makes it clear that there is also a sickness due to Satan. In Job 2:7 we are told, "Satan went forth from the presence of the Lord, and afflicted Job with loathsome sores from the sole of his foot to the crown of his head." Basic historic Christianity has recognized that some illnesses are traceable to demonic activity. Some are sick due to satanic *oppression*. The evil one has

238

backed some people into a corner, tempted them, and the individual has fallen to that temptation so often that he is enslaved. It could be some compulsive habit that is unhealthy. It could be something that has brought on neurotic behavior. Whatever the case, the individual needs deliverance. (I might add here, that satanic oppression is not always due to sin. Job, a righteous man, was sorely oppressed by Satan. There was no particular sin in Job's life. Satan seemed to have oppressed him arbitrarily.) Scripture also affirms that there is a sickness caused by possession. Satan can not only *tempt* and *oppress* an individual, he can also *possess* someone. Here, exorcism is required to clear up physical and emotional maladies.

So, there is a sickness due to sin, a sickness due to Satan, and, according to scripture, there is a sickness to the glory of God. In John 9:1-3 a group of men saw a blind child and inquired of Jesus, "Who sinned, this man or his parents, that he was born blind?" Jesus answered, "It was not that this man sinned, or his parents, but that the works of God might be made manifest in him." I think many of us are like the disciples. We like to trace all illnesses to Satan or some secret sin in someone's life. But this is not always the case. Jesus said that some sickness is for the glory of God. We live in a broken world. We can be born with deformities like blindness, hormonal imbalances, and mental deficiencies. Furthermore, this broken world can break us. This is seen in childhood diseases, accidents, and natural disasters. Saint Paul had his own famous "thorn" in his flesh. He suffered with it throughout his adult life. Of course, Jesus endured crucifixion. Both of them, Jesus and Paul, suffered for God's glory. They suffered with God as he worked to restore this broken, sinful world.

Are you sick? It could be a sickness unto sin or Satan or the glory of God. It could also be a sickness unto death. Isaiah said to King Hezekiah, "Thus says the Lord: 'Set your house in order; for you shall die, you shall not recover' " (Isaiah 38:1). Look at it this way; there has to sooner or later be a sickness in your life that is fatal. If there were not, how would you ever get to heaven? Can you imagine two unborn twins in their mother's womb? What if they could talk? When the time of birth comes they struggle against

239

it. Where they are is warmth and food and security. The outside world is new to them. They are afraid to be born, and they fight it. We do that with death, too, don't we?

Here we have our loved ones, a home of sorts, and a familiarity with the way things are. When a sickness unto death comes upon us, we struggle against it like an unborn child. Yet our death is but a birth into heaven.

Your Response To Sickness

There are many different kinds of sickness and there are many ways of responding to sickness as well. James says, "Is any among you sick? Let him call for the elders of the church." Here, we are told to seek spiritual assistance in our afflictions. Here, we are told to call for the church authorities. Pray for yourself, sure! But call for the elders as well.

I've noticed what people are accustomed to doing when they become ill. It's a kind of game they seem to be playing. Some creep off to the hospital very quietly. They don't want anyone to know about it. Others shut themselves up in their home and quietly put the elders to the test. "How long will it take them to miss me?" they ask. Sometimes several weeks pass and the sick person feels injured, insulted! "Why, I'm so important in this community they should have missed me the second day," they rage.

Why is it that many expect the elders to know of their illness when they haven't been notified? Perhaps it's an attempt to find something to criticize. There are some people like that, you know. Maybe it's a test to see if the elders are omnipotent. The reasoning goes like this usually, "They're elders and they should know." In case you missed it, that's like saying, "They're God and they should know everything or they're not doing their jobs."

The scripture puts an end to all this foolishness! The sick have more responsibility than just being sick, for the Bible very clearly says that when you are ill it is your responsibility to call for the elders. If your house were on fire you'd call the fire department. You wouldn't wait for them to smell smoke or by chance happen by. You'd call them right away! The same with your elders. Call them! Go by their house. Use the phone or a letter, but

240

you personally call them! Say, "Pastor, I'm ill. Could you please come by with the elders and pray for me?"

In case you are wondering why the text stresses your calling for the elders, I'll tell you. It's an act of faith. When Jesus walked in Galilee the sick called out to him! They traveled to meet him. They were let down on beds through the roof. They cried out as lepers. "Lord, heal me!" They sought to touch the hemline of his garment. And to the many that Jesus healed, he said, "Go your way. Your faith has made you well."

What Do The Elders Do?

So far we've discerned four varieties of illness and seen how it is the responsibility of the sick to exercise faith, to take the initiative and call out for mature assistance. Now the text explains the elders' roll. It instructs, "Let them pray over him, anointing him with oil in the name of the Lord."

Some background here: In the Greek, the word "elder" is *presbuteros*. We get the word "presbyterian" from that. It literally means the "gray-bearded ones," the older, more mature spiritual men. In the Old Testament the temple priests were the original physicians. In them was what medical knowledge there was. Priests quarantined lepers, taught people to wash in running water, burned contaminated bed clothes, and prayed for Israel's general welfare and health.

When the text says elders "anoint with oil," the word "oil" could be translated as "medicine." Psalm 23 soothes, "Thou anointest my head with oil." Sheep, you see, incurred all manner of bug bites and scratches. It was easy for these to get infected. So the good shepherd made an antiseptic salve and rubbed it on his little lambs. Not only did it act as a bug repellant. It also helped heal.

Luke's Gospel, likewise, shares the parable of the Good Samaritan. When the beaten victim was left for dead, the kind stranger poured wine and oil on his wounds. Same idea. Wine was an antiseptic. Oil was a form of medicine.

Today's elders may prescribe the oil of modern medical know-how for your sickness as well. You might be asked to get a good

241

check-up. (Did you know an abscessed tooth can cause depression?) Science, you see, is a gift of God. Modern physicians have studied the ways of God's laws and are so often able to bring relief.

"Elders," "oil," — these are weighted words that require background study to fully comprehend their meaning. Now let's consider the laying on of hands, the touching, that is a very real portion of the elder's healing ministry.

A touch makes a connection between two people. It shows concern — a nurse holding a frightened child's hand during a procedure, a grandchild kissing his grandpa as he recovers in bed. It's a way of saying, "I'm here. I care."

Research is discovering that a touch does so much more than transmit good will. There is also an intangible surge of power that flows through a touch. A woman who for many years suffered from a serious hemorrhage reached out to Jesus one day. Her thoughts were, "If I but touch the hemline of his garment, I shall be made well." Jesus, the Bible says, perceived "power went forth from him."

The largest organ in the human body is the skin. Many sick persons are so seldom touched except to administer a shot or to roll over in bed. They develop what scientists now call "skin hunger." A combination of depression, lack of stimulation, and longing for bonding. Only the kindness of touching can bring relief.

Oil, elders, touching — this is the focus of an elder's healing ministry. Now, one thing more — prayer. "Let them pray over him," the text says. This is simply when we pray asking Jesus to love the sufferer with his presence, his will, and his healing power. Two phrases qualify how our prayers should be. "In the name of the Lord." That is — in God's will. And "the prayer of faith" — of trust not doubting. This is our prayer.

What's The Result?

So far we've looked at different types of sicknesses. We've looked at your responsibility to call for the elders. We've looked at the elder's task of counseling, touching, prayer, and sometimes referral. Now, let us examine what the result of all this is. What is

God's responsibility? The text says, "And the prayer of faith will save the sick man, and the Lord will raise him up."

If you follow Jesus around in his New Testament ministry, you will find him healing many people of various diseases. He healed those who were sick due to some sin (Matthew 9:1-8). He healed those oppressed or possessed by Satan (Mark 5; Luke 13:10-16; Job). He healed some that were sick for the glory of God (John 9:1-33). In some cases God even healed those sick unto death (John 11:1-44; Isaiah 38).

Yes, the Lord healed many. But it is not true that Jesus healed in every time and in every place. He did not heal Saint Paul's thorn in the flesh (2 Corinthians 12). Nor did he heal young Timothy's stomach disorder (1 Timothy 5:23). He didn't even heal his own wounds of crucifixion on the cross. And in John 5, Christ walked off leaving an entire crowd unhealed except for one.

Now, understand this, dear people: The Lord always heals, either right now or in the resurrection. He can choose to heal us, or he can choose to give us the grace to bear it until death and the resurrection when we receive a new body. God can work in many and marvelous ways. A lady named Mrs. Williams became ill with cancer. She took treatments of chemotherapy, but only got worse. Her church held a prayer meeting just for her. They laid hands on her and all prayed. When she returned to the doctor, x-rays showed no further evidence of cancer whatsoever. God can heal us still! He can heal through doctors and prayer, through many channels. He can still heal our spiritual, mental, physical, and social illnesses.

But the Lord does not always offer the easy cure. He does not always offer a way out. Sometimes he offers a way through. He offers the grace to bear the sickness for his glory.

In a church I formerly served, was Cindy. Wife, mother, busy volunteer, professional clown — she was an all-around good, lovely woman. Then Cindy got cancer. I still don't understand it, but cancer ate her alive! And Cindy prayed! Oh, how she prayed! The elders anointed her with oil. People fasted. I was absolutely certain Jesus would heal Cindy. Still she died. But, oh! How Cindy died! She died one of the most triumphant deaths I've ever seen!

243

Before she perished, Cindy read a poem one Sunday morning to the entire church. Here is what she wrote...

ALMOST PERFECT

Only two Chemo's left!
PRAISE GOD!!!
It's almost over
Soon I'll be back to my old self
Going to work
Selling cosmetics
Cooking for family and friends
Doing all the things I've put off doing ...
Because of the "Big C."
Yes, I'll be ALMOST PERFECT.
Then I look in the mirror at the scars
Two where my breasts were
One where my catheter was
One where my colostomy was
One where a drainage tube was inserted
One where my hysterectomy was, and last but not least...
One that runs the length of my stomach ... that's been used twice.
Quite a picture of beauty!!
I didn't realize how important a woman's body is to her until now.
I still avoid looking in too many mirrors because I still can't believe I'm seeing ME!!!
Who is that person devoid of almost all hair on her body
And those horrible red gashes all over her soft white skin?
How can this be???
What did she do to deserve this mutilation of her healthy flesh?
How could GOD let this happen to one of His own?
Then I realize these are the scars of a warrior. A warrior strong in battle.
Only warriors get battle scars.
I straighten up and proudly admire the scars in the mirror.

244

These are my badges of honor.
I earned every one by the grace of GOD!!!!!
I am proud to be a member of the ARMY OF GOD!

Not a day goes by that I don't think of Cindy's victorious life. Her courage, her faith, her grace is a tonic to me. For God doesn't always offer an easy way out. Sometimes he offers a way through.

In Isaiah 43:1-2 we read, "Fear not, for I have redeemed you; I have called you by name, You are mine. When you pass through the waters I will be with you; And through the rivers, they shall not overwhelm you; when you walk through fire you shall not be burned, and the flame shall not consume you."

Living The Promise!

Jesus sent the disciples out with a sense of urgency to bring about healing of soul and body alike. The harvest is still plentiful and the need for willing workers remains. Realize that God is still sending his people out to hurting people everywhere ... and that he may be sending you to a healing ministry or a preaching of the Good News in the places and with the people you know the best.

Suggested Prayer

We give thee thanks, O God, for your healing ministry. We thank you that you not only care for the health of our spirit, but for our minds and bodies as well. Help us to make it a habit to call on you and your church for all our health needs. For Christ's sake. Amen.

Stephen M. Crotts

245

Proper 7
Pentecost 5
Ordinary Time 12
Matthew 10:24-39

God, The Enemy

Do you remember when Timothy McVeigh, the man responsible for the bombing of the federal building in Oklahoma City, was executed? As the time of his execution drew near, McVeigh gave a handwritten statement to the warden, intending it to take the place of any verbal comment. In that statement, McVeigh quoted a section of the poem "Invictus," which is Latin for "unconquered." That poem, by nineteenth-century British poet William Ernest Henley (1849-1903), reads, in part, "I am the master of my fate: I am the captain of my soul."

In case you haven't heard the poem, here it is:

Out of the night that covers me,
Black as the Pit from pole to pole,
I thank whatever gods may be
For my unconquerable soul.

In the fell clutch of circumstance
I have not winced nor cried aloud,
Under the bludgeonings of chance
My head is bloody, but unbowed.

Beyond this place of wrath and tears
Looms but the horror of the shade,
And yet the menace of the years
Finds, and shall find me, unafraid.

It matters not how strait the gate,
How charged with punishments the scroll,
I am the master of my fate:
I am the captain of my soul.

From what we had learned of McVeigh's attitudes and opinions, those lines probably came as close as any to a philosophy of life for him. Even to the point of ending the appeals process, McVeigh sought to be the master of his fate.

But of course he was not. And in a letter written just a day before his death, he demonstrated how little he understood that. He wrote that if it turned out that there was an afterlife, he would "improvise, adapt and overcome."[1] As if he or any of us will have the ability to affect our environment after arrival in the world to come! Once we are at the judgment seat of God, none of us is any longer master of our fate.

One man, hearing of McVeigh's reference to "Invictus," said that it made him recall Mrs. Johnson, his eighth-grade English teacher. That was the year they read "Invictus" in English class, as part of a unit on poetry. The man said that although he could not remember what other poems they studied that year, this one stuck with him because it was the only one where Mrs. Johnson took issue with the poet. After reading the whole poem, she challenged her class to look again at the last lines, "I am the master of my fate: I am the captain of my soul," and to discuss whether they could indeed reflect the true state of affairs. She even asked whether in any sense, those words could be considered bravado, a posturing of courage in the face of frightening things humans cannot control.

It's worth noting that when the poet Henley wrote those words, he probably was not thinking of setting his own standard of morality, as McVeigh appears to have done. Far from claiming the right to be judge, jury, and executioner of others, Henley was vocalizing his attitude toward the hurts and setbacks of life. At the age of twelve, Henley developed tubercular arthritis, and his left foot was amputated in his teens. He had other health problems later on and actually wrote "Invictus" while once again in the hospital, too ill to work. He was, as his poem says, "bloody, but unbowed." For

Henley, "Invictus" was an expression of courage in the face of life's difficulties, not a license to kill.

Henley had a long, close friendship with the great author, Robert Louis Stevenson, who in fact, based part of the character of Long John Silver in *Treasure Island* on his one-footed, hearty friend.

Stevenson wrote of Henley's poem that, "[Henley] wanted me to understand that 'I am the master of my fate: I am the captain of my soul,' not my teachers, family, friends, money, or the 'powers,' that may be. To come 'out of the night that covers me,' I must be 'unafraid,' 'unbowed,' and 'unconquerable.' "[2]

What might Jesus have said about the sentiment expressed in the "Invictus"? Actually, we could say that he has already rendered a judgment about it. We find it in Matthew 10:28: "Do not fear those who kill the body but cannot kill the soul; rather fear him who can destroy both body and soul in hell."

This is a troubling verse, for Jesus is not talking about Satan, but about *God*. Jesus presents God as the *enemy* — the ultimate enemy — in whose hands our final fate lies. Those who would kill the body — a body that cannot survive forever in any case — are one thing. But to put ourselves above the moral reality God has planted within us is another matter altogether, for we stand to lose that which not even death itself can take away.

To grasp the starkness of what Jesus was saying here, consider the experience of Victor Frankl, a survivor of the Nazi death camps. If ever there was an earthly enemy — one with the power to kill the body — there it was. But Frankl writes about the things that the Nazis, with all their evil power, could not take away. He recalls men living in the camps with him, who despite starving themselves, nonetheless walked through the huts comforting others, and giving away their last piece of bread. He saw that as evidence of one human freedom that no earthly power can take away: the freedom "to choose one's attitude in any given set of circumstances."[3] So even the worst that this world can throw at us cannot take everything.

But there is one, if we understand what Jesus is saying, who can take even that final freedom — and everything that we are.

Perhaps that is why Frankl writes that for those like him who had not yet been killed when the Allies liberated the concentration camp inmates, there was "the wonderful feeling that, after all he has suffered, there is nothing he need fear any more — *except his God*"[4] (emphasis mine).

Admittedly, we don't often think of God as an enemy, but when we are refusing him entry into our lives, barricading our spirits against his admission, he becomes for us the enemy at the gates. The noted philosopher of an earlier era, Alfred North Whitehead, once wrote that, "Religion is the transition from God the void to God the enemy, and from God the enemy to God the companion."[5] Life without awareness of God is meeting God the void; life confronted by God is meeting God the enemy. What it takes to get to God the companion is *surrender* — exactly what one does when an enemy wins.

For many of us, our first surrender to God came not because God gently asked permission to come into our lives. More likely he used a battering ram to punch an enormous hole in our emotions or some other aspect of our being. He came in like an invader, commandeered space, and made it clear that we'd better learn to live with his presence, at least for a while.

God, it seems, is not one to pussyfoot around, patiently waiting in the background until we choose to invite him in. When he decides he's coming, he comes, using any one of several portals into our soul. The fact that we may have them fortified seems not to matter.

We then have a choice — either make peace with him or turn him out by force. If we insist on being invictus, an unconquered soul, then there are grounds for thinking of God as our enemy.

God is also the enemy in that he draws lines in the sand and says, "You shall not...." You shall not step over these. And if you do, there are consequences.

When the people of Judah crossed those lines, they heard God's word through the prophet Hosea. It was a call to repent, but it also recounted the judgment that had befallen them specifically at God's hand: "Come, let us return to the Lord; for it is he who has torn, and he will heal us; he has struck down, and he will bind us up"

(Hosea 6:1). We tend to hear only the positive parts of that verse — "Repent ... he will heal us ... he will bind us up." But the words in between speak of an equal reality — "it is he who has torn ... he has struck down."

Luke also records this story we read from Matthew. Luke too reports Jesus describing God in adversarial terms, but Luke also adds Jesus' comment about the sin that cannot be forgiven, the blasphemy against the Holy Spirit (Luke 12:10). The work of the Holy Spirit is to reveal God's truth to us and to convict us of our sins. The only way to blaspheme against the Holy Spirit is to reject what the Spirit reveals to us, to refuse the conviction and deny God's truth. Thus we do not repent, for we say, "I have nothing to repent of." If we will not repent, we cannot be forgiven. If we persist in that way long enough, we eventually lose the ability to hear the Spirit. We can't be forgiven because we see no reason to repent.

Given that definition, it would seem that Timothy McVeigh, with his self-proclaimed unconquered soul, might be a poster child for the unpardonable sin. But of course, ultimate judgment is up to God, not to us. And although McVeigh said he was an agnostic (as, by the way, was Henley), during his final hours he reportedly accepted a visit from a Catholic priest, who gave him last rites.

Of course, Jesus did not warn of the danger of losing our souls just to scare us. He wants our fear to serve us well, to drive us to God, to cause us to live with the good fear of the Lord within us. The same God who knows the hair count of our heads and who cares for lowly sparrows wants our allegiance and our love, for we are of more value than many sparrows, Jesus says.

Jesus tells us that God does not want to be our enemy, but until we have surrendered first place to him, the outlook for inner peace is bleak. Christ wants us to be able to say, "God is the master of my faith, the captain of my soul."

That affirmation has a great bearing on this life, but where that may count most is in the life beyond the grave. Where it is decided, however, is right here, by each one of us, on this side of eternity.

251

1. Jon Bonne, "Unrepentent McVeigh is executed" MSNBC.com, July 11, 2001.

2. www.bowdoin.edu/~azimman/henley.html

3. Viktor E. Frankl, *Man's Search for Meaning* (New York: Washington Square Press, 1963), p. 104.

4. *Ibid.*, p. 148.

5. Quoted in *The Interpreter's Bible*, vol. 8, p. 157.

Stan Purdum

Proper 8
Pentecost 6
Ordinary Time 13
Matthew 10:40-42

In Our Pastor's Success,
So Is Our Own!

Did you hear about the farm boy who always wondered what would happen if he twisted the tail on the mule? One day he tried it. And now they say about him, he's not as pretty as he used to be, but he's a whole lot wiser.

When I was a young man, I wondered what my life would be like if I became a pastor in answer to God's call. Now, thirty years later, I'm not as pretty as I used to be, but I am a lot wiser.

Ministry is not for cowards, the lazy, the easily discouraged, the thin-skinned, or those without endurance. It is a tough occupation! And it's getting tougher!

I love the cartoon that shows a man saying, "I don't get America's fascination with the television show 'Survivor.' I've occupied an island of strenuous and dangerous activities with hostile cohorts with a chance of getting voted out. I've been a pastor for thirty years!"

It used to be, people came in the door of the church over here, and for a small amount of energy, you could grow them in Christ to the farthest side. Now people come in the door way over there, and for an inordinate amount of energy you can grow them the smallest bit. So the pastorate is more demanding, less fulfilling, and burnout, quitting, getting run off, and despair are on the rise as the quality of discipleship and church life plummet.

Over 25 percent of pastors will be put out of the church, fired, or run off at least once in their career. If ten men begin the ministry at age 25, by age 65 only one will still be in the pastorate. I tell you, a crisis is brewing in the church! For there is coming a shortage of good pastors, and with that, a famine of the word of God.

There is an old legend about Satan one day having a yard sale. He thought he'd get rid of some of his old tools that were cluttering up the place. So there was gossip, slander, adultery, lying, greed, power-hunger, and more laid out on the tables. Interested buyers were crowding the tables, curious, handling the goods. One customer, however, strolled way back in the garage and found on a shelf a well-oiled and cared-for tool. He brought it out to Satan and inquired if it was for sale. "Oh, no!" Satan answered. "That's my tool. Without it I couldn't wreck the church! It's my secret weapon!"

"But what is it?" the customer inquired.

"It's the tool of discouragement," the devil said.

Indeed!

In the text Jesus is talking to the church about their attitude and deportment toward the prophets God sends among us as shepherds. He speaks frankly about acceptance and rejection, about kindness and trust. In short, he promises that in the minister's success among us shall come our own reward.

Receive

First of all, Jesus tells us to be careful to receive from God's prophets. Eight times in the brief three verses Jesus used the word, "receive." "He who receives you receives me."

I've noticed that when I preach, certain people in the crowd look up and begin to listen intently. Sometimes they take notes. Sometimes they smile at me. But on a vital level, they receive from me God's word.

Others, however, find fault. They may grimace, they may cross their arms and look out the window, impatient for the preaching ordeal to be over. Then they go out and talk, not about the Word or Jesus, but about me. You see, they will try to find a fault, blow it out of proportion, and crucify with it.

For the one, Jesus and the Word and their own selves are the issue. But for the other, I am the issue.

The one is open. The other is closed. The one is humble. The other quite proud. The one appreciates any pearls from the Word

254

you cast at their feet. They grab them up and treasure them. The other are swine that trample the pearls underfoot with no sense of their value.

I once worked for a tough church. I couldn't do anything right. The grumbling and gripes were never-ending. So were the politics. After four years of patience, I shook the dust off my feet and moved on.

The next church was so kind, so receptive. I kept wondering why they liked me and the other did not.

Then I understood. It's in the first four beatitudes of Matthew 5. The one church was not poor in spirit, mournful, meek, or hungry and thirsty. The other, however, was all these things.

And the conflict is as old as the Pharisees and the disciples. For the both are still in our world.

Over the years I've heard a lot of sermons. And I always meet the pastor if I can at the door of the church. I never say, "Preacher, I enjoyed it!" For sometimes we're not meant to. That's like telling your surgeon you enjoyed his operation. Rather, I look him in the eyes and say, "I receive from you. Thank you. I heard God's Word to me from the text through you."

Rest

The text also urges us to see that our ministers get rest. Jesus talked about giving our prophets a break, time off for a cup of cool water.

Let's face it; a minister's job is never done. There is always another sermon to write, a book to read, prayers to pray, a person to meet, a wrong to right, a meeting to attend. Even the pace of ministry is accelerating thanks to e-mail, faxes, and cell phones. And a pastor, to survive, must learn to work under a load of unfinished work.

Why, today's pastor is like a man juggling a dozen balls well. The people of his congregation keep tossing him more balls until he's up to 64! Then he drops them all and people walk away, shaking their heads in disbelief, they spit in disgust or worse.

Jesus knew the busy pace of ministry. But he had replenishing friendships that gave him breaks from his labors. A friend with a sailboat, a meal with no agenda at Mary and Martha's, a long walk in the great out-of-doors ... these were restful to him.

I challenge you to approach your ministry staff in your parish. Take them out to lunch. Look them in the eyes; ask them how the work is going. Inquire if they're doing too much. Insure they're taking a day off. Ask if they're tired. Ask them what they're doing for fun.

My friend Robert weekly asks me if I'll take a boat ride with him. He constantly invites me to a concert, to live theater. He never "pulls" on me. In his presence, there is no depletion, only replenishing friendship. God may not call you to do that for your minister, but he does call you to see that someone is doing it!

Sharing Materially

Jesus, in the text, urges us to receive from his prophets, to see that they get some rest from their labors. But he also calls on us to pay them for their work.

I once drove 700 miles and preached six times at a weekend church seminar. Afterward, a cranky-looking deacon walked up to me and rudely blurted, "How much do we owe you, preacher?" You could look at his face, his body language, and his white-knuckled grip on the church checkbook and see that he was stingy.

For years I've heard moronic churchmen say dourly of their pastor, "God, you keep him humble and we'll keep him poor!" Don't do that! The Bible says, "The workman is worthy of his hire." Scripture tells us not to "muzzle the ox while he's treading out the grain." A minister lives in the same world you do. His car runs on gasoline. His family needs to eat. His daughter wants piano lessons.

Poor pay can be a form of control. It can spell unfaithfulness in tithing on the part of the church. It is a sure sign of disrespect.

The text urges us to give a cup of cool water to our prophets. It doesn't say give a sip, but a cup! And it says cool water, not room temperature! So, why not refresh your pastor with a salary that shows you value his services and want to make certain you refresh him by the provision of his material needs beyond any question of stinginess.

256

Conclusion

How do we treat God's prophets? We *receive* from them. We give them *rest*. And we faithfully *reimburse* them materially. For this Jesus says we get a *reward*. Three times in these three verses Jesus mentions God rewarding those who are kind to his servants.

The reward can be in the wisdom that comes from hearing good sermons over the years. It can be the reward of an effective staff that has a long and fruitful pastorate in your church. Thus the parish is stable. It can come in friendship with God's prophets in a deeply satisfying and vulnerable relationship.

But many rewards are literally "out of this world." For there are rewards for sure Jesus himself will give out in heaven.

One unsung hero of the Bible is Onesiphorus. He is forever known as a minister to the minister, the one who kept the Apostle Paul on his feet. In 2 Timothy 1:15-18, Paul confided, "You are aware that all who are in Asia turned away from me, among whom are Phygelus and Hermogenes. May the Lord grant mercy to the household of Onesiphorus, for he often refreshed me and was not ashamed of my chains, but when he arrived in Rome, he searched for me earnestly and found me — may the Lord grant him to find mercy from the Lord on that day — and you well know all the service he rendered at Ephesus." Just listen to the action verbs:

> *He often refreshed me.*
> *He was not ashamed.*
> *He searched for me.*
> *He found me.*
> *He rendered service.*

May we be that sort of person to one another, and especially to our prophets!

Stephen M. Crotts

Try This On For Size!

One church has an organ that many sweated, sacrificed, and slaved to buy. Its cost was astounding! But when one hears its tone, sits under the influence of its quality, one begins to believe it was worth it all. It is a special musical instrument. It will serve God and man for many decades.

But what will happen when something goes wrong with this musical instrument? Who will be called in to repair it? Perhaps there is one of you who tinkers with old organs and antique pianos. Would we allow him to fix the organ? No! You would want the best organ repairman you could find. You would probably call the organ manufacturing firm itself and say, "Send us your master repairman. Our organ needs fixing."

Many of you have gold watches that have great sentimental value for you and your family. Your great-grandfather brought it from Ireland perhaps. It is a priceless heirloom. When it stops ticking for some reason, you wouldn't even touch it, even though you yourself have tinkered with old clocks and watches. In fact, you wouldn't even take the back off. You want an expert craftsman to examine this watch and fix it professionally.

Similarly, when your wife is ill and needs surgery, you take her to the best specialist locatable. Oh, you may have biology or anatomy as a sideline hobby. Maybe you successfully dissected a frog in high school biology, made an *A* in college anatomy. Still you would not even think of performing surgery in the kitchen on your wife. You will trust her only to a specialist.

But how about us! How about ourselves! When something goes wrong with our lives, whom do we turn to for repairs? When our lives are damaged or broken and we are left lonely, depressed, bitter, or divorced and afraid, whom do we take our lives to for the fixing? Do we go to the master, to a specialist, a professional? No! We go to Bob or Jim or Sue or Carol across the street. We trust some amateur's advice or the stars or a television psychic or Dear Abby.

Jesus said, and still says, "Come to me! Come to me all you who labor and are heavy laden, and I will give you rest."

If your life is broken, if you are hurting and in need of repair, bring your life to Jesus. He is the divine physician who can heal. He is the master repairman representing your manufacturer. He will examine your life. He will fix it.

The poem, "The Touch of the Master's Hand," shows us what can happen when we commit ourselves to stronger, more skilled hands than our own:

> 'Twas battered and scarred
> And the auctioneer thought it scarcely worth his while
> To waste much time on an old violin,
> But he held it up with a smile.
> "What am I bid for the old violin?
> Who will start the bidding for me?
> A dollar, a dollar, then two, only two?
> Two dollars, and who'll make it three?
> Three dollars. Three dollars, once, do I hear four?
> Three dollars twice ... going, going," and almost gone,
>   but no;
> For from the room far back, an old gray-haired man
>   arose,
> And coming forward and taking the bow,
> And wiping the dust from the old violin
> And tuning the loosened strings,
> He played a melody sweet and pure as the caroling
>   angel sings.
> The music ceased and the auctioneer with a voice
> That was quiet and low, said,
> "Now, what am I bid for the old violin?"
> And he held it up with its bow.

"A thousand dollars," someone cried.
"Two thousand" and "Who'll make it three?
Three thousand once, three thousand twice, and
*   gone!" said he.*
And the people cheered and oh, how they cried,
"What changed its worth?'" Quick came the reply,
"'Twas the touch of the master's hand."
Many a man with life out of tune, all battered and
*   scarred by sin,*
Is auctioned cheap to the thoughtless crowd
Much as the old violin.
A mess of soup, some cheap advice, a game and he
*   travels on.*
He is going once, going twice, going, almost gone.
But then the Master comes, and the foolish crowds,
They don't understand, the worth of a man's soul
And the change that's wrought by the touch of the
*   Master's hand.*

— Myra Welch

Yes, Christians, our hurts, our brokenness, all our problems are best taken care of by the Master. Others may give us encouragement, a listening ear, or a word of truth, but it is to Jesus, to the Master, that we primarily go. He says, "Come to me!"

Let The Weary Come!

Let us look a second time at our text for today. It says, "Come unto me, all who labor and are heavy laden, and I will give you rest."

A German tourist was asked, "What impresses you most about the United States?" He answered, "The fact that you are a tired people impresses me a great deal; clerks, wives, friends, teachers, youths, leaders — you are all so tired!"

Could it be that he was right? Is America tired? Have we stewed and schemed and studied and slaved only to win the badge of guilt and fear, ulcers and psychiatric appointments? Let us look at our society and see if he was right.

First, let us look at our homes. Here we find divorce destroying thousands of homes a day. Marriages that began as optimistically

261

as a running romance end in hate or indifference and two quitters. It would seem that we are not too easy to live with. Other homes that manage to remain intact display no real zest or creativity or pizzazz! The mother and father both work so they can give their family the best, so they can have all the "extras." But they come home at the end of the working day tired and ill. There is a loss of communication. The home begins to deteriorate into just another laundry, hotel, and filling station. Arguments occur more and more frequently. Children run away. Suddenly all those "extras" that the Joneses have do not mean so much anymore.

The drugs we take also accuse us of being tired. "Pick-me-ups" are a morning must, a little "toddy for the body" in the afternoon, and, of course, the "tension reliever" at night. Did you know that it takes about 51 million sleeping pills to put America to sleep each night? Tired of coping with ourselves, we rely on pills to see us through. Or bored and worn out with reality, we escape with heroin or marijuana or some other chemical.

Isn't it a paradox that Americans now have more leisure time than ever before, and yet we are so bone-weary we cannot face life, get involved and reach out to others? Our prisons are filled to overflowing. But our society has no time for the rehabilitation of problem people. We neatly stuff them away in cages. We throw away the key! We are busy riding our motorcycles, fishing, vacationing at our second home, golfing. Yes, we are busy, and we are tired!

A more affluent society has never existed. A healthier people has never lived. And a more tired race has probably never breathed. Suicide is probably the most extreme form of national criticism. And did you know that suicide is now the number three killer of teenagers? It ranks high in adult deaths, too. Listen to the words of a young college student — a suicide.

> *Dear America,*
>   *I'm tired. Tired of puppets instead of people, of people with green hair and pierced tongues, rave parties and casual sex, people who drop soliloquies carefully labeled intelligence. I'm tired of people who play the dating game like tips at the racetrack. I'm tired of*

*seeing people used because its only a game, of people
who turn love into a social grace and woman into a
piece of beef, of watching sincerity fester into smooth-
ness. I'm tired of cynics who label themselves realists,
tired of minds rotting into indifference, of people bored
because they are afraid to care, of intellectual games
of ring-around-the-rosy. I'm tired of people who have
to be entertained; tired of people looking for kicks with
a bottle in one hand and a condom in the other; of girls
proud of knowing the score and snickering about it, of
girls intent on learning the score. I'm tired of sophisticated slobs, tired of drunkards and dopeheads who are
never more than spaced or tight, of people who tinker
with sex until it's smut, of people whose understanding
goes no deeper than* neat, sharp *or* cool. *I'm tired of
people who scream they hate it, but won't leave it because they are lazy, tired of people with nothing better
to do than glue their days together with alcohol or dope.
I'm tired of people embarrassed at honesty, at love, at
knowledge. I'm tired, yeah, very tired. So long, America.*

Could it be that any of us are tired like the young man in the
letter? How about you? Are you tired? Are you hard to live with?
Too tired to get involved, to do your work well, to live righteously?
Then come to him! Come to Christ! He will replenish your strength.
In the text today he promises, "Come to me, all who labor and are
heavy laden, and I will give you rest."

The prophet Isaiah was speaking to people much like us when
he said,

*Have you not known? Have you not heard? The Lord is
the everlasting God, the creator of the ends of the earth.
He does not faint or grow weary, his understanding is
unsearchable. He gives power to the faint, and to him
who has no might he increases strength. Even youths
shall faint and be weary, and young men shall fall ex-
hausted; but they who wait upon the Lord shall renew
their strength, they shall mount up with wings like
eagles, they shall run and not be weary, they shall walk
and not faint.* — Isaiah 40:28-31

263

Yes, it looks like America is tired. Our homes, excessive alcohol, drug abuse, suicide, and short tempers all point an accusing finger at us. The question is, will we realize that we have a problem? Will we admit that we are tired and need help? A psychiatrist recently stated that man's greatest problem is in realizing that he has a problem. We are so proud. We try to be so self-sufficient. Yet on the inside we are weak and trembling. It is true that no one can help an alcoholic until he admits he has a problem and he asks for help. It is also true that God will not help you until you admit your need and ask him for help.

This is why in the text for today Jesus asks only those to come to him who admit they are tired. He did not say, "Come to me all who are self-sufficient." He did not say, "Come to me all who are getting along quite well without me." He asks only that those come who recognize their need. He says, "Come to me all who labor and are heavy laden, and I will give you rest." Who does he want to come? "All who labor and are heavy laden!" Do you fit into this category? Do you admit that you have a need? Then come to him. "I will give you rest," he promises.

"Take My Yoke!"
Now let us look at the text again, especially the last part. Jesus said, "Come to me, all who labor and are heavy laden, and I will give you rest. Take my yoke upon you, and learn from me, for I am gentle and lowly in heart, and you will find rest for your souls. For my yoke is easy and my burden is light."

Here, Jesus is speaking as a skilled tradesman. He is flashing back to his boyhood days. You see, Christ was a carpenter for twenty years or more before he turned preacher. His father Joseph taught him the carpenter's trade. Together they ran a little shop in Nazareth. It was located in the poor side of town, down some inconspicuous dusty little avenue. It was a pleasant shop, however, well kept and nestled beneath the shade of olive trees. From it could be heard frequent peals of laughter amid the sound of hammering and sawing. The smell of fresh cut lumber filled one's nostrils as one entered the vicinity. Out front, according to legend, there hung a sign that read, "Our yokes fit well."

Legend has it that Joseph and Jesus made the best yokes to be found. Even though their shop was inconspicuously located, people came from villages all around just to have their yokes made by Joseph and Son. They would tie their big oxen to a tree, step inside for a few moments, and soon emerge with a young boy named Jesus. He would walk over to the oxen and take careful measurements. Then a lightweight wood was chosen, carving and filing was done. Finally there would be trial fittings. The yoke must fit just right. It could not be too tight, too small, or heavy or rough. Otherwise, it would gall the oxen's neck. That would never do, for it would cause the oxen to suffer; it would inhibit their work. With Joseph and Jesus, you see, it was a matter of reputation, a matter of quality. The yoke must fit perfectly.

And now in the last years of Christ's life, we find the carpenter no longer fashioning yokes for animals. He now fashions them for men. Likewise, these yokes still fit well. They are smooth and light of weight. In fact, they, too, are tailor-made.

All of us have known the discomfort of ill-fitting garments. When a shirt is too tight, it restricts us. Trousers that are too large get in the way. "Hand-me-down" shoes seldom fit perfectly, but when you are small and in need, you must suffer the looseness or tightness that pinches or blisters your feet.

Jesus has a special kind of garment for you to try on for size. It is called the yoke. He promises that it will not be a hand-me-down. It is especially made for you. It is tailor-made. Therefore, it will fit just right. It will not be too large or too confining. He challenges you, "Take my yoke upon you." He promises you, "My yoke is easy, and my burden is light."

This yoke that Christ wants you to wear represents your calling in life. It is true that God has work for you to do. Better than anyone else in the whole world you are qualified to do it. God takes into consideration your strengths and weaknesses and he matches you with a calling, a vocation in life. This becomes your yoke. It is well fitting in that it will not under-challenge nor over-bear you. To carry this yoke means to carry out God's divine plan for your life. And when you carry out God's plan for your life, when you are submissive to his will, you experience the peace and joy and freedom known among Christians as "the abundant life" (John 10:10).

When I was a freshman at Furman University I played football. The coach issued me the necessary pieces of equipment. Each protective pad fit well except for my helmet. It was too small. After several days of practice I began to get headaches and performed poorly. I asked for a new helmet, one that would fit properly. I was told, "That's the best we can do. We have no more." Several days later I suffered a concussion. My football career was ended.

Professional football teams take better care of their athletes than do small college teams. When a player reports, he is suited up with pads that fit perfectly. Helmets are especially important. Many times an athlete's helmet is tailor-made just for him. Such helmets can cost as much as a thousand dollars. The cost is worth it, however, because the well-fitting uniform insures the player's maximum safety and performance.

God is likewise concerned with your safety and performance. He wants you to achieve your maximum capability as a person. This is why he offers you a yoke that is a perfect fit. He knows that if you work the right job, marry the right person, make the right salary, live in the right neighborhood, and so on, you will be at your best physically, emotionally, intellectually, and spiritually.

We look at America today and see tired people. They are under-challenged or overborne by their walk in life. Sexual perversion, financial stress, self-contempt, and divorce are but a few of the symptoms that life is being lived out of the will of God. Their yokes do not fit well and they suffer. Like my college football helmet or a hand-me-down, their jobs are not right for them. Their vocation is too tight and confining or loose and callous. They are getting hurt.

America needs to come to Jesus! You need to come to Jesus! You need to take his yoke. Here, try this on for size! See if it doesn't fit just right. Hundreds of years ago, Saint Augustine tried God's yoke for his life and he remarked, "In his will is our peace." We of the Christian faith are still finding God's will for our lives. See our joy! Feel our peace. Witness our smiles. Attest to the fact that we are loved and can ourselves love. We are not tired. We have strength for every task. We have tried his yoke on for size, and behold! It fits just right!

A young dog was spinning round and round in circles when an older dog sauntered up. "What are you doing?" he asked. "I'm chasing my tail," the young dog replied. "You see, happiness is in my tail. When it wags, I'm happy. When it drops, I'm sad. Happiness is in my tail. If I catch it, I will always be happy!" So again he spun round and round trying to bite hold of the elusive tail. Finally, all out of puff, he sagged to the ground, tired out. The old dog, still watching all this, said, "You know, I used to chase my tail. But one day I found that if I just went on about my business, happiness followed right along behind."

Today, God's Word calls out to any and all tail-chasing, happiness-seeking, worn-out people. Jesus says, "Come unto me. If you are tired, I will give you rest. But I will also give you a yoke. Do not worry. It will fit you just right!" Yes, Jesus will not only save you from your sins, he will save you to your yoke. God knows that man needs to be saved from something to something. He wants to deliver you from the things that make you tired, those things you are doing which are outside his will. They are sins, and he will save you from them. He wants also to give you a yoke, to busy your life with the things of his will. When you follow God's will, happiness will follow along right behind!

Stephen M. Crotts

267

Proper 10
Pentecost 8
Ordinary Time 15
Matthew 13:1-9, 18-23

The Garden Is Doing Fine?

Remember the nursery rhyme about little contrary Mary? It asks the question, "Mary, Mary, quite contrary, how does your garden grow?" This parable of Jesus asks the church the same question. It's all about seed and four different soils that receive it. It's a parable of how different people respond to the gospel.

Stolen Seed

Jesus said, "A sower went out to sow his seed, and as he sowed, some fell along the path and was trodden underfoot. And the birds of the air devoured it." Anyone who has ever planted a garden knows the ruin of crows. And here we have a great mystery of the faith. In his explanation of this parable, Jesus said, "The ones along the path are those who have heard; then the devil comes and takes away the word from their hearts, that they may not believe and be saved" (Matthew 13:19).

Did you know that the late atheist Madelyn Murray O'Hare was reared a Presbyterian? New York's Son of Sam, the serial killer, was a former Baptist.

After buying a new home, the owner began to landscape the lawn himself. Since it was his first attempt to plant a lawn, he was careful to do everything according to the book. He prepared the soil, put in a sprinkling system, and then waited for the right day. When that day came he seeded the lawn, rolled it, and watered it. For the next three weeks he watered the lawn daily, shooed away the birds and his cat, and waited eagerly for the first blades of grass to peek through. Except for a few weeds, nothing happened.

Then one Saturday morning he discovered the sack of grass seed — still in the garage. "What in the world did you plant?" his wife asked. With a sigh, the man replied, "Kitty litter." You might wonder, looking at some people, if bad seed, sort of kitty litter, weren't sown in their lives instead of the gospel. Jesus assures us that there is nothing wrong with the biblical gospel. It'll grow if given the chance. The problem is that Satan comes along and snatches away the seed.

You know how it is. You begin to share your faith with someone. You mention salvation, sin, faith, peace, repentance, and the Holy Spirit. And the other person looks at you rather blankly and says, "Whatever are you going on about?" and changes the subject. Or they say, "Yes, yes, all in good time!" and they promptly forget.

Rocky Soil

A second type of response, Jesus said, is likened to rocky soil. Seed falls on this ground, springs to life, but since it has no depth of soil for roots, it withers away in the heat of summer.

You've seen, no doubt, a bonsai plant. A cedar tree is planted in a small bowl. It grows but remains dwarfed because the gardener clips its taproot. So many come limping into the church hurt, divorced, bitter, broke, confused, and, hearing the gospel, jump for it with all the eagerness of a drowning man grabbing for a life rope tossed his way. And for a few months they can't get enough!

Then the gust of emotion dwindles. They find out God doesn't always come when you whistle. Bible study is a chore. They want to be selective about obedience. And the next thing you know, they're out the door.

Remember! Jesus said it'd be like this! "No depth of soil," Jesus said. Shallow.

Thorns

A third soil Jesus called thorny ground. Christ put it this way: "And some fell among thorns, and the thorns grew with it and choked it." Indeed! Every gardener knows the menace of crabgrass, kudzu, and thistle. Jesus, in his explanation of this parable,

270

said, "As for what fell among thorns, they are those who hear, but as they go on their way they are choked by the cares and riches and pleasures of life, and their fruit does not mature."

I once saw a barn overgrown with kudzu. One rainy day the added weight caused the building to collapse. It's like that in post-Christian Europe today. Churches are everywhere. Splendid cathedrals! But they are mostly empty. The people are out working, playing, sleeping, holidaying — with zero time for the things of Christ. Again, there is no fruit.

Good Soil!

Ah! But not to despair, for Christ spoke of yet a fourth soil, fertile and deep. "And some seed fell into good soil, and grew, and yielded a hundredfold." These are persons, Jesus explained, who receive the Word and carefully allow it to take root in their lives so that fruit is born.

And what is fruit? Galatians 5:22 calls it *love*. This is a reminder of the great commandment in Matthew 22. God asks us to love him with all our intellect, emotion, and will. And to love our neighbor as ourselves.

Conversion

None of the first three soils can in any sense be called conversion. Each of the three ends with no life in the seed, no response to the Word.

Clearly in this parable Jesus points out the three enemies of the faith: the world, the flesh, and the devil.

The *world* is like the weeds, Jesus said, choking the life from our soil. It must be handled according to 1 John 2:15-17, "Love not the world."

The *flesh* is like shallow soil, Jesus said, allowing for no enduring roots. It must be handled according to 1 Corinthians 6:18 and Romans 12:18, "Make no provision for the flesh, to gratify its desires."

The *devil* is like the seed-pilfering birds, Jesus said, pecking away at the Word in our lives. Ah! But 1 Peter 5:8-10 says, "Resist the devil and he will flee from you."

271

Anyone in Christ who desires to mature, must learn how to deal with the enemies of faith — the world, the flesh, and the devil. Each can be successfully met, but each is handled differently.

The *world* is not loved. We do not set out affections upon it. It does not last.

The *flesh* we run from, like Joseph when tempted by Potiphar's wife. He fled the house (Genesis 39:12).

Ah, but Satan we stand against. In the armor of Christ, we are strong before him.

Ephesians 6:10 and following verses challenge us not to flee the devil but to stand against his wiles. "Resist the devil and he will flee from you" (1 Peter 5:8-10).

Trouble is, too many Christians get confused. We cling to the world in desperation as if there is no better world to come. We flee in terror when Satan attacks. And when it comes to the flesh, we take a firm stand, saying, "I can handle it!" Like Samson, who put his head in the lap of Delilah and napped.

In other words, we zig when we should have zagged. We run when we should stand. And we stand when we should run!

Conclusion

I love the minutes of the local garden club published in the weekly news. "The day lilies we planted around the courthouse all died for the third straight year. The club voted to replant the lilies and also to adopt as our club motto, 'To dream the impossible dream!' "

Hey! In the midst of so much chaos and poor response to the gospel in our world and churches today, let's remember the four soils and how Jesus said it would be like this! Let's also remember that all conversions are miraculous, that there is hope so long as Jesus keeps sowing his word in the world.

Perhaps there is one of you reading this who is primed for conversion. Somehow the word has gotten past me through this text to you. And you choose to receive it.

God wants you to know he loves you. He has paid the penalty for your sins in Christ's death on the cross. He simply asks you to receive him by faith into your life. Believe him! Trust him! Welcome him!

And like a seed falling into soil, he will dwell in you and take root to bear the fruit of love.

One doesn't have to understand it all right now. Just get started. Say, "Yes," to Jesus who is saying, "Yes," to you!

Suggested Prayer
Lord Jesus! Yes! Yes!

Stephen M. Crotts

Proper 11
Pentecost 9
Ordinary Time 16
Matthew 13:24-30, 36-43

Two Harvests

All of the Bible is inspired. But just as some parts of a turkey have more meat on them, so some parts of the Bible are meatier than others. For example, the genealogies of Leviticus versus the Sermon on the Mount.

Matthew 13 is one of the meatier portions of the scriptures. It is unique as an identifiable sermon of Christ Jesus, a series of seven, maybe eight parables that seem to be prophetic, to foretell the history of ministry ahead of time.

The parable of the wheat and the tares is the second in Jesus' sermon. Let's look at it now.

Two Sowers

Jesus tells of two sowers, "a man who sowed good seed in his field" (v. 24) whom he interprets for us as "the son of man" (v. 37). And "while men were sleeping, his enemy came and sowed weeds among the wheat" (v. 25) whom Christ interprets for us as "the devil" (v. 39). The Greek word for devil is *diabolos* or *liar* or *one set against.*

From the earliest pages of scripture, we are taught of the almighty God, the ancient of days, who created life, who upholds justice and righteousness, and who is to be worshiped and loved. But we are also taught of Satan, the evil one, the tempter, the deceiver. It is for us to realize that ours is a world in conflict between God and the devil, good and evil. That is the message of the two sowers.

Two Seeds

The "son of man" plows his field and sows "good seed" (v. 24). They are the "sons of the kingdom" (v. 38). In the first parable of the four soils, "seed" was interpreted as "the Word" of God. Now, in the second parable, the seed has taken root in certain persons so that they, like Jesus, are further incarnations of God's Word. Colossians 3:16 bids us, "Let the word of God dwell in you richly." By trusting in his word, doing it, fleshing it out, we become "sons of the kingdom."

Ah, but while good men slept from the rigors of sowing the farm fields, the devil came and sowed bad seed, or "weeds," among the wheat (v. 25). These weeds grew up to become "the sons of the evil one" (v. 38).

The "weeds" sown were undoubtedly tares or "darnel." Jews called it "bastard wheat." Today farmers often refer to it as "cheat." Examining the seed of wheat and tares, it is difficult for the untrained eye to distinguish between them. Even in the early stages of growth one cannot tell them apart. It is only at harvest time when the wheat ripens that tares can be easily singled out as fakes.

According to ancient Roman Law, it was illegal to sow darnel. Such a deed of treachery was punishable by death, for it could ruin a harvest and leave a field weed-infested for years. The crime was made further malicious because eating darnel causes nausea, vertigo, and sometimes death.

Two Questions

So we have two sowers, two seeds, and now two questions. The farm hands, closely caring for their crop, begin to detect weeds among the wheat as the crop ripens toward harvest. So they ask their boss, "Didn't you sow good seed? How then has it weeds?" (v. 27). This is the question of humanity echoing across the ages! Why evil? Jews asked it in Egyptian slavery while watching their fathers lashed by cruel taskmasters. Young women asked it after being raped by Assyrian soldiers looting the land. Nazi death camp prisoners asked it before they were shot. And we asked it again on

September 11, 2001, when Arab terrorists turned passenger jets into missiles, killing several thousand men, women, and children. "How then has it weeds?"

The fact that Satan sowed his cheat while men slept is no sign of negligence, but rather a sign of the devil's sneakiness and cowardice. It also is a hint of his evil ploy to deceive humanity. I call it "opposition by imitation."

The next question the farm hands ask their boss is in verse 20: "Do you want us to gather them?" In short, "Shall we go fix it for now? Shall we pluck out the evil? Rid the field of tares today?" The wise boss says, "No, lest in gathering the weeds you root up the wheat along with them." It seems tares have a well-developed root system that entwines itself around nearby plant roots. So, in plucking up the cheat one inadvertently plucks up the wheat as well. So the wise farmer, though vexed, determines to "let them both grow together until harvest" (v. 30).

This means Christ's kingdom has a mixed character until judgment day. Jesus had his Peter but he also had his Judas. The early church had Barnabas but also Ananias and Sapphira (Acts 5). We have our sheep, but also our wolves in sheep's clothing. Paul warned the Ephesian elders of false brethren, even "savage wolves" who would come in among them (Acts 20). The two letters to the Corinthian church certainly evidence this. Along with the righteous singles and marrieds are the incestuous, the homosexual. Along with the sober are the drunkards. Along with apt teachers are the doctrinally false.

This same mixed field of wheat and tares is represented in our church pews, in schools, often on elder councils and beyond — persons not of Christ but sown of the devil. Darnel. Cheat. Tares. Imposters.

The Bible says we must learn to live with it for a while. Impurity, corruption, deceit are a part of our very real struggle to live by faith in Christ in a world of two sowers and two seeds. Like the text, it will undoubtedly leave each of us scratching our heads and asking a lot of questions of God.

Reminds me of a needlepointed quote on Mrs. Harvey Milton's kitchen wall in Virginia. I first read it there as a newly minted and naïve 25-year-old pastor. The sign said, "In dealing with men's souls, one has to put up with a few heels."

Two Harvests

Ah, but not forever will Satan deceive and weeds pollute God's garden! There is coming a harvest, a judgment day! And sooner than we think! Then Jesus says, "At harvest time I will tell the reapers, 'Gather the weeds first and bind them into bundles to be burned, but gather the wheat into my barn.' " Jesus interprets the meaning of the harvest for us most graphically in verse 39 and following. "The harvest is the close of the age, and the reapers are angels. Just as the weeds are gathered and burned with fire, so will it be at the close of the age. The Son of Man will send his angels, and they will gather out of his kingdom all causes of sin and all evildoers, and throw them into the furnace of fire. There men will weep and gnash their teeth."

Jesus said this. I didn't. There's coming a harvest, a judgment. On that day the weeds will be pulled up and burned with fire, but the wheat will be stored in barns.

Revelation 14:13-20 further illuminates this:

> Then I heard a voice from heaven say, "Write: Blessed are the dead who die in the Lord from now on." "Yes," says the Spirit, "they will rest from their labor, for their deeds will follow them."
>
> I looked and there before me was a white cloud, and seated on the cloud was one "like a son of man" with a sickle in his hand. Then another angel came out of the temple and called in a loud voice to him who was sitting on the cloud, "Take your sickle and reap, because the time to reap has come, for the harvest of the earth is ripe." So he who was seated on the cloud swung his sickle over the earth, and the earth was harvested.
>
> Another angel came out of the temple in heaven, and he too had a sharp sickle. Still another angel, who had charge of the fire, came from the altar and called in a loud voice to him who had the sharp sickle, "Take your sharp sickle and gather the clusters of grapes from

278

the earth's vine, because its grapes are ripe." The an-
gel swung his sickle on the earth, gathered its grapes
and threw them into the great winepress of God's wrath.

Conclusion

For over thirty years people have looked me in the eye and asked with urgency, "Are things getting better or worse?" And I have long struggled for an honest response. Mostly I have tried to be optimistic, pointing at some hint of revival or purity or act of courageous statesmanship by some leader. Now, however, I think I've come up with a better answer. When queried are things getting better or worse, I quickly answer, "Both!" For indeed, both God's seed and the devil's seed are being sown, both growing. Ah! But harvest day is coming. Not forever will the world be polarized as we know it. Take hope! Continue to receive and grow in Christ's Word! For there is a cleansing on the dawn!

Suggested Prayer

Sweet Jesus, my Lord, sow your gracious word in my life that I may grow for your harvest. Amen.

Stephen M. Crotts

Sermons On The Gospel Readings

For Sundays
After Pentecost
(Middle Third)

The Incomparable Christ

Stephen M. Crotts
and
George L. Murphy

Things To Come!

I'd quit the ministry were it not for what Jesus said in Matthew chapter 13! Here Jesus is brutally honest in telling his ministers both then and now what to expect. In the best of times ministry is difficult. In the worst of times it is downright intolerable. But there is hope! For in Jesus Christ, nothing is wasted!

Matthew 13 is a unique Bible chapter. It is all but the first time in Matthew's Gospel that Jesus used parables to teach. And, clearly, these parables comprise a single sermon, at that! The first four parables were taught to the disciples, as well as the world, using the prow of a small boat as a pulpit! (Matthew 13:1-3). Then Jesus left the crowd, went into a house with his apostles (13:36), and finished out his message with three more parables.

In the Greek, the word *parable* means "to cast alongside." They are similes or metaphors, literally, earthly stories with heavenly meanings. But do not be confused. They are not sermon illustrations meant to elucidate the gospel, as is commonly thought. For in Matthew 13:10, the disciples ask Christ point blank, "Why do you speak in parables?" And Jesus says, rather amazingly, "I speak to them in parables because seeing they do not see ..." (Matthew 13:13). Parables are like those hidden pictures from your childhood *Highlights* magazines. It's easy to miss many things hidden in plain sight! To unbelievers a parable is but a simple story. Ah, but to the believer there is more, so much more, the very gospel of God itself!

Today's reading contains a mix of the "outdoor" and "indoor" parables. Let's get into them and see what light there is for the living of our days.

283

Mustard Seed

This parable is found in verses 31-32. The kingdom of heaven is like that tiniest of seeds, the mustard seed that is planted and grows into a shrub. Up until this point, the apostles are with him. But when Jesus said the shrub grows into a tree, they must have done a double take. "Say what!" It'd be like saying an azalea bush grew into a forest giant. The mustard shrub is the *kardah* plant. It is never bigger than six to ten feet, and it bears thousands of tiny seeds in its branches that when harvested and properly prepared, yield what we know as mustard, the spice.

Alas! As Jesus mentioned in the text, birds love to snatch these seeds! (Sounds familiar from the first parable!) Why, I have seen mustard shrubs in Israel swarming with birds that devour every single seed of its spice!

The popular interpretation of this parable is quite optimistic. The tiny gospel seed takes root in the world and becomes such a great sheltering tree the birds, or nations of the world, come to rest in Jesus! Yet if the birds in the first part of this seven-parable sermon represent the thieving devil, why would Christ suddenly change his symbol's meaning here in the third parable?

Consistency, my Bible scholars! Consistency! And remember that the popular interpretation of scripture is not always correct. Why, the popular interpretation of scripture crucified Jesus in his day! Jesus is saying the gospel church is like a spice shrub, but unfortunately it outgrows its divine purpose and becomes treelike. In its new organizational structure it allows the birds of the devil to come strip it of its own divinely appointed spices.

How many colleges were founded in rustic simplicity to be a Christian influence! Dartmouth College to evangelize the Indians, Princeton University to train biblical preachers, but now they have metamorphosed into endowed, politically correct, bureaucratic organizations devoid of anything of Jesus Christ. Why the birds of humanism, institutionalism, materialism, liberalism, and pride have literally pecked the church seed bare!

Read for yourself Revelation 18:15! There you'll find the birds pecking away! This is the abortion of the divine design.

Leaven

Jesus then told four more parables which he leaves for us to interpret ourselves. So, how are we doing? Rather poorly, to be frank. For these last five parables suffer from gross misinterpretation.

For instance, the parable found in verse 33 is but a one-sentence parable. "The kingdom of heaven is like leaven which a woman took and hid in three measures of flour until it was all leavened." The popular interpretation is that the gospel is like leaven, which conquers the whole of the world as leaven does dough!

Yet leaven is used 71 times in the Old Testament and 17 times in the New Testament. And in every place it symbolizes evil!

For instance, in Luke 12:1, Jesus said, "Beware the leaven of the Pharisees" which is *legalism*. In Matthew 16:6 and 12 he bids us watch out for the leaven of the Sadducees, which is *liberalism* and *rationalism*. Then in Mark 8:14-15 we are warned of the leaven of the Herodians, that is *materialism*.

So the church, meant to be unleavened bread, actually has the person in charge of the household introduce leaven directly into the process!

This is the corruption of the divine agent.

Not a very pretty picture of the church and what ministry would be like, eh? Oh, the frustration of wasted seed, the galling bitterness of a mixed harvest, the bureaucratic nightmare of a proud and savorless denomination and the evil right inside the church!

Like I said at the outset, I'd quit if this is all there was to the crucible of ministry! But it is not! For Jesus, having finished these four parables before a mixed multitude on the seashore, walked into a house with his apostles, then told three more parables. Check it out in verse 36.

It is these last three parables that give us hope that something worthwhile is happening as we minister, something rich and beautiful, something nourishing, ah! But things hidden, not yet revealed. Things that must be trusted by faith!

Treasure

The parable in verse 44 is of a man who discovers treasure buried in a field, covers it over, then rushes out to buy the property.

Again, the popular interpretation is that Jesus is the treasure we inadvertently discover buried in our world. Excitedly, we rush off to buy him, or something like that.

If one returns to Jesus' interpretive key, the field is the world, the man is Jesus, and the treasure? Again and again in the Old Testament Israel is God's rich possession, his treasure! (Exodus 19:5; Psalm 135:4; Malachi 3:17). God found the Jews in the world, loved them, and quickly sought the covenantal business arrangement that they might be his!

But what is this covering over of his treasure? In Matthew 23:37, Jesus weeps over Israel's rejection of his love and laments, "You will not see me again until ..." It was 70 A.D. when Roman armies sacked Jerusalem and Israel was covered over until she began to regather in the twentieth century, actually becoming a nation once more in 1948.

Pearl

Next comes the merchant of pearls, who finding one perfect pearl sells all to own it. The popular notion of Christ being our pearl is quickly debunked since it is works/righteousness. Since when do we have anything with which to buy our salvation? (Ephesians 2:8, 9).

Fact is, the sea, where of course pearls are found, is very unfamiliar to the Jewish nation. It is a place of evil in the Old Testament, and there will be no sea in heaven. Exodus 28 describes the priest's ephod covered with twelve precious stones, none of which is a pearl. Jews simply did not value them.

Watch carefully here: so far Jesus has spoken only of the familiar — fields, seed, yeast, weeds, mustard. Now he introduces an unfamiliar element — pearls. This gem is not mentioned in the Old Testament. But it is mentioned in the New Testament in Revelation 18:12. The pearl is the only precious stone produced by a living organism, and it comes from a wound. They were a prized treasure for the Gentiles.

Here it is fitting to think of Christ as the merchant seeking pearls, seeking treasure the Jews did not value, that is, the gentiles. As in the book of Jonah, God was extending his love beyond

Israel to the Ninevite, yet Jews were slow to understand. God was intent on a relationship with the gentiles and he was willing to give everything on the cross for it.

Dragnet

The final parable is in verses 47-50 where Christ says his kingdom is like a dragnet pulled beneath a fishing vessel and catching all sorts of creatures. The day is coming when the net is hauled in and the catch is sorted, good and bad.

One sees here men dragging the nets ashore. Grace does not work alone. We co-labor with God. The catch is a mixed haul, some good fish, others worthless. A time of sorting comes.

Do you see the hope Jesus is sharing in these last three parables? Now watch this: In verse 51, Jesus asks the twelve, "Have you understood all this?" And they readily respond, "Yes!" They hadn't the slightest clue, even as we today often do not!

Scribe

Verse 52 begins with the words, "Now therefore." Anytime one comes to the word *therefore* he must inquire, what is the *therefore* there for? It is a capstone, a summary argument. As with an octave of musical movement where the first sets the theme, two through seven develop it, and the eighth resolves it, the first four parables set the conflict theme forth clearly, the next three give hope, and this eighth and concluding saying of Jesus brings the resolve.

Christ calls us *scribes*, in the Greek *grammar* or *words*. Ezra was the first scribe, a man devoutly dedicated to study, doing and teaching God's word (Ezra 7:10). Jesus says every scribe trained or discipled for God's kingdom is like a householder, literally a house despot or lord, who brings out, literally lavishes upon others the things of his treasure old and new. In other words, regardless of the world's tastes or demands, rejection or applause, we lavish God's word on the world ... and leave the results to God. Yet all the while knowing there will be a treasure in Israel, a pearl of the gentiles, a net full of fish! Just you wait and see!

Suggested Prayer
Oh Lord God, the duty is mine, the results yours. Keep me true, keep me true. For Christ's sake. Amen.

Stephen M. Crotts

Proper 13
Pentecost 11
Ordinary Time 18
Matthew 14:13-21

Will You Give Christ Your Supper?

The world scene today is as frightening and desperate, as needy and inexplicable as I've ever seen it. There is a bewildering global economy that's sucking jobs overseas and lengthening unemployment lines. India and Pakistan are on the brink of war and armed with nuclear warheads. There is a threat of terrorism in every subway, stadium, and cockpit. A younger generation is adorned with spiked hair and grunge clothing; they are pierced, painted, and ready to party. Add that to Korea's intransigence, Africa's AIDS epidemic, and mix in over six billion people! We're left with a sense of overwhelming inadequacy.

What difference can one person make?

In the life of Christ is an episode that so impressed the twelve disciples that it is the only miracle of Jesus besides the resurrection that is recorded in all four gospels. And it is the story of a small group of people facing an overburdening need.

The Bible tells us Jesus retreated to an isolated hillside for some rest. But it was not to be, for a crowd of 5,000 men followed. And that's just the men counted in the tally. If you add a wife and two children to each man, the crowd could easily have numbered 20,000 souls or more!

So how does Jesus handle this massive interruption of his rest plans? He teaches them, heals them, loves on them.

It is a tradition for a rabbi to feed those who come to his house for learning. The disciples knew this, so as the day grew nigh to supper, they grew edgy. "Lord, this is a desolate place, and the day is now over, send the crowds away to go into the villages and buy food for themselves." Jesus startled the twelve by saying, "You give them something to eat!"

John 6 tells us Jesus said this to test the disciples. Philip had already run the numbers. "Eight months' wages wouldn't even begin to finish the job!" This is not the voice of faith. It is the voice of despair. It is the voice of every church treasurer who looks at the world's crying needs then opens the church financial account to look upon paltry balance sheets.

Enter Andrew. He, too, had been doing some ciphering. "Lord, there is a lad here who has five loaves and two fishes," he explains (John 6). But then, too, he laments, "But what is that among so many?" Which is to say, such a sparse dinner cannot possibly make a difference.

That's when Jesus takes over. He receives the small boy's offering, blesses it, and causes the multitude to be fed miraculously. But that's not all. When supper was over and all had eaten their fill, the leftovers were taken up. And there were twelve baskets full. Which, I suppose, is Christ's clear statement to the twelve that if you give to Jesus, there will still be enough left over for you.

Today, as we stand on our own hillside amidst overwhelming need, I ask you, "What's in our picnic basket?" For, indeed, as the lad of old, we have something to offer.

Availability

One loaf in all our baskets is availability. As with the small boy who simply made his supper available, so we too can do the same. For it is forever not one's ability but his availability that matters with God.

In Virginia, a small church was hosting a bake sale and crafts fair to raise money for missions. The best cooks presented their pies, jams, and cakes. Men offered exquisite woodworkings. But Ellen, old and arthritic, took old clothing and cut the cloth to sew it into a patchwork quilt of red, turquoise, and yellow. It didn't sell, its bright colors so garish. So at the end of the day the money and leavings were boxed up and shipped to Africa to the waiting missionary. He opened the box of tools and money and thanked

God for the needful things. The odd colored quilt he draped over a tree limb.

That's when the tribal chief who'd been particularly difficult to deal with came by and admired the quilt. He draped it over his shoulders like a cape and admired the effect. "What will you take for this?" he asked the missionary. "A piece of land on which to build a church," the missionary bargained. And the deal was made. One never knows what God can do with an out-of-fashion quilt sewn by an 86-year-old widow with arthritic hands and offered to Jesus in faith.

Prayers

A second loaf we all have in our possession is intercessory prayer.

This summer I stood in the nave of St. Nicholas Church, Leipzig, Germany. This was J. S. Bach's old parish. It happens to be where the East German Christians gathered in growing swells to pray for the fall of communism.

Later, I walked the streets of Berlin, the dead zone of the old Wall. I thought of how brutal repression is no match of kneeling saints with folded hands persisting in prayer.

Read of it in Daniel the prophet's prayers. When he prayed something happened in heaven, something happened in the demonic world, and something happened on earth. It is still the same today.

Faith

Yet, a third loaf we each have in our picnic is faith.

Andrew couldn't see God for the size of the crowd. Philip couldn't see Christ for the enormity of the hungry and the feebleness of his purse. Ah, but the wee lad saw not the multitude, nor even his own small dinner. He saw Jesus. And somehow he understood as Paul the Apostle was to write, "For he is able to accomplish abundantly far more than all we ask or think."

So I inquire of you as Jesus did in the testing of the twelve. Do you see the crowd or Christ? Do you see the cost or God? Do you look upon your own reserves or the resources of the almighty God?

Do you have faith?

Suffering
Yet another crust of bread we all carry is our pain. The Apostle Paul wrote, "Blessed be the God and Father of our Lord Jesus Christ, the Father of mercies and God of all comfort, who comforts us in all our affliction, so that we may be able to comfort those who are in any affliction, with the comfort with which we ourselves are comforted by God" (2 Corinthians 1:4). It is true as Hemingway put it, "Life breaks us all. But then we are strong in the broken places." No one can counsel an alcoholic like someone who has been there. It is the same with divorcees, the bankrupt, and the sick and lonely. The Lord wastes nothing. Our pain, and the comfort we've derived from Christ, is one of our best ministries.

I grew up in the affluence of the '50s and '60s in small-town America. My church was weak though my family was strong. In college during the hippy radical rebellion I had questions about God, the Bible, meaning in life, sex, Jesus, God's will, and authority. There was no one teaching on these things. Mostly I had to dig out the answers myself. That's why I return to the university for ministry so often today. I know the pain. I go to offer students "the comfort with which I've been comforted in Christ."

Experience
A fifth and final loaf each of us has in our dinner pail that we can hand to Jesus is our experience. Four out of the twelve original apostles were fishermen and when Jesus called them he said, "Henceforth you shall be catching men." Just as they'd learned to read the fish, to wait in patience for a large haul, so their experience would serve them well in evangelism.

At an opera in Belarus this winter, I met a man running for president of his country. He confided in me how the communists had ripped the entrepreneurial spirit out of his people. And he begged me to urge retired businessmen to his nation to mentor young Russians in how to start and run a business. "We need disciple-makers," he said with real feeling.

And so it is, if you've a skill, God can use it on the mission field — teacher, nurse, computer technician, well digger, physician, radio operator, pilot ... your skill matches a need somewhere.

It was Stephen Jobs of the computer industry trying to lure the head of Coca-Cola away from his high paying job so he could work for the computer industry. His man was reluctant until Jobs said urgently, "Do you want to spend the rest of your life making fizzy sugar water or do you want to change the world?" So it is Christ calling us with our skills from the easy chair and television remote to come change our world and eternity.

Conclusion
Yes, it is a big world. And the needs are immense! We ourselves are so frail. Ah, but our Christ is able! Won't you give Christ your supper?

Suggested Prayer
Lord, here am I! And here is mine. In Jesus. Amen.

Stephen M. Crotts

Proper 14
Pentecost 12
Ordinary Time 19
Matthew 14:22-33

Deep Water!

I don't know anyone who's not in over his or her head today ... A plant manager struggling to make payroll in a down economy ... A parent of a rebellious teenager ... An elderly person trying to pay hospital bills out of his tiny pension checks ... A marriage trying to overcome adultery and trust again....

Modern life is a deep and stormy season that can swallow us whole. So thank God there's a Bible story just for us today!

Christ was tired. He'd been grieving over his cousin John the Baptizer's death. But as he sought to be alone, the crowds sought him more. He'd spent the time teaching and healing and feeding them. He is really fatigued. He sends his disciples packing.

They put to sea in the boat. Jesus goes up on the mountain to pray, to rest in the night's solitude. Somewhere in the wee hours of the morning, Christ seeks to regain the company of the twelve. And he does something totally unimaginable, yet so God-like. He walks out upon the billows. He literally walks on water.

Meanwhile, the apostles have had a rough sail. The wind had been against them all night, so they had been rowing hard for hours. Now they are wet, hungry, and bone-weary. That's when they spot Jesus.

"It's a ghost!" the sailors cry out. They are limp with fear.

Have you ever had a day like theirs? Eighteen hours, grabby crowds of the needy, sleeplessness, your transportation has broken down, you are wet and afraid because God seems more like a ghost than a savior. Or you received the worst possible diagnosis from the doctor. Or your telephone rings in the middle of the night and you hear your son's voice, "Mom, Dad, I've been in an accident...." Days like that come upon us with little warning and we are consumed with fear. It's dark and we have no idea of what to do next. How will we ever get through this?

That's when Jesus speaks, his word soothing across your rankled nerves, "Take heart, it is I; have no fear!"

Peter spoke first. As usual.

Remember, it was dark. The wind was howling, sea spray stinging his eyes. Only the voice of Jesus was at all clear. Still Peter's heart leapt within. And it was with a mixture of bravado and timidity that Peter blurted out, "Lord, if it is you, bid me come to you on the water!"

And Jesus said, "Come!"

The rest of the apostles have a white-knuckled vise grip on the gunnels of the boat. The storm, the waves, the dark, the wind, the uncertainty — they're not about to move. And, as with the most of us, they are quite happy to stay in their comfort zone and watch as Peter makes his move.

Thank God for the Peter's among us. When life grows stormy, when we cannot see, when all is tired and wet and fearful and nobody knows what to do, usually God sends us a Peter.

These are those who can think outside the box. Those who haven't been told it can't be done. Their middle name is "Adventure!" And they can come to us from the unlikeliest of places. A word from a stranger who has no idea of what's going on in your life is a clear word to you from God. Or your young child sees you crying and, with a child-like faith, encourages you to ask God for help. Suddenly, what you need to do is clear ... just as it was for Peter.

So Peter stands up, puts a foot over the side, and steps out on the sea. His eyes are riveted upon Jesus. And he's doing it! He's actually doing it! He's walking on water! So it was, the text says, "He came to Jesus."

Indeed! There are times Christ bids us walk on water, to throw off the comfort zone of the familiar, to venture out onto the realm of the impossible. And unless we have the impulsive audacity of Peter, we'll never be qualified for church leadership of the visionary sort. That fundraising project, that city-wide evangelism venture, that impossible family situation — those wet, windy, dark, fearful challenges keep us in the boat, keep us glued to our seats.

Yet Jesus says, "Come!"

So Peter did the impossible. He walked on water with Jesus. But now, watch what happened. Peter looked down. He saw the waves. He heard the wind howl out of the darkness, and he began to sink. Screaming out to Jesus, "Lord, save me!" Jesus reached out to a beleaguered Peter with a sustaining hand.

I tell you, there is a powerful point made here, one we should never forget. For as long as Peter *gazed* at God and only *glanced* at the danger, he was sustained. But when he *gazed* at the waves and only *glanced* at Jesus, he sank.

Peter was not the only one who got his *gazing* and his *glancing* wrong. The Bible is filled with examples. The spies who went into the promised land came back and gave their reports: Ten of them said they had gazed at the inhabitants and they were like giants ... and that the Israelites were like grasshoppers by comparison. Two of the spies glanced at those same "giants" and gazed at God and said that the Israelites should go and take possession of the land.

David gazed at Bathsheba and gave God only a quick glance before he entered the darkest part of his life.

Ananias and Sapphira glanced at how others were giving their all to the early church and they gazed at how easy it would be for them to look good and cheat God.

The list goes on ... it's a matter of perspective and faith.

Is it not true for us? Jesus said there would come a day when "men's hearts would be weighed down with fear and foreboding of what is coming down upon the world." We read of crime statistics in the papers. We see the ugly snarl of humanity on the evening news. Friends disappoint us. Suddenly, we comprehend the world as a desperate sinking place.

I know there are times when I must abstain from television news, the papers, and magazines. They sometimes arrest my gaze and fill me with despair. So I eschew them for a period of time while I restore my faithful gaze at Jesus. If I don't so this, I sink into the world's miseries.

297

The answer to those times of despair and misery is to be very intentional in looking to God. Time spent in reading the Word, time spent in prayer and meditation, time spent with fellow believers ... all of these help us to keep our *gaze* where it ought to be. It is only when we look up to God that we seen any difference — the sustaining hope of all nations. The One who is able. The One who sustains me.

Indeed! For those who tackle a cause, a work, a labor with God, so big, so impossible, so unthinkable, that it is doomed to failure unless God is in it, we must remember, it is only by God's strength that we can do what we do — preach, convert, sustain, and grow the church.

That means less self-ego, more divine worship. Less looking to ourselves, more looking to Jesus. Less gazing at the world, more riveted faith in God.

When Jesus and Peter got back in the boat, the whole lot of them, the disciples, worshiped. "Truly you are the Son of God," they whispered.

And so may it ever be with us as we only glance at the impossible world, but gaze at our Savior, Christ, the Lord of all possibilities.

Stephen M. Crotts

The Cry For Help

In the Gospel of Mark, the woman in our story is called a "Syrophoenician." Matthew, however, calls her a "Canaanite." That's easier to say than "Syrophoenician" but there's something more important going on with that change. The Canaanites are not just Gentiles but *enemies*. They are the people who were to be driven out of the promised land by the Israelites and who fought against God's covenant people. There could be peace with other people of the Near East, but not with the nations of Canaan. In the Old Testament the people of Israel often got seduced into the worship of Ba`al and other gods of the Canaanites.

Jesus is a Jew who knows about those old conflicts between his ancestors and the people of Canaan. Now he has left his home territory of Galilee and gone north toward Gentile country, the region of Tyre and Sidon, where this Canaanite woman lives. Somehow she has heard of his reputation as a healer and comes to him to beg for help. She wants Jesus to heal her daughter. What will he do? Some of his people — and that apparently includes some of his disciples who are present — would say that he shouldn't even speak to the woman.

There are a couple of possible responses that Jesus might make. We might like to think that the obvious thing for him to say would be, "Of course I'll be glad to help. God loves everybody." We are the beneficiaries of centuries of the Christian church saying, "God shows no partiality" — it's in the book of Acts. Well, we know that in theory. But if we remember that we get a little nervous when we have to drive at night through an area of the city populated by people of a different race, or that we felt uncomfortable when that Arabic looking person got on the plane right after us, we'll realize that that nice enlightened attitude doesn't come so easily.

The other way to respond would be to say, "You belong to the wrong group. I can't help you." That's the way Jesus does in fact answer. "I was sent only to the lost sheep of the house of Israel." That may surprise and even disappoint us, but attitudes like that were part of the culture Jesus grew up in — just as, in different ways, they are part of our culture.

We can see the story of this encounter with a Canaanite woman as one of the things that made Jesus aware of the scope of his mission — that it wasn't just limited to the Jewish people. But let's concentrate for now on the way the woman deals with this rejection — because that's going to tell us something about our own situation. She doesn't get angry and insist that Jews are no better than Canaanites, or demand her rights. Instead she just repeats, "Lord, help me!"

That doesn't seem to do any good. "It is not fair to take the children's food and throw it to the dogs," Jesus says. That is — "You and your daughter are dogs, not children of God." Jews didn't get enthusiastic about dogs — there's nothing about them being "man's best friend" in the Bible. Jesus' words are obviously not complimentary.

But those words spoken to the Canaanite woman are mild in comparison with some of the language that we find in the Bible. The divine judgment against sin strikes all people without partiality — Jew and Gentile, black and white and yellow, man and woman. None of us has, because of the family we were born into or our genes or our hard work, any prior claim on God. Jesus uses far sharper language for some of the religious leaders of his own people than he does for any Gentile — hypocrites, the blind leading the blind, and so forth. In the next chapter of Matthew the leader of the disciples, Peter, will try to deflect the one he calls Messiah from taking the way of the cross and Jesus says "Get behind me, Satan." Being called "Satan" is a good deal worse than being called a little dog.

300

In Romans, Saint Paul uses some harsh language directed not just at certain individuals but at everybody. "There is no one who is righteous, not even one." "All have sinned and fall short of the glory of God." And if we're inclined to argue with those judgments on ourselves, we can use Jesus' summary of God's Law to do a reality check: "You shall love the Lord your God with all your heart, and with all your soul, and with all your mind." Do you — *with all your heart*? "You shall love your neighbor as yourself." Do you — *as yourself*?

What do I do when the law says, "You're a sinner"?

Well, I can say, "No, I'm not." I can lower the scale and argue that I love God more than some things and usually try to obey him, and that I treat my neighbor decently, even if not as well as I treat myself. I can always find someone worse than myself and say that there's the real sinner, or I can be very modern and deny the relevance of the whole concept of sin.

I could say, "Yes, I'm a sinner but I'll clean up my act and make up for my past mistakes." I have the ability to be a righteous person in God's sight and to make the entrance requirements for belonging to God's people. Maybe I'll need some assistance from God but it's not something that's beyond my capacities. This is the response of standard brand religion.

Or I could say to God, "Yes, I am a sinner. Help me." That is the kind of response the Canaanite woman gives to Jesus' words. She could have angrily denied what he said or promised to live a better life if he helped her but instead she simply repeats her plea for help. Perhaps I am a dog but even the dogs get fed. I have no claim on God but appeal entirely to the divine mercy.

Jesus does give her what she asks because, as he says, "Great is your faith!"

How she may have heard of Jesus and the rumors that he was the Jewish Messiah we don't know, but she began her appeal in faith with the words: "Have mercy on me Lord, Son of David." Her trust is not placed in some general idea of deity but in the God of Israel and his Messiah. She continued to trust in him and his ability to help even when it looked as if her appeal were going to be turned down rudely.

God's character is fundamentally one of love and mercy. That is stated often in the Old Testament and is revealed most fully in the life of Christ. The demands of the law and divine judgment are realities but they are not the deepest truth about God. When the law convicts you of sin, its purpose is to make you realize your need of the forgiveness and salvation that are freely available in Jesus Christ. That is what God wants. "I have no pleasure in the death of anyone" he says through the prophet Ezekiel. "Turn, then, and live."

I'm sure that it wasn't easy for that woman to believe that a Jewish teacher would have any interest in helping her. Especially when we are conscious of something we've done wrong and are feeling guilty for our sin, it isn't easy to believe that God is gracious and merciful. After all, we've already had to ask for forgiveness so often! God can forgive us even if we find it hard to forgive ourselves. We can "reassure our hearts before him whenever our hearts condemn us," says the First Letter of John, "for God is greater than our hearts."

The simple truth is that God really does love all people and finally doesn't make any distinction between Jews and Canaanites, between those who appear to be righteous externally and those who don't. God "desires everyone to be saved and to come to the knowledge of the truth" — and not just "everyone" as an abstraction but you and you and you. God's salvation is there for the asking, for all who ask it in faith.

George L. Murphy

The Incomparable Christ

While sightseeing in Boston last fall, I entered the narthex of a church building. Much to my surprise I discovered a gallery of marble busts, images of some of history's great leaders. Socrates and Aristotle were there. So was Alexander the Great, Charlemagne, Joan of Arc, Shakespeare, Confucius, Moses, Mohammed, and Christ. I personally found the display troubling, mainly because Jesus was just one of the crowd. And that just isn't historically or theologically accurate! For you see, Christ is so unique as to be incomparable!

In the text, Jesus asked the question, "Who do you say that I am?" Was he just another on of the crowd? Did his disciples have any idea of who Christ was? Peter, of course, responded, "You are the Christ, the Son of the Living God." While it's pretty clear that Peter did not fully understand all that meant, he was absolutely right. Jesus is the Christ. There is no one like him. There is no one else who is the Son of the Living God. Peter was right and Jesus blesses Peter and makes a prophetic pronouncement over him. Jesus still blesses those who come to the realization that Jesus is the Christ.

So, to be accurate, the narthex should be redesigned so that Christ is lifted up on a level by himself, with the remainder of history's host far below. Let's take a look at the record and see why this is so.

God's Action

The major religions of the world agree on two facts: 1) The human race once had a close relationship with God; 2) Somehow

303

we lost it. Where religions disagree is on how that relationship is restored. This is where religions divide into two main categories — active religion and reactive religions.

An active religion teaches that a person must do something to restore his relationship with God. Judaism warns we must obey the law. Hinduism persuades us to meditate, diet, and squelch passions. Islam bids us give alms to the poor, pray five times daily, and fight Allah's holy wars. "Do something!" religion bids. "Take the initiative. Reach out!"

The other sort of religion is "reactive," and Christianity is its only representative. This sort of faith says there is nothing I can do to restore my relationship with God. Only God himself is capable of doing such. In Jesus Christ, God has acted decisively, capably, once and for all. All I can do is react, and repentance and faith are the proper response.

See this in Genesis 1-3. Adam and Eve turn from God to Satan and sin. Then they know fear and shame and hide themselves. But God acts. In the cool of the evening God walks in their garden. "Where are you?" he queries. Finding them, he begins to unfold his divine redeeming strategy. At God's initiative an animal is slain, the first blood sacrifice, and the promise of a savior is prophesied — one who would crush Satan's head.

Confucius, Mohammed, and Buddha are but the initiative of man. The uniqueness of Christ is that he is the initiative of God.

Prophecy

Yet another distinctive of Jesus Christ is that his life and ministry were predicted long before he was born. The Old Testament was written over a 1,500-year period. In its 39 books a savior is predicted over 300 times.

These prophecies are quite specific. The Savior sent from God would have a virgin birth and know poverty. He'd be born in Bethlehem, be called a Nazarene, and yet God would call him out of Egypt. He'd come from the tribe of Judah, the house of David. His would be a ministry of miracles, yet he'd be rejected by his own people, be a suffering servant, and die like a sacrificial lamb, yet not one of his bones would be broken.

304

There were over 300 such prophecies. And Jesus Christ fulfilled every one of them literally. So, indeed, he is the one promised of old — Jesus, the Christ.

"Jesus" is the Greek version of the Hebrew "Joshua." The name means "savior" or "health-giver." "Christ" is Greek for "the anointed one of God." So, his very name means, "The anointed one of God to bring health."

His Teachings

When one turns from the initiative of God and prophecy to Christ's teachings, a further distinctive is found. Other religious leaders said, "I have taught you the truth." Jesus said, "I am the truth."

There are those who like to say that Jesus Christ was a great teacher, but he was not God. I hasten to point out that Christ has not left that option open to us. A man who said the sort of things Christ said about himself is either absolutely correct or he is a liar or a lunatic.

"If you've seen me you've seen the Father." "I am the way, the truth, and the life; no one comes to the Father but by me." "I am the door." "Before Abraham was, I Am." "I will come again and receive you to myself." Such is the boldness of Christ that either he is right or wrong. Either he is telling us the truth or he is lying or deluded.

Yet — amazing thing — Jesus taught with such authority, his lifestyle never contradicted his words. Merciful love, sterling character, and extraordinary miracles accompanied his utterances.

The Witness Of History

In 1896, after fifteen centuries, Athens renewed the Olympic games, thus fulfilling the dream of Baron Pierre de Coubertin of France. You can imagine how proud the Greeks were to host the first modern Olympics. You can also imagine how disappointed they were at their athletes' lack of success in event after event.

The last competition was the marathon. Greece's entrant was named Louis, a shepherd without competitive background. He'd trained alone in the hills near his flock. When the race started, Louis was far back in the pack of marathoners. But as the miles passed he moved up steadily. One by one the leaders began to falter. The Frenchman fell in agony. The hero from the United States had to quit the race. Soon, word reached the stadium that a lone runner was approaching the arena, and the emblem of Greece was on his chest! As the excitement grew, Prince George of Greece hurried to the stadium entrance where he met Louis and ran with him to the finish line.

In this sports tale we have something of the history of the human race. Most historical figures make their impact, achieve a measure of fame, books are written about them, but as the years go by they begin to fade. Less and less is written or spoken of their lives until they rest in relative obscurity.

With Jesus Christ, however, one finds quite an opposite phenomena! Christ started from way back in the pack. He was born in relative obscurity, never had many followers, commanded no army, erected no edifices, wrote no books. He died young, was buried in a borrowed grave, and you'd think he'd be quickly forgotten.

But, no! His reputation has grown so that today he is worshiped on every continent, has more followers than ever before, sixteen times has his picture been on the cover of *Time* magazine, and his sayings have been translated into more than 200 languages.

Consider: Socrates taught for forty years, Plato for fifty, and Aristotle, forty. Jesus Christ only taught for three years. Yet which has influenced the world more? One hundred thirty years of classical thought or three years of Christ's?

In the Library of Congress there are 1,172 reference books on William Shakespeare, 1,752 on George Washington, 2,319 on Abe Lincoln, and 5,152 on Jesus Christ. Perhaps H. G. Wells best summed up the runaway difference in interest. "Christ," he wrote, "is the most unique person of history. No man can write a history of the human race without giving first and foremost place to the penniless teacher of Nazareth."

From poverty and obscurity to teacher to death on the cross, to ascended Lord — Jesus Christ is the growing figure of history. Unique — while all others decrease, he increases — until, as the Bible predicts, "To him every knee shall bow and every tongue confess that Jesus Christ is Lord."

Human Unity

Yet another rich distinctive of Christ is the social unity he brings. The world to which Jesus Christ came was a divided world — rich against poor, slave and free, Jew and Gentile, male and female, Greek and barbarian. Other religious leaders entered this arena and compounded the problem with strict caste systems, classes of desirables and undesirables, infidels and faithfuls.

Jesus Christ, however, was the only religious leader tall enough to see over all the fences we have erected to divide ourselves. At his birth, wise men and shepherds, animals, the rich and poor, male and female, king, peasant, young, old, Jew and Gentile came and worshiped as one.

As an adult, Jesus continued to draw all humanity unto himself — rich Lazarus, a poor widow of Nain, harlots, Pharisees, soldiers, scholars, priests, and businessmen. It is written of Jesus in Ephesians, "He has broken down the dividing walls of hostility and made us both one." Galatians announces, "In Christ there is neither Jew nor Greek, male nor female, but one new man in Christ." Indeed, no one has done more to unite the infirm, the orphan, the student, the poor, the rich, and the various races than Christ himself!

Salvation Of The Whole Person

Another uniqueness of Jesus is his emphasis on the well-being of the whole person.

If I become a Muslim, my religion promises to make me right with Allah, god. But it offers me no relationship with myself or creation. Arabs raped Palestine ecologically, and their religious leaders make them into car bombs constantly.

If I become a pantheist, I get right with nature but ignore my relations with God and other people.

If I become a Hindu, through diet and meditation, I achieve a relationship with myself, but have nothing with God, people, or creation.

In Christ, however, I am promised a relationship that is based on love that intellectually, emotionally, and willfully includes God, self, neighbor, and creation. This is the exceeding breadth of the great commandment of Christ — to love God and my neighbor as myself. See in 1 Thessalonians 5:23 God's interest in the whole person: "May the God of peace himself sanctify you wholly; and may your spirit and soul and body be kept sound and blameless at the coming of our Lord Jesus Christ."

No one cares for all that I am and for all my basic relationships like Jesus Christ!

Philosophical Epistemology

Epistemology is the philosophy of knowing. It asks the question, "How do I know something is true?" And basically, it works out to four means:

1. *Experience:* "I know fire burns because I touched it."
2. *Reason:* "I know 2+2=4 because it is reasonable."
3. *Authority:* "I know man walked on the moon because *NBC News* told me so."
4. *Revelation:* "I know there is a God because my conscience bears witness."

The interesting thing about world religions is that they all appeal to epistemological verification in at least one of these four areas and to varying levels of quality. Jesus Christ, however, can be verified in all four areas and to the highest levels of quality.

As James 3:17 teaches, "The wisdom from above (Christ) is first pure, then peaceable, gentle, open to reason...."

Consider:

1. *Experience:* All varieties of people on every continent have experienced Jesus Christ for 2,000 years.
2. *Reason:* Jesus and his Bible are the most scrutinized of all. There has been more debate, writing, thinking, and teaching about him than any other. Christian apologetics is well documented. And the most intelligent of history have believed in him — T. S. Eliot, Shakespeare, Rembrandt, Handel, Tolstoy, C. S. Lewis, and the like.

3. *Conscience, revelation:* I read this word and I am strangely calmed. We keep coming back to him, rediscovering him. He's the man we cannot avoid, the one revealed from heaven.
4. *Authority:* Here there is the Bible, the church, Christian universities, families — human authority and beyond — all chorusing, "Jesus is truth!"

Oswald Spangler called Jesus "an incomparable figure." Ibsen said he is "the greatest rebel who ever lived." Will Durant called him "God's highest incarnation." Charles Lamb observed, "If all the illustrious men of history were gathered together and Shakespeare should enter their presence, they would arise to do him honor; but if Jesus Christ should come in they would all fall down and worship him."

It was Napoleon who wrote of Christ: "I know men, and I tell you, Jesus was more than a man. Comparison is impossible between him and any other being who ever lived because he was the Son of God."

Incarnation

The Bible says Jesus is "the word" that "became flesh and dwelt among us."

I asked a young Oriental student at the university why he had become a Christian. "I was in a deep pit," he testified. "I wanted out but was in too deep and was entirely too weak to climb out. Confucius looked in and said, 'You are in a deep pit. You should have been more careful. If you ever get out, come and see me and I will teach you wisdom.' Next Buddha looked in on me. He said, 'Quit struggling, my son. There is peace in the pit. Only meditate on my words.' Next Moses visited. He gave me ten rules and told me to build my life around them. There followed, then, the man Jesus Christ. He looked down into the pit, saw me and didn't say a word. He simply climbed down into the pit, embraced me and carried me out on his back. Now, every day he walks with me teaching me how to love like him."

Such is the incarnational love of Jesus. He comes among us, feeds us, heals us, numbers the hairs of our head, calls us by name, dies in our place, and bids us, "Cast all your cares upon me because I care about you."

His Miracles

Yet a final distinctive of Jesus Christ is his miracles. What did he do? What didn't he do! He turned water into wine, healed the lame, the blind, and the deaf. Calmed a storm, multiplied a little food to feed 5,000, raised the dead, even resurrected himself from death!

Look at it this way. If you were walking down the road in life, and the road came to a fork and you didn't know which way to go, you'd ask directions. Let's say four people are there, three dead and one alive; who will you ask?

Buddha, Mohammed, and Moses are dead, but Jesus Christ is alive. He is unique among religious leaders of the world in that he alone has no tomb. He alone is alive, eternal, and reigning!

Conclusion

Almost 2,000 years ago a man was born contrary to the laws of nature. This person lived in poverty, was reared in obscurity. Never did he travel extensively. Only one or twice did he cross the boundary of Israel. He possessed neither wealth nor influence. His family had little education. In infancy, he startled a monarch. In childhood, he puzzled scholars. In adulthood, he ruled nature walking upon the sea and hushing a storm.

He healed the multitudes of blind, lame, mute, possessed, and he did it without medicine and made no charge for his services. He never wrote anything down, and yet the libraries of the world bulge with the volumes written about him. He never wrote a song or painted a picture or molded clay and yet he has furnished the theme for more art than all others combined.

He never practiced medicine and yet he has healed more broken spirits and hearts than modern medicine far and near. He never started a university, yet all the colleges of the world cannot boast of having as many disciples.

He never commanded an army, fired a gun, drafted a soldier, or ran for political office. Yet no officer or king ever had more volunteers who have, under his orders, marched into every valley of human need to begin orphanages, schools, hospitals, to right wrongs, and institute justice.

Every Lord's Day, the wheels of commerce cease their churning and multitudes assemble in churches worldwide to worship him as Savior and Lord.

The names of athletes, senators, artists, emperors, and soldiers have come and gone; but the name of this person grows with time. Though nearly 2,000 years from his birth, yet he still lives! Herod could not kill him. Satan could not seduce him. Death could not obliterate him. The grave could not hold him.

He stands forth upon the earth as God Incarnate, the King of glory, Jesus Christ, Savior and Lord.

Proclaimed by prophets, heralded by angels, worshiped by saints, feared by devils, he asks, "Who do you say that I am?"

Stephen M. Crotts

Do You Get It?

"Is that really necessary?" It's a question that we may ask when something unpleasant or disturbing has been said or done. If someone brings up a topic like capital punishment or abortion at the dinner table, you might ask rhetorically, "Is that really necessary?" In that situation it probably isn't, but there are times when such issues do have to be discussed. We can't always insist on keeping things light and comfortable.

When somebody does refuse to face some of the tough realities of the world, we might say that that he or she "just doesn't get it." The implication is that the person ought to be able to grasp whatever it is that's in question and see the necessity of dealing with it, that enough opportunity has been given, but that for some reason he or she just doesn't — or won't — understand.

In today's gospel, we could say that Peter "just doesn't get it." It seemed last week that he knew what was going on. In answer to Jesus' question about who the disciples thought he was, Peter, as their spokesman, said "You are the Messiah, the Son of the living God." Jesus commended him for that and told him that he was "blessed" because God had revealed that to him. Peter was on a roll and so, it would seem, are Jesus and the other disciples. To this point in Jesus' ministry all the crowds that have gathered to hear him and the people that he's healed have been very impressive. If Jesus is the long-awaited Messiah and Son of God, we can expect for those successes to continue. He'll be "Number One." Peter and the others are happy to be following him because everybody loves a winner.

313

But today, when Jesus immediately starts talking about being rejected by the leaders of the nation and says that he's going to suffer and die, it doesn't fit with the confession of faith that Peter had just made. Jesus' words seem to contradict what it means to be the Messiah and don't make any sense. When Jesus starts talking that way, Peter figures that he's mistaken and wants to correct him.

That's a very natural thing for Peter to do. When Peter said that Jesus was the Messiah, he meant that Jesus was the Lord's anointed, the long-awaited king who would finally liberate the people of Israel from oppression. If that were the case, it wouldn't make any sense for the Messiah himself to be crushed by the oppressive powers that enslaved Israel. If he is "the Son of the living God," how *could* he be killed?

The Jewish people had been waiting for a liberator, a Messiah, for a long time. They'd gone through religious and political turmoil for generations and now were suffering under the Roman occupation. The hope was that when the Messiah, God's true king, came, it would be the end of all that. They wouldn't have to be pushed around any more. The Messiah would put them back on top of the world, the way their traditions told them that it had been under David and Solomon.

Well, what would you expect an oppressed people to think? Preachers sometimes say things like, "The Jews were expecting the Messiah to be a military conqueror, not a suffering servant," as if that had been a quite unreasonable hope of theirs. Of course oppressed people want liberation. It's far too easy for comfortable Americans to criticize them for that.

We have our own ways of expressing the same feelings that Peter had — "God forbid it, Lord! This must never happen to you." We can put the cross in a corner — there's a reason why far more people come to church on Easter Sunday than on Good Friday, and it isn't just because they have to work on weekdays. We can make the cross into a shiny piece of jewelry, of course without any body hanging on it, and when Easter does come we'll cover it with lilies.

Being on top of the world? We like to say "God Bless America" — and of course there's a way we should pray that. But when we say it, do we mean, "God, keep America *number one*" the way some Jews of the first century looked for the restoration of the Davidic empire? Do we want America to be blessed without any corresponding sacrifice on our part, or without having any concern about being a blessing to others? If we do have that attitude, what does a crucified Messiah have to do with our hope?

Do we get it? When we hear about the cross, do we say, "Was that really necessary?" That was the reaction of a lot of people to the Mel Gibson film *The Passion of the Christ*. Certainly there are criticisms that can be made of that movie, but when people suggested that an intense focus on the passion was somehow inappropriate, we really have to wonder if they got it.

"From that time on, Jesus began to show his disciples that he must go to Jerusalem and undergo great suffering at the hands of the elders and chief priests and scribes, and be killed, and on the third day be raised." The statement is carefully worded: "He must go." The little Greek word that is used there, *dei*, means "it is necessary." In the Bible it's often used in the sense of something that God has decided upon, a "divine necessity." These verses are sometimes called a "passion prediction" but they do more than just say what is going to happen. It is something that *needs* to happen.

"Jesus began to show his disciples" — to reveal the plan to them, and to say "it is necessary" means that it is *God*'s plan.

Can we see that it was necessary? Let us not imagine that we're smarter or more spiritual than Peter and the other disciples. If we've begun to grasp the necessity of the cross, it isn't because we're more insightful than they were. It's because Peter and the others eventually were brought to understand what had happened and passed the message on to us. On the Day of Pentecost Peter told the crowd in Jerusalem that Jesus had been crucified "according to the definite plan and foreknowledge of God." We owe our faith and knowledge to the witness of the apostles who didn't get it to begin with. If you haven't gotten it yet, there's still hope for you.

Why was the cross necessary? It was to deal with the problems of sin and evil in the world — really to deal with them and not simply to cover them up. It was to deal with the problem of sin

315

for us. Sin means being out of touch with God, having our lives centered on the wrong thing, something which distorts our understanding of ourselves and our relationships with others. That is what ultimately leads to the kind of oppression that the Jews of Jesus' time experienced, to the poverty and sense of helplessness and anger of so many people in the world today, and to the fruitless searches of well-to-do people to fill their inner vacuum with chemicals or sex or toys.

If our basic problem is our relationship with God, then only God can really fix it. That's why the one who is on the way to Jerusalem is the Son of God: God isn't going to leave the job to an assistant or somebody in celestial middle management. But it is *our* problem, and so has to be handled from within, as part of the human race. God comes to heal us by sharing our life — including the consequences of sin and death.

"Surely he has born our infirmities and carried our diseases," the prophet said. If you're going to lift a heavy load, you have to get under it. God goes as far down as possible, taking on what was considered the most agonizing and disgraceful kind of execution, what one early Christian teacher called "the utterly vile death of the cross."

When he cried, "My God, my God, why have you forsaken me?" he was at the very bottom of reality, where sin would eventually take all of us if God did not act to save us. But he went there — and the words, "And on the third day be raised," mean that the whole catastrophic plummeting of humanity into the depths will be reversed.

We shouldn't imagine that we're privy to all God's secrets or can say that God *had* to do something, but in very general terms that sort of explanation *may* help us to understand why the cross was necessary. It still may not answer all the questions that you have. How does it work? How does the cross save us from sin? Theologians have suggested various answers — that Christ paid our debt, or suffered our punishment, or defeated the powers of evil. But the main question isn't "How?" If you're wheeled into the emergency room with a heart attack and the doctor says that

316

some procedure is necessary in order to save your life, you probably won't ask first for a detailed technical explanation of how all the medical instruments and technology work. That can come later if you're really interested.

What Jesus did was necessary for our salvation. More than that, it was what a mathematician would call a "necessary and sufficient condition" for salvation. Believe it, accept what God has done, and get on board. There is no need for you to add anything to it in order be one of God's people.

But be sure to listen to Jesus' words. He doesn't just speak here about what's going to happen to him, but about what it means to be a disciple — to be one of God's people. The fact that that status is given to us freely doesn't mean that it's going to be easy. "For those who want to save their life will lose it, and those who lose their life for my sake will find it. For what will it profit them if they gain the whole world but forfeit their life. Or what will they give in return for their life?"

We will have real life if we recognize what it is and distinguish it from an illusory kind of life. Those who think that life is defined by enriching themselves at the expense of others and who cling to power and wealth will lose real life. Those who can let go of lesser goods, who put them in second place, will be able to open their hands to receive the life that Jesus promises. Those who lose life not just for anything but for his sake will find it.

Taking up the cross means to follow Christ and to be given real life. It means that we can begin to know what the world is really all about. It means that we get it.

George L. Murphy

Church Discipline: A Cure
For What Ails The Body

When a sixteen-year-old stays out all night drinking, then drives home, a father disciplines him with grounding. When a student cuts class, is late with papers, and turns in inferior work, a college professor disciplines him with failing marks. When an employee is lazy and is caught pilfering company goods, his boss disciplines him by firing him. At the businessman's club a member who skips meetings and refuses to join in service projects is disciplined by dismissal from club membership.

A church member having an adulterous affair — what happens? Nothing.

A church member who has not attended worship in six months and has no legitimate excuse except a busy social schedule — what happens? Nothing.

A pastor, hard-working and faithful, yet being slandered by a mean-spirited and disgruntled church member — what happens? Absolutely nothing.

Indeed!

> *Living together above*
> *With the saints that we love,*
> *O, that will be glory!*

> *Living together below*
> *With the saints that we know,*
> *That's a different story!*

Why Not?

The question is, why does the church refuse to provide discipline for her members? One reason is that we are ignorant of what the scriptures say, verses like the text in Matthew 18:15-20. We either do not know the verse, or we pass over it in unbelief.

✓ There are other reasons, like bad incidents in history: the Spanish Inquisition, the Salem Witch Trials, the Crusades ... and more.

When I was a young pastor in Virginia, I read the minutes of the elders for the past 100 years, and there was an attempt at church discipline. It seems that in the 1920s a church member was selling "moonshine" liquor. The elders accused him of "putting temptation to the lips of his neighbors." The man refused to quit and left the Presbyterians to join another local church!

We also are afraid to discipline sin in the church because of popular verses that are taken out of context and improperly interpreted. "Let him who is without sin cast the first stone." "Judge not that you may not be judged." Indeed, we surmise, how can a sinner correct a sinner?

✓ The result is, there is precious little discipline in the typical church today. People do as they please. Folks can get away with anything, and we have an unholy anarchy of gossip, sexual immorality, inattendance, false teaching, and lies. None of this glorifies Jesus Christ!

So, how is it that we can find the proper application of church discipline? Several points made in the text can aid us.

Learn To Hate Sin

First we must learn to hate sin as God does. The text mentions someone who "sins against you." It is like the madman who entered the Vatican in the 1970s, took a sledgehammer, and began to strike Michelangelo's Pieta. Sin is to deface God's will. It is to destroy the works of his creation by disobedience. Lies, slander, theft, greed, murder, and more of our behavior accomplishes this quite nicely.

And we smile about it.

My! My! How light an attitude we have toward sin today. Why, it is no longer betraying the wife of one's youth by breaking covenant vows of matrimony, it is but a discreet divorce. It is no longer ruinous adultery and lust, it is a dalliance, a mere trifling affair.

Yes, it is to us in our slackness. But read Psalm 5:4-6. "For thou art not a God who delights in wickedness; evil may not sojourn with thee. The boastful may not stand before thy eyes; thou hatest all evildoers. Thou destroyeth those who speak lies; the Lord abhors bloodthirsty and deceitful men."

Clearly God takes sins — big and small — seriously. If you do not believe me, just look at the cross! So, too, we must learn to hate sin in our own lives and in others.

Avoid Nitpicking

The next step in church discipline is to avoid negativity, to avoid walking into a room and focusing on what's wrong while passing over so much that is right. Twice Matthew 18:15-20 uses the word *brother*. We are not to pull specks out of other's eyes (Matthew 7:3). We are to "forebear one another in love" (Philippians 2:3).

Like a well-waxed car in the rain, water falls on the hood and quickly glides away. So with us when we live in God's mercy at peace, we are prepared to allow the little bumps and scrapes of sin against us to go without notice. Simply put, "Love is not touchy" (1 Corinthians 13). "Love covers a multitude of sins" (1 Peter 4:8).

Face To Face

For sins that cannot be overlooked, that are particularly bothersome, Matthew 18 says to go to your brother face-to-face. Involve as few people as possible. Make a private appointment. Pick a convenient time when your fellow is not hungry or stressed out and pushed for time. Go humbly, and say, "I could be wrong. I'm willing to listen. What happened between us the other day hurts me, and I'd like to talk it over." Then come out with your grievance.

The Bible says that if your brother listens to you, then you've gained your brother. "Oh, I am so sorry. I did not realize. Do forgive me. I'd never want to hurt you!"

Other times the tack might be similar, but tapered to the need. "I just want you to know privately, the word is out you are having an affair. If it's true, we need to talk. If it is not true, we need to look to your reputation."

To The Elders

What happens though, when your brother dismisses you coldly? When your attempts are rebuffed? When you are told to get out of their face?

Then you widen the circle. More responsible people are brought into the conflict. Go to the elders, the text says. Lay your grievances before them, and ask them for help.

The elders then are to call the quarreling parties together and arbitrate the matter. Hopefully, both sides will listen to reason and the matter can be settled.

I recall a family building a house with a contractor. Matters went poorly. Money was involved, and they couldn't settle it between them. The elders were called in, a solution was found to everyone's agreement and relationships were maintained.

Church Discipline

But again, what if matters still aren't resolved? What if the elders' advice is disavowed? Then church discipline must be invoked.

It is never issued by one elder, or by a pastor. The text says the *elders* (plural) are to do it.

The mildest censure is a simple admonishing or rebuke. "John, how can a man of your stature allow this issue to fester?" So much in the church can be settled with a look, a private word with someone, a warning, and such.

These failing, however, the elders may issue, after some time of patience and prayer, a *suspension*. This is a public or private ban on the offender's right to vote, to serve, to give, and to receive communion.

The offender, still failing to repent and follow the course of reconciliation, is finally *excommunicated*. This does not mean the person is no longer saved; it simply means he is unwelcome in the church until he heeds the elder's discipline.

322

We once had a young man selling heroine in the parish. We strove with him for ten months — warning, later suspending, and as a last resort, publicly telling the church why he was no longer on our rolls or welcome in our midst until he repented.

It took six years, so much prayer, and a pile of hurt. But he came back, asking for help and to be restored.

Be assured! The purpose of such church discipline is never to destroy, but to heal. By disciplining one another we are to honor Jesus Christ. We are to restore what was lost. We are to maintain a higher level of purity. And we are by so doing to discourage others from sinning.

Conclusion

In my study, I have two rocks. One is from a field at Gettysburg battlefield. It is rough and ugly. The other is from a river where it empties into the sea. It is smoothly polished and lovely. One tumbled with other stones in the river and so got its rough edges knocked off. The other lay alone in a field uninvolved with others.

As Christians, we are called in Matthew 18 to our brothers, to fellowship, to interaction, to speaking the truth in love, to accountability. When we obey, our lives grow, the rough edges on us all are smoothed and polished until we become like Jesus himself!

Suggested Prayer

Lord, help me to value relationships. Amen.

Stephen M. Crotts

Proper 19
Pentecost 17
Ordinary Time 24
Matthew 18:21-35

A Severe Mercy!

French author Victor Hugo has a short story titled, "93." In the midst of this tale a ship at sea is caught in a terrific storm. Buffeted by the waves, the boat rocks to and fro, when suddenly the crew hears an awesome crashing sound below deck. They know what it is. A cannon they are carrying has broken loose and is smashing into the ship's sides with every list of the ship. Two brave sailors, at the risk of their lives, manage to go below and fasten it again, for they know that the heavy cannon on the inside of their ship is more dangerous to them than the storm on the outside. So it is with people. Problems within are often much more destructive to us than the problems without. Today, God's word would take us "below decks" to look inside ourselves concerning the whole matter of forgiveness.

Everybody's In Debt!

In the text, Jesus tells us of a king who decides to settle accounts with his servants. One man is brought before him who owes 10,000 talents. The modern equivalent would be about ten million dollars! So this subject was hopelessly enslaved to debt!

Yet another fellow in the text is mentioned as owing a hundred denarii, which today equals nearly twenty dollars. So everybody in the text is in debt. Some owe a lot. Some are indebted a little. But all owe somebody!

The text also makes it clear that the terrible consequence of being in debt was debtor's prison. Why, when a bill became past due and one couldn't pay, the creditor had the right to seize you

325

and throw you into the rat infested, dark of a dungeon. And there you remained until you paid every cent or died.

You've been in debt, haven't you? Remember the fear, the worry? Things get bleak, don't they? One holds his head down and avoids all eye contact. Frustration compounds fatigue and leaves you drained. God is saying that unforgiven sin in our life is like those unpaid debts. They weigh heavily upon us whether a little sin or a huge amount of sins.

Dostoevsky's novel *Crime and Punishment* is about this. The novel is little more than the tale of a young, fascist, poor student who murders a rich, old lady so he can get her money and continue his studies. But the student, hounded by guilt, pursued *by* his sins, finally confesses his crimes and is punished. Eloquently, so eloquently, Dostoevsky shows us what the real world is really like, a world where sin comes due like all debts and must be paid in full as the creditor comes calling us to account.

The same is true of Shakespeare's play *Macbeth*. A man is killed so Macbeth can usurp the crown, and Lady Macbeth, tormented by her part in the murderous sin, is driven to insanity. She pitifully raises her hands imagining them still to be stained with blood, and frets, "Will these hands ne'er be clean?"

Can't we identify with Dostoevsky and Shakespeare's characters? We are sinners like they were. Some of us owe a lot. Some are sin indebted a little. But each of us, like the debtors in the text, must settle accounts with the king, God Almighty himself.

Forgiveness Is Available

So, in the text everybody owes everybody. Now this: According to this parable Jesus told, forgiveness is available.

The king in calling his subjects before him finds one who owes ten million dollars. Surely Christ is exaggerating here! According to Roman tax records of the time, all Israel's taxes for one year amounted to about $800,000. So Christ was saying this man was hopelessly indebted. His bills were impossible to pay. Yet the debtor grovels before the king and says, "Please be patient with me. Just give me a little more time." He declares, "I will repay you in full!"

326

The king had pity on him, the text says. Rather than throwing him in jail, he simply forgave him his debts and let him go.

Jesus is saying God is like a king who has pity on us. He is willing to cancel out impossible debts and he is willing to forgive.

Did you know that the Greek word for *forgive* means *to let loose*? That's right. It's like a terrible knot that suddenly gives and is completely untied. It's like a dark bondage from which there is sudden release.

Try this experiment when you get home today. Take a trash can lid and lay it on a healthy portion of your lawn. Leave it there for a week. Afterward, lift the lid and look under it. See the pale, sickly grass? See the roaches and worms nesting in the dark decay of the withered grass. That's what sin does to us!

Put the lid back down on the grass. Does the grass have the power to remove the lid all by itself? No. That's impossible. And again, we are like the man in our text with an impossible debt to the king. We are helpless to free ourselves.

Finish the experiment. Take the lid away. The bugs flee. The grass begins to receive sunshine and moisture. Its health is revived, restored. It is literally *forgiven*, let loose from bondage and decay. Forgiveness is just like that. What we can't pay, God pays. God lets us loose from debts of sin and frees us to new life!

The Forgiven Should Forgive

Back to our fascinating parable. We have already seen that everybody owes everybody in the text, and that forgiveness of debts is available from a merciful king. Now this: When forgiven our debts, we should forgive others their debts also.

In the parable, the king forgave a man his ten million dollar debt. He let him loose, let him out of it! And what does this free man now do? He goes out and happens upon a fellow who owes him a measly twenty dollars. He seizes him by the throat! And he demands, "Pay what you owe me!" When the fellow says he cannot and asks for patience, the man throws him in debtors' prison. And someone goes and tells the king.

What does the king do? He recalls the man, derides him for his wickedness and explains, "Should not you have had mercy on

327

your fellow servant, as I had mercy on you?" In anger the king delivers the unforgiving man to the jailers until he pays the ten million.

Some story, eh, this parable Jesus told? And the point is clear. If God forgives us we must be about forgiving others.

I once talked with a lady who had been hurt six years ago. During that time she had never forgiven the individual who'd sinned against her. Instead she nursed her grudge, schemed of glorious get even tactics, and meditated on hatred. So now she was tired all the time, her face was hard and wore a mask of bitterness. She was neurotic. My, was she neurotic — such negativism and compulsive criticism as you've never seen! But what do you expect with her mind so focused on evil all the time! We talked. She was a Christian. I suggested she let her debtor loose just as God had let her loose. Finally the woman decided, "Well, I guess I'll pardon her as you suggest, but I don't want anything more to do with her!" "Is that how you'd like God to forgive you," I asked, "To pardon you, but then have nothing more to do with you?" She saw the point, and forgiveness flowed and this withered woman began again to thrive.

Now this is just the point of the text. When we begrudge someone, refuse to forgive, someone goes and tells the king. They tell God, and according to the text we are turned over to the jailers. The Greek word for "jailers" is literally "tormenters" or "torturers." We are tormented in prison when we are unforgiving!

Years ago, on a television show, a comic character was angry with another fellow. He said, "I'm tired of him slapping me on the chest every time he sees me. I've told him to quit and he won't. So I'm ready for him. I've got me three sticks of dynamite strapped to my chest. Next time he hits me it'll blow his arms off!" The first character was about to find out that his grudge was going to cost him as much or more as it was going to cost the other fellow! The fire he'd kindled for his enemy was going to burn him more than the other.

Dear people, when you're playing with unforgiveness, with grudges and hatred, you're playing with dynamite. You're playing with fire. Julie Nixon Eisenhower says, "One of the most deadly things you can do to yourself, is to be unforgiving." It's true. The text says so. It says unforgiveness ruins your relationship with God. It ruins your relationship with people. It imprisons you with torturers! It makes you sick to be unforgiving!

Let Go?

What about you? Have you called on God to forgive you? Your debt is impossible to pay, you know. I hope you're not like the fool in this parable who just wanted a little more time so he could scrounge up ten million bucks. Have you faced God and told him you're helplessly a debtor to sin and prayed for mercy? You can be let loose from your sins in Jesus!

And what about your own debtors? Forgiven, are you now forgiving? Are you bearing grudges, holding debts over others, and thus ruining your own relationship with God while being tormented yourself?

Just like the unlashed cannon in Victor Hugo's story, are there burdens of unforgiveness crashing around inside you tearing your guts out, rending your mind, tormenting you with the rise and sink of every day? "I can't forgive!" you say. Oh, but you can! The trouble is, you haven't wanted to, you haven't asked Christ to help.

Right now, ask Jesus to take your hand and go below decks with you. Tell him you're weak, you're afraid you'll fail. But tell him you're *willing* to forgive, willing to go with him and take care of all the troubling things within. Yes, tell Jesus you're willing, ask him to give you power, to forgive through you, and the healing, oh, the healing, it will begin!

Suggested Prayer

Lord Jesus, let's begin! Amen!

Stephen M. Crotts

329

Proper 20
Pentecost 18
Ordinary Time 25
Matthew 20:1-16

As Long As It Is Day!

The greatest sorrow is to have no cause, no work, no sacrifice for which to live. One is alive, but lives only for himself. Just standing around, twiddling his thumbs, absorbed with his own personal trivia — this is no life at all! And our text introduces us to such a crowd of people as represents many in our generation. They were "standing idle in the marketplace."

Now the fact that they were idle does not mean they were lazy, loafing. Rather, these men were "unhired." The marketplace, you see, was the assembly zone for day laborers hoping to find work. It was there employers came to hire.

And Jesus tells us a parable about such a situation. I've often defined a parable as an earthly story with a heavenly meaning. Literally in the Greek, parable means *to cast alongside*. It is to use the familiar to explain the unfamiliar.

Before we get started unpacking the meaning of this parable, we must put it in context. The disciples were following Jesus. Unlike those who'd not yet been called, or those who refused Jesus' summons, the disciples had left everything to be with Jesus. Their voice found utterance in Peter's question: "Lo, we have left everything and followed you. What then shall we have?" (Matthew 19:27). This parable is Christ's answer to that query.

So, what's here for us? Just this!

The Rich Man Is Harvesting!

A wealthy local farmer, perhaps the owner of a vineyard, has sown a crop, nourished it, and is now desiring to harvest his grapes, and he needs willing workers.

331

Have you ever wondered, "Why am I here? What is my purpose in life?" I saw a student on campus standing mute in front of the philosophy building. He held up a sign: "I would like to know what life is all about before I'm out!"

The Bible explains that God is harvesting people. He is drawing persons to himself, for a faith relationship that is lived out in love. This is the meaning of life. It is our reason for existing.

Furthermore ...

The Rich Man Is Hiring People!

If you've ever been without a job, you know how time oozes by, your resume seems to fall into a black hole, and you feel like half a human. Then you hear a rumor that someone is hiring, you go and market yourself, and you're offered a contract.

This is the good news of the text to idle humanity. God in Christ is calling laborers to his tasks! We have a purpose! There is no need for us to be idle any longer!

One of the most effective advertisements ever written was by Sir Ernest Shackleton, the British Polar explorer. It appeared in the London *Times* almost 100 years ago and read, "Men wanted for perilous expedition. Several years' commitment. Long days, hard work, bitter cold, little pay, bad food. Safe return doubtful." Hundreds of men replied. Shackleton said, "It seemed like all of London wanted to accompany me."

The Bible offers a similar advertisement. "Persons wanted for establishment of Christ's new kingdom. Repentance and faith necessary. Love a requirement. Lifelong commitment expected. Persecution anticipated. Inquire at your local church."

So, the rich man is harvesting, he's calling for willing workers. Now, this:

He's Paying Wages!

Verse 2 must have sounded like a clap of thunderous good news, "After agreeing with the laborers for a denarius a day, he sent them into his vineyard."

I remember my first paycheck. I was 25, a newly-minted minister working for a church. That money seemed such a gift. Why, here was provision, reward! Excitement!

Romans 6:23 explains, "The wages of sin is death." Abandonment. Oblivion. Darkness. Still as the grave. This was to be my plight! Ah! But the grace of Christ Jesus calls me to faith, to redemption. He saved me from my purposeless, self-absorbed existence to his kingdom. I became his co-laborer! Oh, the dignity of it all! And this — he rewards me! The fruit of his efforts in my life, and my effort in him, is "love, joy, peace, patience, goodness, kindness, gentleness, faithfulness, and self-control." And my drab, mundane existence is altered forever! My waiting is over! I have a purpose! I am wanted! I am fairly paid!

Now this:

It's Not Too Late!

Perhaps there's one of you for whom all this comes as good news. Yet you hang your head, saying, "It is too late for me. I'm too old, too sinful, too failed, too ... whatever!" Ah, but look! For the boss sets the first force of laborers to work and then throughout the day returns again and again to the public marketplace hiring any and all willing hands to go into his fields to help with the harvest.

"At the sixth hour," "the ninth hour," "about the eleventh hour," he did this. "Why do you stand here idle all day?" he inquired.

"Because no one has hired us," they explained.

"You go into the vineyard, too," he said.

No, Jesus is saying, it is not too late for you! There's room in God's purposes for you.

There are reasons why many of us come to the marketplace later in the day. Perhaps one has to care for a sick father, or a cow was bearing a calf, or we had to finish our own farm chores first.

In the text, some men had waited eleven hours to be hired. Almost the whole of the day was gone, but to their credit, they had not given up. They came and presented themselves for work. They had hope, and when they were hired they did not complain, "It's too late!" "So little can be done now." Rather, they jumped in and did the best they could with the time available.

I'm thinking of two fellow divinity school students in my class. Both talented. Both zealous for Christ. Both wanting to be pastors.

One graduated and soared to effectiveness and fame in the pulpit. The other suffered a health loss and has struggled for over twenty years before being able to enter a parish, but now only as a lowly assistant.

Yet both are beloved by God and hired in Christ's vineyard.

So, we each start life without a purpose, we are idle, full of unfulfilled longings. But the rich man is harvesting. Yes, God is! He's hiring folks like us. He's paying wages. And it is not too late, even in the eleventh hour!

He Is Just, Sovereign, And Gracious!

And now we come to the crux of the parable. The harvest is in, the workers are summoned to the boss. The last hired, those who've worked the least, are paid a full day's wage! The long-term workers get excited thinking, "Surely the boss will pay us more!" And when the same wage is paid them, they complain bitterly, "It's not fair!"

The boss says, "Did not we agree on your wage? If I want to be generous, isn't it my money to do with as I please?"

If nothing else, this parable teaches us the justice, the sovereignty, and the grace of God.

Remember Peter's question. "What then shall we have?" And Jesus is answering with this parable. He is warning the disciples and us that we can claim no special honor because we came first or worked longer. He is telling the Jews that, indeed, they came first, but the Gentile just as vitally came second. He is saying that some come in their youth, some at middle age, while others in old age. But all are welcome in God's vineyard. And all will benefit from his generosity, his purposes, his grace, his justice, and his sovereignty.

I recall my senior year of football. I thought I had my position made. But Stan, a second stringer, did his best to win my position. Instead of coasting, I had to hustle every day.

Stan never started. He played very little. But he pushed me to do my very best, and when championship trophies were awarded to the team, he got one just like mine.

Indeed, they also serve who sit and wait. God knows. He knows. And he rewards us all.

Conclusion

This parable answers Peter's question, and our own. "What then shall we receive?" Only Christ's justice, his sovereignty, and his graciousness. His is the cause, the harvest, the labor, the capital, the calling, and the wages.

And this story reminds us Jesus is the boss, not we ourselves.

Suggested Prayer

Lord, if you're calling, I'll come. Set me to work with no thought of myself. For Christ's sake. Amen.

Stephen M. Crotts

A Guide To Christmas

If you talk about the blind and guides you are talking about seeing-eye dogs. If you discuss Alpine mountains and climbing, you must think of a Swiss guide. If you are ignorant and in college, your guide is a professor. So it is with foreign lands and tour guides, taxes and tax consultants. But what of Christmas? I think many of us feel that Christmas is so easy to find that we don't need a guide. Yet, let me remind you that there were few that found their way to the first nativity. In fact, most missed it. And even today there are thousands who never find their way through all the glitter and "holidaze" to the Christ of Christmas.

God knows we are apt to get lost in our quest for the manger child, hence he has sent us a guide, our guide to Christmas. His name? John. John the Baptizer! In the text, a group of religious persons is testing Jesus' authority. Jesus stops them in their tracks with a hard question. "The baptism of John, from whence did it come?" The Pharisees couldn't answer him. Can we?

John's Purpose

In the Bible we are told of John's purpose. He was a go-between. He kept pointing to one coming after him, "One mightier than I," he said. (Matthew 3:11). In John 3:22-30, John the Baptizer is described as a "Friend of the Bridegroom." The Hebrew word for this groomsman is *Shoshben*. His job was something like a modern day wedding director. The *Shoshben* sent out invitations, he made arrangements for the wedding feast and presided at it.

337

Then, on the wedding night he brought the bride and groom together in the bedchambers and quickly left, his job done, the couple together, the marriage consummated.

John was this kind of wedding director, too. He was God's *Shoshben*, God's man chosen to bring Israel and Jesus together in the marriage of faith. He was sent to give the invitation, to call Israel to their covenant with God. His purpose was to bring Jesus and people together and then leave.

John's Message

Having considered John the Baptizer's purpose, let us now consider his message. In the scriptures we are told that John preached, "Prepare the way of the Lord!" (Matthew 3:3).

It has never been God's plan to take people by surprise. Amos, the prophet, said, "The Lord God does nothing without giving his servants the prophets knowledge of his plans." The great flood was preceded by the preaching of Noah; and so it is that the coming of Christ was preceded by John the Baptizer. He came saying, "Prepare the way of the Lord!"

In the time of John, a king planning to visit a country would send his messengers before him. These royal messengers would pass through the countryside saying, "The king is coming! The king is coming! Prepare the way for the king!" The citizens would immediately go to work fixing the roads over which the king would travel. It would be unthinkable for the king to get stuck in the mud, for his ride to be disturbed by bumps. What if the roads were so bad the king had to turn around? So it was that the king's messengers went ahead to spread the news of his coming. And so it was that the citizens set to work clearing the roads, patching bumps. This was John's message to Israel. "God, the king, is coming! He will visit his people. How is the pathway to your heart?" The psalmist said, "Blessed are the men in whose hearts are the highways to Zion" (Psalm 84:5). He wrote of how it is that some people grant the Lord easy access into their lives. They provide smooth travel for Jesus to come to them.

However, for most of us, the way to our hearts is all but impassable. You know how ice and snow can hinder travel. So can

338

mud, washed out bridges, barricades, and debris. Sad to say, but many a person will not receive Christ this Christmas because the pathway to their hearts is impossible to travel. There is bitterness. There is unteachability, self-satisfaction. God tried to come to them but he was hindered.

If one wanted to restore a road, the tools of the trade would be bulldozers, highway engineers, and asphalt. But what of the highway of the heart? What are its tools? John the Baptizer tells us in the text. He said, "Repent, for the kingdom of heaven is at hand ... Prepare the way of the Lord, make his paths straight." Central to John's message was repentance.

Let's take a look at the meaning of the word. The Hebrew word for repent is *shub*. It means, "to turn." The Greek word for repent is *metanoia*. It means, "to change one's mind." Actually, repentance is a mental event, a change of mind, that leads to a change of behavior, a turning in one's life. You know how it is to tell someone you're going shopping on Tuesday, but you decide later to stay home and clean up. Your friend sees you and says, "What are you doing here? I thought you said you were going shopping!" You reply, "Yes, but I changed my mind." So it is that your change of mind has led to your change of behavior! This is what John is preaching to us. "Turn! Change your mind!" When you do, your behavior will be different. If you've been ignoring God, turn and pay attention to him. If you've been a rebel, turn and become his servant. If you have been saying, "Get out of my life, God!" turn and say, "Come into my heart!!" If you've been faithless, turn and be faithful. Change your mind. Turn!

What about you? What is the condition of your mind this moment? Does the path to your heart allow God access unto you? If it doesn't, if your mind and heart are turned away from God, then repent! Stop and turn! Change your mind! Ask God to help you clear the roads of clutter. Ask him to fix the ruts of hate and bitterness, to bridge the fears and failures, to smooth out the sins, the pride, the complexes. "Turn to God," John is preaching, "The Lord is coming! Clear the roads!"

The People's Response

From John's purpose and message, let us pass on to the people's response. According to the scriptures, the people came out in swarms. The city of Jerusalem and the country of Judea turned out in great numbers. They listened to John, they questioned him, and often they were baptized. Yet still, the majority refused to take John the Baptizer seriously.

I know how this is as a pastor. You burn over some issue; half kill yourself preaching on it, and someone says, "Don't take it so hard, preacher!" Once I preached on God's judgment and national repentance and some lady at the door tweaked my cheek and said, "That sermon was too cute!" John knew these frustrations as well. He was good entertainment with his fiery voice, his dramatic presentation. It was a nice day trip with the family to carry a picnic and go out and see this unusual sight. Yes, the people responded to John as if he were some kind of sideshow for entertainment. There was much travel and activity, many questions and opinions, but there was no major movement toward repentance.

The results? The king came and there were no roads. God visited and there was no repentance. People had not prepared. They were not ready for the Messiah. Few recognized him. Some actually threatened his life. He had to spend his first years in exile, and when he did return, it wasn't long before he was killed.

Have you ever wondered why people reacted so violently to Jesus and the apostles and pastors and prophets? Why were they persecuted? What did Jesus ever do to make people hate him? Was it because he healed and restored? Because he fed people, raised the dead, and preached the truth? If you try an experiment I think you'll understand man's violent reaction to Jesus. Go into your basement and turn on the lights. What do the bugs do? They run for cover! They seek out the darkness. In John 3:19 Jesus said people are the same way. They are used to living in darkness. They love twilight. Christ said, "And this is the judgment, that the light has come into the world, and men loved darkness rather than light, because their deeds were evil. For every one who does evil hates the light, and does not come to the light, lest his deeds be exposed."

Now do you understand? John told the people God was coming. They did not listen. And the result? Violence! The people ran for the cover of darkness and there in their twilight temples, they hatched their plots, set their traps, and cut John the Baptizer's head off! Later, on Calvary, they snuffed out the light of God himself when they crucified Jesus.

Dear people, history can repeat itself. How long do you think it'd take us to crucify Christ if he came to us again? Are we not just like the people of old? Isn't their nature ours? We, too, have little trouble finding the truth. It's facing it that is difficult! If we are to find God, face him, and live in his light, we must accept our guide to Christmas. We must take him seriously. A man's ability to accept Jesus is directly related to his ability to accept John the Baptizer. If you don't listen to John, you won't listen to Jesus. If a man won't obey John, neither will he be a disciple of Jesus. If John's authority and word are rejected, so is Jesus'. This is the drama of the text.

I've about decided that there is nothing I can do or say that will make a man repent. It's not a matter of preaching a better sermon, deeper counseling, or writing a better book. In fact, preaching and teaching can actually drive a man away from repentance. To say no and to say it so loud and so often is to harden one's heart. It is to become so calloused that one doesn't give a darn if God is born in Bethlehem or this county. In short, a man will repent if he wants to, or he will find any one of a thousand excuses not to repent.

The Connection Made?

Yes, John came. God didn't want to take us by surprise, to catch us unprepared. So John preceded Jesus. He is our guide to Christmas. Yes, John had a purpose, a message. And the people? They all had a response. So do we! What will your response be? I pray it will be repentance. I pray you will make straight the highway of the King. I pray you will receive Christ by faith and live in his light.

My first pastorate was in the rural part of Virginia. You must know what it's like to call long distance from the country. You dial direct, but there is a delay in the connection, the lines buzz and crackle, and the operator comes on the line saying, "Hold on, I'm trying to connect you." When the operator has made the connection she fades out to leave you talking with your party. This is John the Baptizer's function in your life at this time. He is trying to connect you with Jesus. Why not allow him to come into your life, make the connection to Christ, and fade away? Until John has done his job, Jesus cannot do his. There can be no Christmas without John the Baptizer.

Suggested Prayer

Father, I accept John in preparation for Jesus. Grant me a deep repentance, a change of mind that leads to a change of life. Prepare me for the coming of the Lord. For Christ's sake. Amen.

Stephen M. Crotts

Proper 22
Pentecost 20
Ordinary Time 27
Matthew 21:33-46

History: His Story

There have been many who have sought to write a history of the world. Cavemen painted the story of their civilization on the walls of their home. Around 70 A.D., a Hebrew soldier named Josephus surrendered to the Roman army rather than die. Dead men tell no tales, and he said he wanted to live to tell the story of the fall of Jerusalem. Today, his history of the Jewish wars is an invaluable tool to historians.

Many of you are familiar with Will Durant. For half a century, he and his wife wrote the multi-volume *History of Civilization.* The finished product is over two feet thick!

And, of course, there is Hollywood's zany *History of the World* by clown prince Mel Brooks, that depicts man as a bumblesome ninny stumbling his way through history.

But did you know that Jesus Christ is something of a historian, too? That's correct! In our text for today, Jesus adroitly sums up, in eleven verses, all of the pertinent facts in the sweep of human events. So let us now turn to Christ's history and study its meaning for our day.

The Lease Of Creation

The first part of the text tells us that history, the world, is like a man who planted a vineyard and then leased it out to tenants. Christ goes on to point out, the people began to act irresponsibly. They began to act like the vineyard was theirs and refused to give the owner his due. History is like that, Jesus said. The creation is trying to wrestle itself away from its Creator.

If you think about it, the history of the world does strongly parallel this story. Satan did not want to serve God, so he rebelled and tried to overthrow God so he could have it all for himself. Caesar after Caesar loudly proclaimed, "I am god! And all this is mine!" Frenchman and military emperor Napoleon Bonaparte said, "Jesus may rule men's souls, but I rule their destinies."

The Beatles, Britain's pop singing group of the '60s and '70s, preened, "We're more popular than God!" In case you haven't heard, modern humanist scholars have now determined, "The world is nobody's, so I'll take it!" Yes, Jesus said, history is like that. The creation tries to wrestle itself away from the creator.

Did you hear about the visitor to the insane asylum? He walked in the front door and immediately met a man with his hand in his coat who claimed to be Napoleon. "Who told you you were Napoleon?" the visitor inquired. "God did," the man testified. Whereupon a man in the other room said rather angrily, "No, I didn't either!" History is like that. Humans are mad! They claim to be more than they are and in the end, they become less than they were.

Put here to be creatures, we try to be self-made. Put here to be under authority, we try to live answerable to no one. Made as stewards, people become usurpers. Created to be children of God, they become depraved offspring of the devil.

The Rent Collectors

But now, on with history! In the story Jesus said the owner sent his rent collectors to the tenants to collect what was due, but the renters didn't want to pay up. They beat the collector and sent him away empty-handed. When the owner sent another, they treated him shamefully as well. So, finally Jesus said, the owner sent his only son, thinking, "Surely they well respect my son, the heir." But when they saw him, they killed him, gloating, "Now the vineyard will be all ours!" Yes, Jesus said, history is like that.

There is something in our bent, sinful nature that will not be owned, will not be ruled, will not accept orders, will not worship, and Jesus said the history of civilization is but the working out of that sin.

344

Years back, I caught my two pre-school-age sons in my Jeep. They had been told not to get in there. They could get hurt if it started to roll, but they were disobeying me. So I crept close by, they didn't see me, and I was able to hear their conversation. Bryan, my older at five, said, "David, we better get out of here! Daddy said for us not to get in here!" To which David replied, "It's not Daddy's Jeep, it's my Jeep!" That's when I stood up, and grinning, said to David, the wee three-year-old, "Oh, it's yours now, is it?" Startled, he jumped up and tried to push me away, yelling, "Go away! You can't come here!" In that childish outburst we have the character of humanity. History bears it out over and over again as God sends his "rent collectors" to the tenants to collect what is due, to remind them of who they are and who God is, and we treat them shamefully and send them away empty-handed. Isaiah was sawn in two. Jeremiah was stoned. Amos was murdered with a club. John the Baptizer was beheaded. And the Son sent from God? He was Jesus, and him we impaled upon a cross outside the city near a garbage dump.

It still has not stopped. Which of the original apostles escaped persecution and death? Peter was crucified upside down. Paul was beheaded. James was put to the sword. Stephen was stoned to death. History goes on down through the twenty centuries of Christendom. Huss was burned at the stake. Wycliff was exiled. Luther was thrown out of the church. Martin Luther King, Jr., was shot.

In our churches it still happens. I once pastored a church that had a reputation for "eating its pastors alive." This church had a 35-year history of chewing up God's "rent collectors." One they falsely accused of adultery. Another they overworked until he was a broken man, divorced, and defeated. Another they criticized and pressured until he had a heart attack. Like Hosea the prophet said, "All of them are hot as an oven, and they devour their rulers" (Hosea 7:7).

It's a dangerous job to be a rent collector in the employ of the Lord! There's a long history of shameful treatment for such laborers. And Jesus said history is like that. History is God creating the world like a fine vineyard and then leasing it out to humanity. History is God sending his workers into the world to call all

345

humanity to give God respect, to give him his due worship. And history is the chronicles of our shameful treatment of those prophets in God's employ.

The Eviction

There is a fable about the Angel Gabriel who has just come from surveying the earth and its inhabitants when he reports to God. "Lord, it's my duty to inform you that you're the possessor of a choice piece of real estate known as planet earth. But the tenants you've leased it out to are destroying it. In another few years, it won't be fit to live in. They have polluted your rivers. The air is fouled with the stench of their over-consumerism. They frequently kill one another, and all the prophets you've sent to them calling for an accounting have met with violence. By any rule of sound management, Lord, you've got but one option." Then raising his trumpet to his lips, Gabriel asked, "Shall I sound the eviction notice now, sir?"

And God said, "No, Gabriel! No, not just yet. I know you are right, but I keep thinking if I just give them a little more time they'll quit acting like they own the place!"

Aye, that's what the text, Christ's world history, is all about. God owns the place, but we've been acting like we do. That brings us to the end of the text, the part where the owner of the vineyard has had enough, and so it is that he destroys the wicked tenants and leases his vineyard out to others who will keep faith with him.

Again, this is but the tale history bears. Consider, if you will, the history of the Mediterranean nations. One-by-one they have risen to power in the vineyard. One-by-one they have turned their backs on God. One-by-one they have been evicted: Egypt of the pharaohs, Israel of David and Solomon, Greece of Alexander, Babylon of Nebuchadnezzar, Persia of Cyrus and Xerxes, Rome of the Caesars, the Ottoman Turks, Spain, and on and on. Creation, employment, irresponsibility, warnings, more irresponsibility, and finally eviction.

Again, consider yet another recent page of human history. World War II. Mussolini of Italy said, "If the church gets in my way, I'll hang God in Italy!" They found Mussolini dead, hanging

346

upside down from a steel beam. Russia's Stalin said, "I'll run God out of Soviet Russia!" Now they curse Stalin's name, and you can't even find the place where he is buried. Adolf Hitler mocked, "No anemic Galilean is worthy of a German's worship," and they found Hitler a smoking cinder in a German gutter. Fact is, our arms are too short to box with God! Jesus Christ said, "I'll build my kingdom and the gates of hell won't stand against it!" History proves him true: "The meek shall inherit the earth!" They have; the rebellious, bloodletting, God-hating grabbers always, always, always are evicted. But the God-fearing, responsible stewards, the meek, always inherit the earth.

The Smallest Kingdom
One of the world's smallest kingdoms is the nation of Liechtenstein, a constitutional monarchy of only 61 square miles found between Austria and Switzerland on the Rhine River. Yet, I tell you there is a kingdom smaller than that, and that kingdom is your life. I'm talking about the vineyard God has planted in your life and leased out to you. I'm talking about that small mound of flesh over which you have jurisdiction. How are you behaving toward the God who put you here to tend his vineyard and give him his due? Have you mistreated his rent collectors sent to receive what is due? Or more importantly, what have you done with God's Son, the man Jesus? Have you crucified him anew as you've made a grab for it all, or have you honored him with the worship of faith and obedience?

Suggested Prayer
Lord Jesus, teach me to give you first place in my life. Amen.

Stephen M. Crotts

Sermons On The Gospel Readings

For Sundays
After Pentecost
(Last Third)

Rendering To God

Stephen M. Crotts
George L. Murphy
Stan Purdum

Supper's Ready!

Let's pretend! Let's pretend that you've been invited by the Queen of England to attend a banquet at Buckingham Palace. Close your eyes for a moment and think. What would you wear? What would you talk about at the dinner table? Should you arrive ten minutes early, take a taxi, or will you be nervous? Better still, would you turn down the invitation? When John Kennedy was president of the United States, he invited a number of accomplished artists to a White House banquet. Among those invited was the then aging William Faulkner. Faulkner turned down the invitation, saying, "I'm too old to make new friends." It is possible, you know, to turn down an invitation. It is thinkable to do the unthinkable, to excuse yourself from a fabulous opportunity.

According to the text the Lord God, creator, ruler, sustainer, and heir of the universe gives an open invitation to all people to come and feast with him at a banquet table. Now, just stop and think about this for a moment! What kind of God do we have in this cosmos? He is a God who wants to get to know you. He is a lord who offers to sit down and eat with you at table. He is a creator who calls your name with a personal invitation.

"Excuse Me, Please!"

How do you respond to these facts about God? Certainly an invitation to eat with God and to become acquainted with him personally outclasses an opportunity to eat with a queen or a president or your favorite musician. And you wouldn't think of turning the queen down, yet according to the text, that's just what happened.

Those invited said, "Excuse me, please. I cannot come." One man said, "I've bought some land. I must go and see it." Think for a moment. Can you imagine anyone buying a piece of land sight unseen? Since the banquet was to be at night, wouldn't that be a poor time for him to be out inspecting land? Real estate doesn't move; his land would still be there on the morrow. Obviously, the man was not giving reasons but excuses. The fact was, he did not want to go to the banquet.

According to the text, another man refused the invitation because he owned a new team of oxen. My, my! How our possessions can get in the way. There was still a third fellow invited, but he, too, refused, saying, "I've married a wife." Does that sound familiar? Blaming it on your wife? That's as old as Adam putting the blame on Eve!

People have not changed much in the years that separate the first telling of this parable and its telling today. Supper is still ready. God is still willing. The invitations are still going out, and the excuses are still coming in.

"Wait Until I Have Some Fun!"

Have you ever heard this excuse? "I'll come. I'll become a Christian and sit at the Lord's table, but first let me have a little fun." These people associate Jesus with a moral straitjacket. God to them is some sort of celestial killjoy. They say, "Thanks, but no thanks!"

Yet, Jesus said, "I have come that you might have life and have it more abundantly" (John 10:10). He didn't come to take the life out of the party, he came to put life in the party. When I was a student in college, my hall adopted a stray dog as a mascot. One winter this mangy, undernourished mutt wandered into the dorm seeking warmth. The fellows on the hall immediately loved that animal and sought to help him. Can you imagine what went on in that dog's brain as the fellows washed him in the shower? Soap and water were alien to a dog used to ugly, smelly, matted fur. Then there was the mange medicine and the rabies shot and the new taste of dog food. In that animal's eyes, I could see fear and distrust. I didn't blame him when he once tried to run away. But

352

slowly that stray became a pet. He understood that we loved him. We weren't out to hurt him or to take his fun away. Indeed, with the right care his fun became funnier! His coat shone! His health increased. He felt loved. I think humankind often relates to God like that dog related to us. "What is this? Can I trust him? He's not going to spoil my fun, is he? I want to be free!" Which state of life do you think was more abundant for that dog — before or after? That's right! The after. It is the same for man.

"Wait Until I Get Better!"

Another excuse for not supping with Christ is, "Wait until I get better. I'm too sinful right now." I suppose this excuse is akin to the woman who has nothing fitting to wear to a party or the man who feels himself too crude in manners to eat with gentlemen.

The Bible says, "Behold, now is the day of salvation" (2 Corinthians 6:2). The human condition is such that to wait, to put off coming to Christ until we're better, is like waiting to go to the doctor until you are healed. What if all the patients in a hospital revolted and kicked out all the nurses and doctors? What if they locked the doors and said, "We're not going to let you in again until we get better!" Wouldn't that be a ridiculous turn of events? Yet, that is the same foolish thought pattern that a man often takes with God. "I'm too sinful. When I clean my life up, I will come." I like the way the hymn, "Just As I Am," puts it. "Just as I am, without one plea, but that Thy blood was shed for me, and that Thou bid'st me come to Thee, O Lamb of God, I come, I come!"

"I'm Good Enough Already!"

Supper's ready! And, oh! Is it ever ready! The question is: Are you? Are you willing to cast aside your excuses and accept God's magnificent invitation to eat with him? One of the most common excuses for not living faithfully to the claims of Christ is, "I'm good enough already. I'm as good as, or better than, any of those people who go to church!"

Dear people, the question is not how good we are in our own estimation. It is how good we are in God's sight! Did you hear about the two men who were working on a roof? As they began to work on the chimney, one man fell in. The other tried to grab him but he fell in, too. Both of them came tumbling down the chimney like another jolly fellow we know about. Now, one man had black soot all over his face, but the other man didn't. That's because he covered his face with his arm as he fell. Now, the funny thing about this story is that the man with the clean face went and washed his and the man with the dirty face did not, but returned to work. Why? Think real hard! You see, they looked at each other. The clean-faced man saw the dirty-faced man and thought, "I'd better wash my face. Since we both fell down the chimney and his face is dirty, mine must be, too." The other man said, "If he is clean, I must be, too." Now, the moral of the story is that one cannot look at others to judge how it is with himself. We must look in the mirror, and that mirror is God's word. Here in the Bible, God will tell you what he thinks of you. "All have sinned," he says (Romans 3:23). There is no good man on earth. Sure, you might be as moral as the next fellow but no man is moral enough in God's sight. That's why Jesus said, "You must be born again" (John 3:3). You must be given a chance to start over from a clean slate!

"Too Many Hypocrites In Church!"

Have you ever invited someone to worship and they replied, "Ha! I'd never put my foot inside that place. There are too many hypocrites in church!" In a *Peanuts* comic strip, Lucy is standing on a pew inside an empty church building. She is saying, "Hypocrites! Where are all the hypocrites? I heard the church was full of them!" Well, I'm not so sure the church is that full of hypocrites. Sure, we've got some weak brothers. Some of our sisters are immature. But isn't that where they should be? Shouldn't hypocrites be in church where the true light of reality will expose them for what they are?

Look at it this way. Handel is no less a great composer just because someone sits down and does a lousy rendition of his music on the piano. There is nothing wrong with the composer. Only the musician's playing is poor. The same with church. The gospel is glorious. Sometimes man's performance is poor, but that doesn't mean God is.

One goes to a doctor even if that doctor has a bad cold. Even though he is sick, he can still heal. Just because a lawyer got a speeding ticket, doesn't mean he cannot help you with legal proceedings. And it is the same with the church. Just because there is sin here, doesn't mean that the church cannot steer you into a saving experience with Christ.

"God Is Love. He Won't Condemn Anyone!"

Here's another excuse: Some tread on God's grace, saying, "I'm not going to become a Christian. After all, God is love. He won't condemn anyone." Oh, really? The Bible says, "If God did not spare the angels when they sinned, but cast them into hell," what makes you think he will spare you? (2 Peter 2:4).

A child was sick with a terminal disease. The only known cure was in a hospital several thousand miles away. The boy's father sold all his belongings and journeyed to that distant hospital just to buy the medicine. Returning home he joyfully handed the vial of medicine to his son and said, "Here, child, take this and live!" The boy took the bottle, looked at it, and threw it against the wall. Then, looking at his father, shouted, "If I die, it will be your fault!" Isn't that about the most ridiculous thing you've ever heard? Yet, God has gone to Calvary to purchase the medicine for our sin. He offers life to every man. Yet we toss it aside and have the guts to say, "He won't condemn anyone. He's loving." Billy Graham said, "Hell was never intended for man. It was created for the devil and his angels. But if a man insists on going there, God will let him."

Come to the banquet. Here's your invitation. What is your response?

"I Have Doubts!"

Maybe one of you here today is full of doubts. "Did God really invite me? Is the banquet real?" The only way you will ever find out is to come and see for yourself. There are always those who would stay away from the church because of their doubts. "Wait until I learn some more," they say. "Dad, I can't go to school today. I don't know math," a child says. And the father replies, "That's precisely why you go to school, my son, to learn math."

When doubting Thomas was overcome with questions he did not leave church. He stayed in it! It was in church that his doubts melted away. The Lord came and allowed him to verify the resurrection firsthand! God won't insult your intelligence either. If you have questions, bring them to Sunday school, to Bible study, and worship. You will find your answers here. Doubters welcome!

"As Long As You Are Sincere ..."

Let's look at one final excuse that people make for absenting themselves from the Lord's table. Have you ever heard this one? "Any religion is good enough. All roads lead to the top of the mountain. I've got my own religion. As long as one is sincere, that's all that's important." Well, all I've got to say is, bull! Sincerity is no basis for a relationship with God. Jesus said, "The true worshipers worship in spirit and in truth" (John 4:23). He didn't say we were to worship with our own religion and in sincerity. He said we were to worship according to God's terms — "in spirit and in truth."

Remember Charlie Brown standing dejectedly in the baseball park and saying, "How can we lose when we are so sincere?" The answer is, sincerity is no basis for winning a baseball game. You can be sincere in your efforts to drive to Raleigh, but if you take the wrong road, you won't get there. It is the same with God. Your salvation is on God's terms and not your own, sincere or not!

"I'll Be There!"

The Bible is full of invitations to supper with God. Jesus ate with a Pharisee; he dined with fishermen, tax collectors, harlots, and rich men. Once he called to a man up in a tree, "Zacchaeus, come down. I must have supper with you this day!" The Lord got no excuses from Zach that day! Around the table with Jesus, a miracle began to form in the heart of Zacchaeus. "Behold," Zacchaeus said, "the half of my wealth I give to the poor. And if I have treated anyone unjustly, I restore things to him four times over!" (Luke 19:1-9). What a meal that must have been! The miracle was not in the bread and the wine. The miracle was in Zacchaeus.

What of your life? You have been invited to come to God, to sit with him at his table and eat. Are you too busy? Have you got an excuse? I saw a fellow at communion a while back whom I hadn't seen in church for some time. "And you," I said, "What are you doing here?" "I guess I just ran out of excuses," he said. Supper's ready! And, oh! Is it ready! Are you? Are you ready? How I pray that you, too, have run out of excuses!

Stephen M. Crotts

Do Politics And Religion Mix?

It was a trap. The Pharisees set it. Jealous that Jesus was gaining a following, they were eager to destroy him, and they'd do it by using his own words against him.

So they brought Christ a coin, asking him, "Is it right to pay taxes to Caesar?" If he said yes, he'd anger the Jews because they were an occupied nation suffering the indignities of the Roman army. If he said no, he'd incur the wrath of Rome for seditious remarks. Jesus, exhibiting great wisdom, asked to see a coin. "Whose picture is on this coin?" he inquired. "Caesar's," they replied, and in a moment of unforgettable eloquence, Jesus retorted, "Then render unto Caesar the things that are Caesar's, and unto God the things that are God's." Clearly Jesus was saying that his people had something to offer both God and government.

Today the Caesar/God question is still tricky. Our society is still trying to answer the question, do politics and religion mix? The first amendment of the United States Constitution reads, "Congress shall make no law respecting an establishment of religion nor prohibit the free exercise thereof." What the first amendment is saying is that government should stay out of religion, but religious people can exercise their faith in the influence of public policy.

Over the past fifty years, lawmakers have misinterpreted the Constitution. We've majored in the first part of the amendment while abandoning the second part, and in doing so, we have disenfranchised the gospel, politically, socially, judicially, and culturally. Like a sponge with the water squeezed out, ours is a society with Jesus squeezed out, and we are living in a fifty-year experiment of building a nation without God. No prayer. No Ten Commandments. No sermon at graduation. No Sabbath. No respect for marriage.

Those things may be contributing to factors to some of today's problems: We have massive teen drug abuse, a girl at her prom who delivers a baby in a bathroom and trashes the child so she can rejoin the dance, school shooting sprees, and an adolescent suicide rate up 350 percent since 1960.

One wag, commenting on our politically correct times, wrote of a school essay turned in to academia at Thanksgiving. It read, "The Pilgrims came to these shores seeking freedom of you-know-what, so they could give thanks to you-know-who, so we, their descendants, could worship each Sunday, you-know-where." It's entirely ludicrous, eh? It's time to ask, cannot politics and religion mix?

Consider: God called Abraham to be *the father of many nations*. Moses was to emancipate Jewish slaves from an evil empire. The Ten Commandments were civil law for a new nation. The last ten books of the Old Testament, the Minor Prophets, are sermons to a nation that is morally adrift. God once exiled a nation into Babylonian captivity for indecency. Nehemiah, Ezra, and Zerubabel of Old Testament fame rebuilt a ruined country by rebuilding her walls, people, and priests on the biblical model.

Even our own American heritage is full of Christian influence. When the Pilgrims landed at Plymouth in 1620, they paused to write the Mayflower Compact, the first law of American shores. It reads in part: "In the name of God, Amen. We whose names are underwritten ... having undertaken for the glory of God and advancement of the Christian faith ... a voyage to plant the first colony in the northern parts of Virginia...."

George Washington, in his first presidential inauguration, added to his oath, "So help me God" and then kissed the Bible. Ben Franklin, in 1778 at the Constitutional Convention, made motion that proceedings each day be opened with prayer. He said, "I have lived for a long time, and the longer I live, the more convincing proof I see of this truth, that God governs the affairs of men. If a sparrow cannot fall to the ground without his notice, is it probable that an empire can rise without his aid? We have been assured by the Holy Scriptures that 'Except the Lord build the house, they labor in vain to build it.' I firmly believe this, and I also believe that without his concurring aid, we shall proceed in this political building no better than the founders of Babel."

Every presidential inaugural speech, less one, has mentioned God. Our coins have *In God We Trust* on them. The Ten Commandments are mostly still in our law books, forbidding theft, lying, murder, and such. Congress is still opened with prayer.

So you see, politics and religion can and have mixed in our nation's past. Fact is, as Jesus did say, we have something as Christians to render to God as well as something to render to Caesar!

Rendering To Caesar!

First, let's consider what Christ meant when he said, "Render unto Caesar the things that are Caesar's." Certainly, it means we pay taxes. It means we pray for our leaders of government, and it means we obey the law. But it means more. It means we strive to be informed citizens; it means we help others to be informed. It means we vote, we protest, we even seek to hold office ourselves.

James Russell Lowell called the United States Constitution "a machine that won't go of itself." Like a bicycle, its engine is people. We peddle it with steady citizenship. It was Abraham Lincoln who pointed out, "All it takes for evil to triumph is for good men to do nothing." It's easy. Christians just get off the bicycle and leave government to others, and we soon find our politic godless and wrong in its direction.

President James Garfield's words from 1877 still ring true. "Now more than ever before, the people are responsible for the character of their Congress. If that body be ignorant, reckless, and corrupt, it is because the people tolerate ignorance, recklessness, and corruption. If it be intelligent, brave, and pure, it is because the people demand these high qualities to represent them in the national legislature ... if the next centennial does not find us a great nation ... it will be because those who represent the enterprise, the culture, and the morality of the nation do not aid in controlling the political forces."

My friends in Christ, my fellow citizens, Jesus said we must render unto Caesar our salty influence. And in citizenship there are one thousand forms of duty. A military career, prayer, being a watchdog, a career in government service, elected office, teaching, homemaking, and so much more!

Rendering To God!

Yes, we've something for Caesar, our citizenship. That is not just marching in a parade or puffing one's chest out with a tear in the eye and lump in the throat as the flag passes by. Our citizenship must be a steady, patient, faithful work of a lifetime.

But that's not all! We also have something to render unto God. He is our reasonable worship; Christ is our first love.

Using the same imagery that Jesus used, we need to remember that, just as the coin was made in the image of Caesar, humankind is *made in the image of God.* Jesus' words still ring true: "... give to God that which is God's." God calls us to make a complete commitment of life and possessions to him and then he will guide how we use them. The far larger commitment in life must be to God. Using the simple question posed made popular today, WWJD (What would Jesus do?) we begin to get at the heart of what it means to give to God that which is God's. What would Jesus do with my possessions? With my time? With my gifts and talents? With my priorities? With my love of country?

It is far too easy to make an idol out of our country, to put our faith in the party and the economy and the president. Yet, our God is Christ. He is our hope, our savior, our Lord, our ultimate allegiance.

I saw a bumper sticker that read "My country, right or wrong!" I said, "My country, right, and my country put right when she is wrong!" In marriage. In justice. In race relations, ecology, foreign policy, schools, courts....

As Christians, we must not be like some and worship the state. Why, to hear some talk, God is a Democrat, or to another he is a Republican! Our faith is in Christ, not country. What if early believers put their faith in the Roman Empire? Where would they be now? Well does the scripture remind us, "For here we have no lasting city, but we seek a city which is to come."

In short, our worship is Christ, but our service of neighbor-loving is to the state.

Conclusion

Do politics and religion mix? You bet they do! Jesus said they are our dual renderings.

George Washington, in his farewell address, spoke: "The truth is, politics and morality are inseparable. As morality's foundation is religion, religion and politics are necessarily related."

So let the word go forth from this place: Made in the image of God, we in Christ are a salty, gifted segment of the populace, and we have something to give to both God and the nation. In our obedience to Christ, as did our forefathers, we will give the full measure of it all!

Suggested Prayer

Lord Jesus, make me a faithful steward of both church and state. Amen.

Stephen M. Crotts

Proper 25
Pentecost 23
Ordinary Time 30
Matthew 22:34-46

How To Love God

In the rock opera *Jesus Christ: Superstar*, Mary Magdalene sings, "I don't know how to love him." You see, Christ had saved Mary from prostitution and demonic possession, and now she wanted to live to please Jesus, to offer him her lifelong devotion. But how could she express her love? In her earlier years she had easily known how to please men. But Jesus was different. What did he want from her? How could she serve him?

Isn't Mary like most of us? Here we are saved and wanting to be devoted to God, but not knowing how. We are so deeply grateful for all he has done for us, but we don't know how to respond.

Good news! In Mark 12:28-34 and Matthew 22:34-46, Jesus teaches us how to please God. He tells us how we can best serve him. He says, "You shall love the Lord your God."

In calling us to love, Jesus is quoting from Deuteronomy 6:5 and Leviticus 19:18. These verses are called the *shema* or "the first word" in Jewish Law. This commandment to love God was and still is the first text every Jewish child memorizes. Its importance was of such merit that scrolls bearing the command were bound to the wrist and forehead of faithful Jews so they'd not forget it.

"You shall love the Lord your God." That is what God wants from us. Love — the most intimate and warm, creative and committed of human acts — this is God's desire of us.

In inviting our affections, God provides us in scripture with a really memorable picture of our love relationship. Often God refers to himself in Christ as the groom and people of faith and love as his bride (the book of Hosea; Revelation 19:7-9; Matthew 25:1-13). So, our relationship with God is a relationship of love — an intimate, romantic, enduring oneness akin to marriage.

It is interesting that the Greek word in the text for "love" is *agape*, the most exalted form of love a person can offer. God could have asked us for *eros* love. *Eros* is the Greek word from which we get the English notion, *erotic*. This is sexual love, a love that develops between two people who find in one another's flesh a pleasing relationship, but God is not asking for this.

Another form of love God could have requested of us is *philia* or friendship. This love develops between two people who enjoy a meeting of the minds, common values, goals, and hobbies. But again, God is not asking for this.

The word is *agape*. "You shall *agape* the Lord your God," and *agape* love means unconditional love.

You see, much of our human love is conditional. We may love someone because they meet our emotional and physical needs for intimacy, or we may love someone if they are nice to us. But when the conditions on which our love like this is propped are withdrawn, then so is our love.

The trouble with "I love you because ..." and "I'll love you if ..." is that it doesn't last very long. When one of the partners fails to met the other's expectations, then and there love ends. *Agape* love, however, places no stipulations. It simply says, "I love you, period! Nothing you can do or not do can ever change my love!"

It is true that one may love God because he has been good to you, given you a job, a house, a car, a family, and so on. But unconditional love for God will continue even when these things are not ours.

You will recall the book of Job in the Old Testament. It is the story of a rich and healthy family man who lost his children, his possessions, and even his health. But he did not lose his love for God. Sitting atop the rubble of his life Job worshiped. "Naked I came into the world. Naked I'll go. The Lord giveth and the Lord taketh away. Blessed be the name of the Lord!" You see, Job did not love God just "because" he was good to him, nor did he set

366

conditions: "If you make me healthy and wealthy, I'll love you!" Job loved God, period! And circumstances could not alter that.

Yet Job's wife was quite a different story. She loved God because he was good to her. He had given her a husband, a family, wealth, and health. But when all that was gone, so was her love for God. She told her husband, "Curse God and die!"

Agape. Unconditional love. This is what God asks of us. "You shall love the Lord your God."

Interestingly, John 3:16 says that God's love for us is *agape*. "For God so loved (*agape!*) the world that he gave...." God, you see, is asking us to love him as he already loves us.

All that! Now this! What practical expression does our love for God take?

We have already seen that God made us in his own image. And part of what that means is that we are tripartite creatures. We have a spirit, a physical body, and a soul (emotion, will, and intellect). All of this is what God is calling us to love him with!

Just look at the text, "You shall love the Lord your God with all your heart, and with all your soul, and with all your mind. And with all your strength." Here, Jesus is appealing to us to love him unconditionally with our entire tripartite being.

Let's break the verse apart now and look at each piece in turn.

Emotional Love

First of all, the text tells us to love God with all our emotion. Jesus said, "You shall love the Lord your God with all your heart." Many people of the church today strongly feel, however, that emotion has no place in the faith. "We don't want shouting and weeping and enthusiasm in our church," they say. They are afraid of emotionalism.

Yet the picture we get of Christ in the New Testament has its dimensions of emotion. Jesus wept when he learned of John the Baptizer's death. At a wedding party the Lord made more wine for merrymakers. He cried over hard-hearted Jerusalem. He shed tears in the Garden of Gethsemane. He breathed fire at corruption in the temple. And part of the picture of the early disciples is emotion as well. Consider Peter, the big fisherman. He is impulsive, blustering. He is ready to make an enthusiastic endorsement of Christ on the mountaintop. Later he denies Christ and weeps bitter tears. Days later, while fishing in a boat, Christ calls to him from the seashore, and Peter's heart leaps within him for joy! He dives into the water and is the first to reach Christ's side. Emotion? Yes, it had its place in the lives of Jesus and Peter, and it has a definite place in the life of every faithful Christian.

Emotion enriches our faith. It doesn't cheapen it. Which of you would want an emotionless marriage? You find those expressions of joy, of grief, of affection and enthusiasm very meaningful, don't you? They do not weaken your love! They strengthen it, don't they? Emotion can do the same for your Christian life.

A member of a small, informal country church was visiting in a large and formal city church. The pastor was preaching a beautiful salvation sermon and the visitor shouted, "Amen!" The congregation became disturbed. The ushers moved in on the visitor. One sat on either side of him. The preacher continued and again the guest shouted, "Hallelujah!" and he raised his hands. The chief usher whispered, "Sir, you'll have to behave yourself or leave." The man answered, "I can't help it, sir. I've got religion." The usher quickly answered back, "Well, you didn't get it here, so keep quiet." Traditionally some churches have been cold and formal. If you show emotion you're breaking the rules. Influential church reformer John Calvin himself had a strong disdain for emotionalism. (John Calvin also had kidney stones. If you've ever had one, you'll know it's hard to get excited about anything but death.) Yet Jesus said, "Love God with all your heart." And we would be unfaithful not to give God an expression of love from our heart. Whether it's tears, joyous music, hand clapping, or at times a loud shout, "Praise the Lord!" such pleases our Jesus.

The classical composer, Joseph Haydn, was once criticized for the gaiety of his church music. To his critics he replied, "I cannot help it. I give forth what is in me. When I think of the Divine Being, my heart is so full of joy that the notes fly off as from a spindle. And as I have a cheerful heart, he will pardon me if I serve him cheerfully."

Yes, emotion has its place in the love of God. But emotion alone is not enough. Jesus gives us a second way to love God. He said, "Love God with all your mind."

Intellectual Love

A noted surgeon said that the first time he looked upon a human brain he felt as if he were inside a magnificent cathedral. He stood in reverential silence in the presence of what he beheld. Here was the center of the person's intelligence. Here, indeed, was the place where an individual became aware of God. Here was a place from which worship could be directed to Christ!

Consider the Apostle Paul for a moment. Think on this scholar's intellect. Examine the work of his brain, the deep, piercing theological insight he achieved. What a strong mind! And what a service of love he rendered to the Lord! Why, much of the New Testament is the work of his own mind. Books like Romans, Galatians, and Corinthians are ours because Paul loved God with his brain. Today, the Christian church is struggling with a mood of anti-intellectualism. Some people say the mind is of little importance in loving God. Scholarship is belittled. Seminaries are considered dens of liberalism. The mind is seen as hostile to the faith.

Yet God gave us minds as surely as he gave us our emotions, and Jesus told us to use our brains. He said, "Seek, ask, and knock."

Great rewards can come from loving God enough to study. When we give our minds to inquiry we learn more and thereby grow. If you have questions about prayer, love God enough to give your mind to the study of the Bible, books on prayer, serious meditation, and practice. You'll be more mature because of it.

Did you know that this generation in which we live can know more about God and Jesus Christ than perhaps any generation that has ever lived? It is true! We profit by more books, hymns, theology, ministries, and leisure time to study than any generation that has ever lived. If we sit in ignorance, it is only because we have not done our homework. The books are there. The understanding can be yours. All you have to do is love God with your mind enough to study. I like the way an old teacher once put it. He said, "A man should not be afraid to read a book, for in doing so there will be more of him to love God."

Yes, our minds are for the love of God. As the Apostle Paul said, we should "Study to show ourselves approved unto God, workmen that need not be ashamed, rightly dividing the word of truth" (2 Timothy 2:15).

Love Of The Will

So, we can love God with our emotion and our intellect. But is there yet another expression our love for God can take? Yes, there is. In the text, Jesus says, "Love God with all your soul." This means that we can love God with all our will.

For instance, there is a lady who is getting a trifle overweight. She remembers that her body is the temple of the Lord and she knows that overeating and lack of exercise can ruin her appearance and, perhaps, her health. She wants to be at her best for God as far as physical appearance is concerned. So she goes on a diet. It takes great efforts of the will to push herself away from the table. It takes will power to resist those between meal indulgences, and it takes real effort to exercise regularly.

I know myself how important the will can be in loving and serving God. As a pastor I by and large have no day-by-day boss except God. This means I don't really have to be at the study at a certain time every day. When I wake up in the morning sometimes my emotion tells me that I've been working too hard lately. "You deserve a break today," it says. "Go ahead and sleep late." Next my intellect talks to me, helping me to rationalize, saying, "Yes, sleep late. You can't get any work done when you are tired. Sleep late and get up later. You'll be able to work quickly when you're fresh." Finally there is a third voice that speaks to me. It is my will. It grabs me and with a shake says, "Now, see here! There's work to be done. You get out of that bed and get going!" So I get out and shower and eat a good breakfast and go to the study and get a lot of work done.

The power of the will is vitally important in the Christian life. Without will power we'd all be at the mercy of our emotions and intellects. We'd become mental rationalizers and emotional jelly-fish. The will is the backbone of the Christian faith. It is the will turned to God in love that gives us courage and discipline to will and to do.

The Apostle Matthew seemed to have a lot of loving will power for God. He above all other New Testament gospel writers is the most legalistic and stern. He is the one who stresses discipline and obedience above all else, and a firm will turned to God in love is endorsed by Saint Paul as well. He is talking about willful discipline when he writes, "Every athlete exercises self-control in all things ... I pommel my body and subdue it, lest after preaching to others I myself should be disqualified" (1 Corinthians 9:25, 27).

Not All Alike!

So you want to know how to love God? Jesus has told us. Love him with the emotion, the mind, and the will that you have. Now you will be careful to observe that all of us are unique blends of emotion, will, and intellect. Some have a strong dose of will-power and lack in emotion and mental capabilities. Others are very emotionally prone people. God made them this way. It is nothing for which to be ashamed. Others are evenly balanced between the three. The beautiful thing about the Christian faith is that it does not stereotype us. We are not cookie-cut out of the same mold. No two Christians are ever alike. You see, each one of us is peculiar in his blend of emotion, will, and intellect. When we turn our lives to the love of God, each one of us comes out unique.

Harry Emerson Fosdick used to say, "If we could get religion like a Methodist, be sure of it like a Baptist, preach it like a Pres-byterian, and enjoy it like an African Methodist Episcopalian, then we'd really have something!" How true it is! If we could learn, as Jesus asks in the text, to love God with all our "strength," to turn all our lives to the love of God, and not just parts of it, we would really have something. If we could just learn to love him fully with our unique blend of emotion, will, and intellect, we'd show the world we really mean business.

Your Neighbor

Wait a minute! We're not through with this text just yet. There is a fourth way to love God. Jesus said, "Love thy neighbor as thyself." And as if to remove all doubt, Christ told the parable of the Good Samaritan, which explains who our neighbor is (Luke 10:25-37). He is anyone, regardless of color, creed, or economic standing who needs our help. "You shall love" ... there's that word *agape* again ... "You shall love your neighbor" without qualification. Not "I'll love you *if* ..." or "because," but "period."

Last winter in Birmingham, Alabama, a woman was walking down the main street. She was shopping for Christmas presents when she saw a small boy about seven years old. He was poorly clothed, barefooted, and standing over a heater vent in the sidewalk trying to keep warm. He had a bundle of newspapers under his arm and was trying to sell them to the pedestrians. The woman went up to him and said, "Son, where are your shoes and socks?"

"Lady," he said, "I ain't got none."

She took him to a department store up the street and bought him a thick pair of socks and a heavy pair of shoes. The young lad skipped happily out of the store without so much as a thank you, when suddenly he returned to ask, "Lady, are you God?"

"No, son," she said, "I'm not God. But I am one of his children."

The little fellow turned to leave, saying, "Well, I knowed you must be some kin to him."

It is true that love for people is a mark of our relationship with God.

The Bible makes it clear that our love for the Creator is measured also in our love for his creation, which includes people, yourself, and the environment. 1 John 4:20-21 teaches, "If anyone says 'I love God,' and he hates his brother, he is a liar; for he who does not love his brother whom he has seen, cannot love God whom he has not seen. And this is the commandment we have from him, that he who loves God should love his brother also." That's powerful, isn't it? It really does not beat around the bush to say love for God must also express itself in love for people.

Let us make an experiment, okay? Let us test ourselves to see how much we love God. Think of the person you love least. Now, that is how much you love God! If you want to measure the gasoline in your car, you look at the gas gauge. If you want to measure the temperature you look at the thermometer. If you want to measure your love for God you look at the person you love least. That is an indication of how you love God. John the Apostle said it correctly when he said, "If anyone says, 'I love God,' and hates his brother, he is a liar."

Power To Love

Right about now you are probably saying, "I can't love like that! *Agape* love! Emotional. Willful. Intellectual. For the Creator, with all my strength. And for *all* of his creation? No sir, I don't have that much love!"

I agree with you. I can't love like that either, at least not in my own strength. But in the power of God I can love! In Romans 5:5 Paul wrote, "God's love has been poured into our hearts through the Holy Spirit which has been given to us."

My daughter once showed me a sticker from her grade school collection. It was a gray butterfly, one of the plainest looking of her entire holdings.

"Touch it, Daddy," she said.

I did, and the butterfly became a lovely iridescent rainbow of colors. Something about the ink reacted to the heat of one's fingers and unleashed hidden beauty. This is something like what happens to us when the power of God touches us.

We've got the emotion, the will, and the intellect, but it's all a dull, loveless gray. Yet when we choose to respond to God's love for us, to allow Jesus to touch us and fill us with his Holy Spirit, then supernatural love is unleashed in our lives, and a unique, multicolored emotional, willful, and intellectual love for God and his creation is expressed in our lifestyle.

This is what the Apostle John meant when he said, "We love because he first loved us" (1 John 4:19). This is what the Apostle Paul meant when he wrote, "The fruit of the spirit is love" (Galatians 5:22). Love, you see, isn't something we generate within ourselves. It comes from God's initiative in our lives. The Lord is the source of love, and when we are rightly related to Jesus by

373

repentance and faithfulness we ourselves are hooked up to the source of unending *agape* love.

You know, friend, people come to pastors in great numbers, people who are concerned about their Christian experience. Some complain they are bored. Some have difficult questions to deal with. Others are crying out in loneliness. How about you? Are you troubled with your Christian experience? Is something missing? Do you feel like life is not all it could be? Why not try loving God completely? Love him with all your heart and all your soul and all your mind. Love your neighbor as yourself. Do that and see if you aren't satisfied. After all, Jesus said this is the greatest commandment. To obey it will bring the greatest life!

Suggested Prayer
Lord, fill my life and teach me to love like Jesus. Amen!

Stephen M. Crotts

Influence!

If you think a mosquito is small and has little influence, try sleeping in a hot room at night with but a single blood-sucking insect. Its high-pitched whine and sharp proboscis can leave you sleepy, itchy, and whelped.

On the other hand, consider the lowly honeybee. One single winged creature lurching flower to flower can make the heart leap for joy as it brightens your day, spreads pollen about, and makes honey in the hive.

We mortals, not unlike mosquitoes and honeybees, have our own influence. We can be the bane of a room or the blessing of a family. Here in the text, Jesus talks about it all with a group of religious leaders of his own day. Let's listen in and be careful to apply his words to our own lives.

Don't hide behind the false security of the fact Christ Jesus is talking to temple leaders, church staff as it were. You might say Christ is an equal opportunity troubler of professions. In Mark 5:26, he spoke of a sick woman who had suffered much ill health and spent a considerable fortune on hospitals, doctors, and medications, and was no better but growing worse. In Matthew 5:25-26, Jesus expresses wariness at the judicial system telling us to settle matters quickly and out of court lest you be sucked into the system and not get out until you pay your last penny.

Yes, Jesus knows what mosquitoes we humans can be in our dealings as lawyers, as physicians, and in the text, as pastors, elders, and church leaders. So lean close, one and all, and heed well! Verse 1 informs us Jesus spoke these words to "the crowds," to his "disciples," and to "the scribes and the Pharisees." And after he made these remarks, he broke down and wept! (v. 37ff).

Why was Jesus so fervent? Why so emotional? Because he wants his people to be different, to exert a positive leadership. Notice in his words the contrast between what we are as opposed to what we can be.

Preach/Practice

First Jesus points out the gulf between what we say and what we do. "Practice and observe whatever they tell you, but not what they do; for they preach, but do not practice" (Matthew 23:2-3). In the movie *The Godfather* the mafia don attends the baptism service of his grandson. He stands piously to worship and recite the creeds of the faith as the movie flashes back and forth between the baptistry and the brutal hits he has ordered against his enemies.

Hey, I can live like that, can you? I can speak patience from the pulpit at 11 a.m., but cut you off in the church parking lot at 12:04. I can write of kindness in marriage in a sermon one day, but act with boorish insensitivity the next. I can espouse eternal values in my small group, but in reality a scratch on my car bothers me more than a child starving to death in Africa.

Jesus is saying his leaders must close the gap between preaching and practice. If we talk the talk we must walk the walk.

Pompousness/Humility

Next Jesus points out the dichotomy between showing off and humility. In verse 5, he speaks of the deeds we do to be seen by men. In verse 12, he talks of how we "exalt" ourselves.

Such spiritual peacocks we can become! Geoffrey Chaucer, writing in *The Canterbury Tales*, observed that preachers and roosters have a lot in common. They are both given to strutting and preening themselves in public and crowing about the same hour each day! Oh, how self-important we can become — like Shakespeare's character who shouts, "I am Sir Andrew Augercheek. And when I speak let no dog bark!"

Jesus reminds us only God is great. The rest of us are equals. In verse 8, he says, "You are all brothers." And in verses 11 and 12, twice he mentions humility.

I know a minister who took down the sign that privileged him to park near the church building. "I'm no better than anyone else," he whispered. And as a humble servant leader to the people he parks in the most distant parking space, even in the rain, and walks in like so many of the rest of his congregation.

"Me-focused/You-focused"

Next Jesus talks about our focus.

There are two ways to walk into a room. I can walk in saying, "Here I am!" Or I can walk in with the attitude, "There you are!"

Many people in today's world are "church shopping." They consider themselves spiritual consumers out bargain hunting for the things of Christ. They walk into a church saying, "Here I am! Court me! Entertain me! Meet my needs! Or I won't be back!"

Some of us are addicted to the process. We love being singled out, pursued. We thrive on the new and being in control — "Maybe I will. Maybe I won't."

Jesus discussed this type of "Here I am!" person in the text. "They bind heavy burdens, hard to bear, and lay them on men's shoulders; but they themselves will not move them with their finger." You bet church shoppers expect gracious childcare when they enter, but don't ask them to help (v. 4). They are here to "be seen" (v. 5), but not to commit and serve. They crave the "place of honor" but not the basin and towel of washing dirty feet.

The better way to enter a room is with the attitude "There you are!" Jim Leet is an elder. For years I watched him walk into Sunday night fellowship and turn on his "people radar" and scan the room. He'd lock onto a visitor, a lonely teen, a troubled mother, a nervous elderly gentleman, then he'd sit and eat with them and meddle in their lives. "Perhaps I can do them some good," he'd say.

Such is Jesus' servant leadership. "The Son of Man came not to be served but to serve."

Titles/Service

In leadership Jesus warned us of the gulf between what we say and what we do, between pompousness and humility, between

377

being me-focused and you-focused. Now he addresses titles and genuine service.

In the seventh verse Jesus points out how we love to be properly saluted in the marketplace. "Rabbi!" "Teacher!" "Father!" "Master!" Today's translation? "Doctor!" "Reverend!" "The city's most dynamic pastor!" "Attended the Washington Prayer Breakfast!" and so on.

At a recent pastors' seminar a group of African-American ministers were complaining, "How can I get my church leaders to serve? They act like an advisory board, but seldom get down to the business of ministry. They've got the title but not the towel. They've got the authority but not the basin of water to wash dirty feet." In the text Jesus urges his leaders to "practice" (v. 3). "He who is greatest among you shall be your servant" (v. 11).

Read how the Apostle Paul introduced himself to the church at Rome in Romans 1:1. "Paul, a servant of Jesus Christ...." Not Doctor Paul, or Reverend Paul, or published author of sixteen books, or pastor of the country's largest parish, or even the most sought-after speaker of our day. Simply, "Paul, servant of Jesus Christ."

I'm thinking of a church that had a huge Christmas cantata Friday and Saturday nights. When the last production ended Saturday night, the pastor walked to the lectern, said how wonderful it was, pointed out how the chancel had to be cleared for the morning worship services, called for volunteers, then took his coat off to do his portion of the work with others. That's servant leadership!

Appearance/Reality

A fifth leadership dichotomy Christ points out is in appearance versus reality. Jesus spends considerable time in these twelve verses discussing our penchant for wanting to keep up appearances. We sit on Moses' seat (v. 2). We make our phylacteries broad and their fringes long (v. 5). We sit in the place of honor at church affairs (v. 6). But is there any reality behind all this showmanship, this pageantry?

"And your name?" I'd asked of a distinguished gentleman, lithe, in his later sixties. I was speaking at a military conference in the Norfolk area. He was at my table.

378

"Charlie Duke," he responded. Though the name sounded vaguely familiar, I couldn't place it. That's when another man at the table leaned over and whispered, "He's a general in the Air Force, one of only twelve men to walk on the moon!"

I became like a kid in the candy store. Here was history! Here was a chance to talk to Columbus, Magellan, Vasco da Gama, Leif Eriksson, one of the great explorers of our time! He didn't just cross the Atlantic! He went to the moon!

It soon became obvious General Duke was a real gentleman, humble, friendly, an easy man with whom to converse, and we did talk; four times.

He grew up in Pageland, South Carolina, just south of Wingate University. He has a twin brother. Though he graduated from the Naval Academy, an eyesight problem busted him out of Navy pilots' school. The Air Force took him, and soon he was in the astronaut's corp.

He trained two years for the next to last Apollo mission. When launch day arrived in April of 1972, he was a 36-year-old who eagerly jumped into the three-man capsule for the ride of his life.

Two and a half minutes to blastoff, a crane removed the white room from the rocket. Countdown began in earnest. Over one million pounds of rocket fuel would be burned, boosting them into space. Pulses quickened.

Through a tiny porthole high up in the capsule, they could see the moon, making its daylight appearance. One of the pilots quipped, "Well, Charlie, they have us pointed in the right direction!"

Then they were off like a shot! Within minutes they encountered the blackness of space. Within hours he saw the earth floating like a jewel, reduced to three colors — brown land, blue water, and white clouds and snow.

Duke was second out of the lunar lander. They stayed on the moon three days.

"We felt perfectly at home," he said. "We weren't afraid of aliens with ray guns. Everything was just like we'd seen in pictures hundreds of times."

If you look up at the face of the moon, they landed right in the center of what you see.

I recall Charlie Duke's antics. Likely you do, too. On earth with a space suit he weighed over 360 pounds, but on the moon, in near weightlessness, he weighed only 61 pounds. So they had a contest to see who could jump the highest. That's what I remember: two astronauts bouncing up and down like schoolboys on a playground.

"The only time I was ever afraid," he confided, "was when I lost my balance, began to flip over backward, and realized I might land on my head and possibly crack my spacesuit. I managed to twist to the side and break my fall with my arms and legs. When I got up I thought I'd made it. That's when I saw the camera pointing toward me. Chris Craft at Houston control chewed me out for my antics."

"When it came time to leave, we didn't want to go. We begged to stay two more hours." But orders were orders. So Charlie Duke flew home to earth. He made colonel and he'd only been fifteen years in the Air Force.

While his professional life flourished, his personal life was failing. His wife began to talk divorce. "I was an engineer. I knew how to fix a machine. But how do you fix a marriage?"

In a small group Bible study, someone shared Christ with him. And General Charles Duke believed. As he matured, so did his marriage.

Today he lives in Texas, enjoys wife, children, grandchildren, and travels extensively as a goodwill ambassador of both Christ and the United States.

The last day of the conference we sat together and shared communion in worship. He is a man who has been to the moon and back. Now in Christ he has learned to live on earth. His is not just appearances but the reality of a life lived out in servanthood to Jesus and others.

Conclusion

What sort of spiritual leader are you? Are you the mosquito or the honeybee? In the mirror of this text, what do you see?

Stephen M. Crotts

What If The End Is Near?

Someone handed me a note at the door of the church building a few Sundays ago. Here is what it said:

Absolute knowledge I have none,
But my aunt's washer woman's sister's son
Heard a policeman on his beat
Say to a laborer on the street
That he had a letter just last week
Written in finest classical Greek,
From a Chinese coolie in Timbuktu
Who said the Negroes in Cuba knew of a man in a Texas
*   town*
Who got it straight from a circus clown,
That a man in the Klondike heard the news
From a gang of South American Jews,
About somebody in Borneo
Who heard a man claim to know of a well-digger named
*   Jake,*
Whose mother-in-law will undertake to prove
That her seventh husband's sister's niece
Had stated in a printed piece
That she had a son who has a friend
Who knows when the world is going to end.

Seriously now, the end of the world is on a lot of people's minds these days, isn't it? Yet no one really knows when the end will come. But what if the end is near? What if Jesus Christ were to return today? Are you ready?

Our text is a parable that Jesus Christ told. It's about a group of people who ran out of oil. It would seem that that alone would make it relevant to us moderns. Even more relevant is the fact that this parable has to do with judgment day. Let's get into the story and see what it has to say to you and to me about life in Christ.

A Job To Do

The parable begins by telling us that there's going to be a wedding. Ten ladies have been chosen to be light-bearers at the feast of nuptials. You see, there were no streetlights then. So if there was going to be a nighttime party someone had to be in charge of the lights. Ten women, according to the text, were given this responsibility. As a group it was an honor to be asked to perform such a task.

In the scriptures we find God often assigning such tasks to people. Jonah was asked to take his lamp and go put it in a dark place we call Nineveh. Amos, the sheepherder of Toccoa, was asked to leave the quiet rural life and get involved in the tumultuous affairs of prophecy and politics. Mary, a teenager, was asked to birth a son. Paul, a Jewish rabbi and tentmaker, was asked to take the gospel to Europe. I believe that God still involves his people in his work. I believe he still asks us to take our lights and put them in dark places. But I also believe he doesn't usually ask us to do it alone. In the text, ten people were asked to provide light. As far as God's work is concerned today it is still a community project. He calls groups of us together to be the light of the world!

What task does God have for you? For us? What does the Lord want us to do? According to the Bible, he is calling us to repent of our sins and believe the gospel. He is calling you to love God in the power of the Holy Spirit, to love him with all your emotion, will, and intellect. And he is also calling you to love creation whether it's yourself, the environment, or other people. That love begins with your family, it continues with your neighbors and spreads out to your job, your church, even the entire world. Do you see how God's task begins with you and continues with us, until it embraces the entire world?

382

Yes, God has a job for his people. He has a job for you and for me. "You are the light of the world," Christ said. Now this:

Time To Prepare

Not only does God assign us tasks to perform such as putting our lights in dark places, he give us the resources and the time we need to prepare. The text says that the ten women each held a lamp and each had oil in them, some even had the forethought to bring an extra flask of oil. There was even time to take up their positions along the wedding route and to watch eagerly for the coming groom.

Just notice how much alike these ten ladies were. All responded to the summons and agreed to serve. They all showed up. All had lamps. All were dressed alike. All had oil. Even as the groom was delayed, they all grew weary from their work of preparation and watching, and they all slumbered.

There is one big difference between some of these women. Five used their time of preparation to acquire extra oil. They were preparing for any eventuality. Five did not

If you read the scriptures carefully, you will find that God's people are almost always thoroughly prepared. Noah didn't wait until it started raining to build the ark. He did that job well ahead of time. David didn't just go out and fight the giant Goliath as his first foe. As a shepherd, he rehearsed his rock slinging for years on wolves and bears that threatened his flock. Then there is the Apostle Paul. For fourteen years after his conversion, the man labored in obscurity sewing tents and sails and pondering the scriptures. Then began his first mission journey.

We each are given resources and time to prepare for our assigned tasks, as well. Yes, here in the church God provides us with Bibles and Bible study, fellowship in which we receive ministry, make lasting friendships, and sharpen our own tools of ministry. There is even a group prayer experience wherein we learn to pray and make the needs of people known to God, and, yes, there are years that God prepares us for future tasks as he teaches us patience, obedience, faith, and steadfastness.

Isn't it entertaining that in the text all of the women are overcome with fatigue? The preparation has been draining, the watching has been boring, the groom has not come yet. Things aren't going along as smoothly and as quickly as they'd planned. So they all begin to doze and nod. My, my, but what a picture of the church today! Haven't the past two years of preparation work been draining? Isn't the work of being in fellowship and Bible study and group prayer becoming a bit tedious? Aren't we all beginning to wonder what the delay is, why more isn't happening? "Where is the groom anyway?" So we begin to doze.

Many a person over the years has confided in me that he finds the things of church boring. Yet, look at it this way. Let's say you're in church fifty times a year and you learn one new fact about God each Sunday. That's fifty facts of God you will have gained in a year's time. In ten years that number will have become 500. In twenty years it'll be a thousand. In forty years 2,000. And if you attend Sunday school and evening teaching sessions, that number can triple in forty years to 6,000! It all adds up, doesn't it? Just like Isaiah the prophet said, the word of God is, "Precept upon precept, precept upon precept, line upon line, line upon line, here a little, there a little" (Isaiah 28:10).

No, it might not look like much here in the church, but this is the grace of God to us who will be called on to place lights in dark places. Here are the resources of God. Here is oil enough and extra for your lamps. And here is time to prepare!

A Time Of Reckoning

A job to do, time to prepare — this is the story Jesus told in the text. Now comes the final part, the story's conclusion. It's the time of accountability.

Have you ever heard Tchaikovsky's *Sixth Symphony*? It's a piece with long serene musical delights that is suddenly intruded upon by a savage theme that shatters all tranquility. That was Tchaikovsky's way of telling us that life flows along placidly until a crisis like death is thrust upon us. The parables of Jesus have this — cute little stories that suddenly end in crisis.

The groom is delayed. You see, in the Mideast, when someone tells you that a wedding will take place Friday night at eight, that means the wedding will take place sometime between Friday night at eight and Saturday or Sunday or even Monday night at eight. Mideasterners still don't punch a clock! Friday at eight simply means, "In the next few days."

Well, as the groom is not yet to be seen, the ladies in the text, having completed what they think to be adequate preparations, begin to giggle and loaf about. Fatigue sets in, and soon they are catnapping.

Suddenly a shout goes up, "The bridegroom cometh! He is near!" And the ten maidens leap up wide-awake, grab for their lamps, and assume their positions.

Now, note the fate of the prepared. Their first filling of their lamps is all but depleted and their lamps begin to flicker. No problem, for hanging from their belts is a flask of extra oil. Their lamps are quickly filled, they light the way for the groom and his guests, and go into the joyous wedding feast to celebrate. A job well done; they are rewarded.

Note also the fate of the unprepared. Their first filling of oil is about depleted also. As their lamps begin to sputter, they have no extra oil. They go to the wise and say, "How about loaning me some of your oil?" The wise refuse and advise them to go to the merchants and buy it. There is a hasty trip, a merchant is inconvenienced by a rap on his door, the maidens return; but now the door is shut and the party is in full sway. A job not done, the door is slammed in their face!

That's a hard verse to hear, isn't it? "And the door was shut." Yet, why not? Weddings can't be held up just because a few guests ran out of gas. Things get started, and, if we're not ready, they are over and done without us.

Did you hear about the Christmas parade in central North Carolina? Many elaborate floats passed by when suddenly a simple hay wagon pulled by a tractor starts by. On the wagon are several fraternity boys from the university. They are madly sawing boards and nailing things together. The puzzled expressions of the onlooker's faces changed to laughter when they read the sign on the back of the wagon. It read: "We thought the parade was next week!" Isn't that just how it is? There is a time to prepare, and there is a deadline after which nothing will do. Either you're ready or you're not!

I see this all too often as a pastor. People don't take God seriously. They dawdle away their time eating, drinking, and making merry. Opportunity after opportunity is missed to learn, to prepare, to grow — to take on oil and enough to spare! These people live as if there is no day of reckoning, no accountability. And suddenly — it comes! It might be death or a grave, lingering illness. It might be a financial reversal or war, or it might one day soon be the actual return of Christ for judgment day!

A few years ago, I was talking with a middle-aged man to whom life had dealt a severe blow in the death of his wife. He was fumbling around trying to find the resources to meet the demands of the hour. "Stephen," he said, "when I went off to college I put my Christian faith in the drawer because I didn't think I'd be needing it. That was 27 years ago and now I need it and can't remember where I put it." Well, even if he had found it, it probably wouldn't have fit. A faith that hasn't grown since childhood isn't likely to fit a 47-year-old man!

You know, when I used to read this parable I would read about those ladies in a panic who asked to borrow oil, and it really bothered me that the five women refused to share and told them to go get their own oil at the market. In fact, just five years ago I might have preached about their selfishness and encouraged you to share with those in need. But now I've come to see this portion of the parable a bit differently. In truth, if the women had shared their oil there might not have been enough for their lamps to light the way and for the feast itself. Why should the five's irresponsibility render the other five's effectiveness invalid also? There are some things you cannot share, you know. You can't share character or courage or inner peace to someone in a crisis, however much they weep and beg of you. You cannot share the thousands of facts you've learned about God over the years, you cannot share all this in one hour or one week or one year. Such must be bought at the merchants in its own time. There is no crash course in prayer that can

386

make up for years of missed application. Just as Noah didn't wait until the day of the flood to build his ark, so we can't wait until the crisis to build our faith and friendships and prayer-life. When the moment of reckoning comes, either you've got it or you don't. There is no borrowing. And sadly, even as badly as some might want to help, to share, to loan, there is no loaning.

What If?

It's simple enough, isn't it? A cute short story with a sudden crisis. A job, a time to prepare, a time of accountability.

Let me ask you some questions. Are you prepared? You've been given a task, a life to live by faith in Christ. Have you accepted that summons? You've been given resources and time to prepare. Are you taking on oil here in the church, learning the Word, growing at prayer, weaving your life into the fabric of friendships and ministry here in the church? Or do you let opportunity after opportunity pass you by as you take life easy and drift along? I'm thinking of a pastor who'd tried his best to win an older man to Christ. The old gentleman kept putting him off with lame excuses. So one day the pastor rang the old boy up on the phone and simply said, "Hello, Mr. Honeycutt, this is the pastor. Just one question for you. What if I'd been death?" Sobering, isn't it? Yet the accountings of life for which we are responsible come, and they come without warnings. They just come ready or not.

If there is one of you here today who doesn't know Christ as your Savior, why not bow your head and ask him to forgive your sins, to come into your life and make you a light to others. If there is another who has forsaken the way and squandered years of opportunity, why not take this moment and rededicate yourself?

The day of reckoning draws near. Are you ready? Will there be enough oil in your lamp?

Suggested Prayer

Lord, give me grace to take my task from you seriously. Let me prepare so that when the crisis comes, the oil will be there on the day of reckoning. In Jesus I pray. Amen.

Stephen M. Crotts

God, The Venture Capitalist?

Epistemology is the study of knowledge. How does one know anything? How can I know what is true?

One means of knowledge is *reason*. Two plus two equals four is an equation of reasonability. The Bible says, "The wisdom from above is ... open to reason" (James 3:17). The discipline of apologetics is the use of reason to defend the faith.

Experience is a second means of knowledge. I know fire burns because I touched it! The blind man Jesus healed was being harassed by the Pharisees over Christ restoring his sight. He defended the incident by appealing to experience. "This one thing I know. I was blind, but now I see" (John 9:25).

Then there is human *authority*. How do I know man walked on the moon? Because summer of 1969 I was home from college and Walter Cronkite, television news anchor, with all his investigative reporting skills said so. "And that's the way it is, June 1969." Christianity appeals to several thousand years of authority in the pages of scripture (2 Timothy 3:16-17).

A fourth means of gaining knowledge is *revelation*. It is sometimes called conscience or intuition. Revelation is God's self-disclosure. A few years ago Pope John Paul went to prison on Christmas Day to share God's love. He preached, "You could not come to me so I came to you!" This is revelation. What we could not learn about God through human speculation, he has himself disclosed. Our feeble reasoning, our limited experience, our lacking human authority, has been surpassed by Jesus coming to us preaching, "If you've seen me, you've seen the Father" (John 14:9).

This, then, is the Bible — a record of human experience with God; a reasonable appeal to the human mind; an authoritative statement of knowledge gained; but most of all, a record of God's self-disclosure.

Read the scriptures with the question "What is God like?" uppermost in your mind. There the Lord gives revelation of himself. The Lord's Prayer tells us he is like a father (Matthew 6:9). The parable of the prodigal son tells us God is a daddy waiting for a runaway boy to come home (Luke 15:11ff). And Psalm 23 explains God as a good shepherd.

Our text for today explains yet another facet of God's character that is surprising to many. He is a businessman investing his resources for profit. He is what we today would call a venture capitalist.

In the parable, Jesus explained how life is like a rich man going on a long journey who called together his servants. He gave them each a sum of money with instructions to trade with it until he returned. After the passing of years he did indeed return to settle accounts with his employees. Some were rewarded. Others punished.

What's here for our edification? First, we must understand that all ...

Ownership Is God's

The text reminds us that all true ownership belongs to God. Psalm 24:1 puts it bluntly, "The earth is the Lord's and the fullness thereof."

A lawyer in Louisiana in the years past was asked to do a title search for a piece of land being acquired by a U.S. Army base. He ran the search back to 1803 and sent the title in. The base commander was not satisfied and asked the lawyer to run the title search back still further. In complying, the attorney wrote, "Said parcel of land was purchased in 1803 by the Thomas Jefferson administration from France, the land commonly known as the Louisiana Purchase. The French acquired it by military victory from Spain; Spain acquired it from the Indians by conquest; and the Indians came to own it from God the Creator. I hope this complies with your request."

Read the Bible and you'll see. All that I have — it came from God, it is God's now, and it will return to God (Hebrews 1:1ff). This is true for my car. It is true of my house. It goes for my clothing, my bank account, even my very flesh and blood. The Apostle Paul reminds us, "For we brought nothing into this world, and we cannot take anything out" (1 Timothy 6:7). You don't see any boat hitches on hearses, do you?

If all ownership is God's, then the second point the parable teaches is that ...

Faithful Management Is Ours

The text says the rich man divided his property among his servants. He commissioned them to work with his resources entrusted to them until he returned. This is what we theologians call *stewardship*. In the Greek it is the word *economia*. The English word "economics" comes from this. Stewardship means I am out of ownership and into management. It means that life is like a great ship loaded with a rich cargo to be delivered to people in many places. And Christ is the owner, but I am the captain.

In Romans 1, the Apostle Paul is clear about his charge from God. He uses three "I am" statements. "I am under obligation." "I am eager to preach." "I am not ashamed" (Romans 1:14-16). It is as if God had given Paul a great wealth that he was in turn to pass along to others.

I read in the *New York Times* of a college graduate who moved to the big city bent on making his fortune in banking. He was driving a very nice car, a graduation gift from his older brother.

One day as he was getting into his car, a poor inner city child of twelve stood admiring the car. "My brother gave it to me," the young banker explained.

The kid said, "I wish...." And immediately the banker thought he was going to say, "I wish I had a car like that!" But, no! The child said, "I wish I could be a brother like that!"

"Do you want a ride?" the banker asked.

"Wow! Sure I do," the lad said and got in. Soon the boy asked if he could stop in front of an old building while he ran upstairs. Thinking the boy was going to fetch a friend to gawk at his car, he was amazed when his young neighbor came down carrying his severely handicapped brother. "Just look at this car! Isn't it fine? Some day I'm going to buy you a car like this!"

Now that's biblical stewardship! Not how much of my money am I going to give God, but how much of God's money do I keep for myself? Not me, mine, I-focused, but God-and-others-focused. Yes, the compassionate use of wealth.

When we get to heaven, Jesus won't ask how nice a car you drove, but did you use it to help others? He won't ask the square footage of your home; he'll ask the number of people you sheltered. He won't ask your net worth; he'll ask about your generosity in helping others.

Stop and think for two minutes. Quick! Name the last three Miss Americas. Name the past ten Super Bowl Champions. Give the names of ten U.S. Senators and the last five best actor Oscar winners. You cannot, can you? Ah, but you well recall the names of those who helped you when you were hospitalized for a week, those teachers who went the extra mile to get you through school that tough year, and the six persons in your small group who've helped you grow this past year.

God, you see, has richly invested in you! Time, talent, money — it's all his! But to you he has entrusted a sum. And now he has strategically placed your life where you can express his love by your kindness in Christ-centered ministry.

So, if all ownership is God's and faithful management is ours, then one final truth yet remains in the text. And that is ...

Accountability Is Coming
The text tells us the businessman returned and called in each of his employees to see what they'd done with his venture capital, and the reward for work well done was more work. But the punishment for lack of vision, laziness, and selfishness was that even what they had was taken away.

In every game there is a buzzer, a whistle, a finish line, a bell that rings signaling the end. Then winners and losers are announced. So will come a day in each of our lives. A trumpet will sound from on high. We will cease all commerce. We each shall stand before the Lord, and we shall give account of our stewardship.

The text says some of us are given five talents, others two, some of us one. We're not all equally endowed. But a man shows who he is by what he does with what he has.

In the parable, the five talent man told the businessman, "Master, you delivered to me five talents; here I have made five talents more." He was commended. The same with the two talent employee, and so on. "Well done, thou good and faithful servant!"

Ah, but one employee took his stewardship to the master and sourly complained, "I knew you to be a hard man, reaping where you did not sow, and gathering where you did not winnow; so I was afraid, and I went and hid your talent in the ground." Translation: "I resent your lordship over me. I'm into possession, not management. I'll work to put money into my pocket, but I won't do it for you!" In short, he rejected his boss. He rejected the entire concept of stewardship. Jesus called him "wicked," "slothful," and "cast him into outer darkness."

Wow! I'm not making this up! This is serious! Ownership belongs to God. Faithful use of resources for ministry belongs to us, and judgment day is coming.

Conclusion

By some reckoning, Jesus told around 48 parables. Five deal with God's character. Eight deal with history. Four encourage us to "Watch" faithfully for Christ's coming. Three bid us pray and not lose heart. Eight deal with obedience. And nine deal with stewardship.

Why did Jesus talk so much about possessions, about management of material blessings? I think he did so because he knew money was his chief rival for the soul of man. After all, what was it that caused the rich young ruler to walk away from Christ? Money. What was it the prodigal son wanted from his father, and getting it, ran away to live the fool? Money. What was it Judas received for betraying Christ? Money.

No, friend, there must be no divorce between business and God, between faith in Jesus and how we manage money, between the Lord's Day and the workweek.

Never forget! Ownership is God's. Faithful management is ours, and the time of judgment is coming!

Stephen M. Crotts

True Reformation

The key idea in this passage in the Fourth Gospel is truth. Jesus says, "If you continue in my word, you are *truly* my disciples, and you will know the *truth*, and the *truth* will make you free."

Truth has taken a beating in the past century. We have come to a supposedly post-modern era in which a lot of people think that there isn't any real truth that's true for you just as much as it's true for me. We're told that there are no grand narratives about reality that are true for everybody — just "whatever works for you." There's truth for women and truth for men, truth for rich and for poor, for Christians and Muslims and atheists and many other faiths and non-faiths — but who's to say that one person's truth is true for another? Sometimes a basis for that idea of the relativity of truth is claimed in Einstein's theory of relativity. "After all," people says, "Einstein showed that everything is relative."

Well, as a matter of fact, Einstein didn't say any such thing. Some things do depend on your point of view. Whether a car appears to be moving or standing still depends on whether *you* are moving or standing still. But even in physics, which is what Einstein was talking about, there are some things that are true for everybody. One of Einstein's basic ideas was that the speed of light in a vacuum is the same for everybody, regardless of their state of motion. That is not relative but absolute. While people may measure different values for the physical quantities, Einstein said that the *form* of physical laws is the same for everyone.

What Einstein said was that the things that are absolute in the world are not the things that our common sense leads us to expect.

395

Some things that our common sense lead us to think will be the same for everybody actually depend on the way an observer is moving. Two clocks that are in motion with respect to one another don't keep the same time, and if that conflicts with common sense, so much the worse for common sense. On the other hand, it's hard to understand how the speed of a beam of light can always be the same, no matter how fast you chase after it — but it is.

The real truths about the world are subtle and often surprising. You have to be willing to abandon preconceived ideas and to work hard in order to find them. Whatever some individual scientists might say about truth, scientists in general do believe that there really are truths to be discovered by studying the world. If they didn't, they wouldn't devote their lives to scientific work.

The Bible certainly leads us to expect that there is such a thing as truth, and that it can be known by us. "Grace and truth came through Jesus Christ" the prologue of our Gospel of John tells us. Today, in the long debate in the eighth chapter of that gospel that we read part of, Jesus promises that his disciples will really know the truth, and that that truth will liberate them.

What is this "truth" that Jesus is talking about? We hear all kinds of claims to truth in today's public square. There are political and scientific and economic claims, liberal and conservative claims, and plenty of different religious claims. For the Jews to whom Jesus was speaking in Jerusalem, the truth was that their descent from Abraham set them apart and made them God's special people. We could spend a lot of time analyzing all the different truth claims of today and yesterday, and can recognize a certain amount of truth in many of them, but we're kidding ourselves if we think that they set us free in the fullest sense. The Jews say that they "have never been slaves to anyone" — as they stand under the watchful eye of the Roman occupation authorities.

Let's cut to the chase. What the Gospel of John, as part of Holy Scripture, presents as the truth is Jesus Christ. If we remain in his word — if we hear him, listen to him, know him, and stay with him — if we continue in his word — we will be knowing him who is the truth. In another place in this gospel, Jesus says, "I am the way, and the truth, and the life." The point isn't so much that he is three separate things — way and truth and life — as that he is the truth who is the way to life.

The truth Jesus speaks of is not a collection of true statements or theorems that have been proved but a person. When he stands before Pilate on Good Friday he will say, "Everyone who belongs to the truth listens to my voice." Pilate, the brutal Roman politician, might have accepted as truth some statement like Mao's "Power grows from the barrel of a gun." But he says sarcastically, "What is truth?" and turns away — as so many have done since — with the one who is the truth standing right in front of him.

It wouldn't have been at all surprising for Pontius Pilate to have said "power grows from the sword" or something like that. The belief that real power requires the domination and destruction of others is one of those common sense ideas that, like it or not, seems to be true of the way the world is. The idea that the one who will be condemned by Pilate and crucified is the truth seems absurd. As with Einstein's theory, so here: The real truths are not those of common sense. Empires and tyrants who have relied on domination and destruction have passed away, while Christ crucified is, as Paul said, "the power of God and the wisdom of God."

Jesus Christ is the truth in a double sense. He is, on the one hand, the fullest expression of what humanity is supposed to be, the truth of what creation is all about. On the other hand he is, as we confess in the Nicene Creed, "true God from true God." We can know the truth about ourselves and about God not in an abstract idea or principle which might be discovered anywhere but in Jesus of Nazareth: "The Word became flesh." It is the person born of Mary, nailed to the cross, and seen alive on the third day, who is the truth in which we are told to remain.

If you know this truth, if you continue in Jesus and keep your faith anchored in him, you are free. Specifically, Jesus says that you are free from *sin*. All the things that keep you apart from God, all the sins that keep your life from being as completely human as God intends it to be, have lost their power over you. You are no longer in slavery. That is the gospel, the good news — that you are free because God has come to be with us, to share our humanity and to free us by his dying and rising.

Today is Reformation Sunday. October 31 is the anniversary of Luther's posting of his ninety-five theses and on this Sunday that historical event, and the whole reformation of the sixteenth century, are often remembered by Protestant churches. Reforming is something that the church has frequently needed throughout the centuries, not least of all today. The church is one, holy, catholic, and apostolic, but its members are human beings who make mistakes. Parts of the church can lose their focus, get fuzzy about their purpose, and get off the right road and find themselves lost in the woods.

It's easy to see how that can happen if we remember what the church is supposed to be focused on, Jesus Christ, and if enough people take their eyes off him things can go wrong. That was happening as far back as the ministry of Saint Paul, even among churches that Paul himself had founded. Some people came to those churches in Galatia and were persuading them that it wasn't enough to believe in Jesus Christ, but that they had to add all the Old Testament laws and rituals as well. Paul's response was uncompromising: "You foolish Galatians! Who has bewitched you? It was before your eyes that Jesus Christ was publicly exhibited as crucified!" *That* is the truth; not circumcision and rules about food.

At the time of what is called *the* Reformation in the sixteenth century, the problem again was a loss of focus on Christ. The western church had become so concerned with the human response to God's grace, with the need for people to do good works and the difficulties of living a holy life, that many Christians no longer felt that they could trust completely, with 100 percent assurance, in Jesus Christ, for salvation. The essential message which the Reformation proclaimed was, "Yes, you can trust in Christ alone." All those other slogans — grace alone, faith alone, scripture alone — have their point in the insistence upon Christ alone. He is the one through whom grace and truth have come, the one in whom we are to believe, the one to whom scripture bears witness.

Reformation Day used to be celebrated in my own Lutheran tradition in a kind of triumphalistic way, as an "Isn't it great to be Lutheran?" festival. But it was never the intention of Luther — or for that matter of Calvin and other reformers — to start a new church. What they wanted to do was precisely to reform, or renew, the church catholic by recalling it to the basic truth of the gospel, the truth of Jesus Christ. There have been Christians called to that work of reformation throughout the centuries — we could think of Francis of Assisi in the thirteenth. However, we may understand what Protestants and Roman Catholics did in the sixteenth century, the state of the church and the state of the world today are too perilous for any Christians to be spending their time refighting the battles of 500 years ago.

The goal of genuine reformation is to bring the church of Jesus Christ to unity in the truth. That does not mean that Protestant and Orthodox and Roman Catholic Christians all have to express the truth in the same way, speak the same theological language, or organize their church polities in the same way. It's a little like the situation in Einstein's theory, in which some things are relative but there are absolutes. Here the absolute on which all Christians must agree is the centrality of Christ. He is the criterion of truth for the ways in which churches organize themselves and speak and act.

The church's unity in the truth is for the sake of its mission in the world, a world which is divided among many different truth claims and assertions that there is no truth. It is a world divided along religious and political and economic lines, a world in which conflict is continually breaking out, and threatening to break out, between people of different religions, different ethnic groups, or with different economic interests. In this world, the church is called to be a light to the nations, to be a means by which divisions are healed by making the truth known.

That will not happen simply by making true statements about Christ. We must, of course, always be ready to speak the truth, but suspicion and hatred are not overcome just by reciting the creed, true as it may be. As the truth is incarnate in Jesus Christ, and as the church is the Body of Christ in the world, we are called to express the truth of Christ in the ways in which we live and treat others and care for God's creation. From the level of one on one dealings with our neighbor to the global level, the people of God are called to be a light to the nations — to share the light of Christ in words and in deeds.

George L. Murphy

Faith's Curious Dynamic

You know that old saying, "Be careful what you wish for, because it might come true"? We see examples of that again and again in life. During the war in Iraq, Hampton Sides, a journalist who had been slated to be "embedded" with one of our frontline Marine battalions, gave an interview on NRP (National Public Radio). At almost the last possible moment, Sides decided not to go with the Marines, but instead to report from Central Command in Qatar.

The interviewer asked Sides when he began having doubts about going in with the Marines, and Sides said that it was when he was receiving training about the use of his gas mask. Knowing that nausea is often one of the first symptoms of a chemical attack, he had asked the military trainer what to do if he threw up in his mask. The trainer didn't have a clear answer, and that's when Sides' second thoughts erupted.

Then the interviewer asked how Sides' fellow journalists, who were going with the troops, reacted when they found he had dropped out. He said they understood completely. He went on then to say that the alleged existence of weapons of mass destruction in Iraq has created a "curious dynamic" in this war: "We are trying to prove to the world that Saddam Hussein has these weapons. We *want* him to have these weapons. He *better* have them, or else in some ways it invalidates the stated purposes of the war. And ... if he has these weapons, [we have to believe] he would use them"[1] — which, of course, is exactly what we *don't want* him to do.

That's a curious dynamic indeed, where you both want and don't want the same thing. Life itself has plenty of curious dynamics like that, though we are more apt to identify them as mixed emotions, contradictions, or paradoxes. Any war brings more of them to the fore, but that war especially had yielded a bumper crop of conflicting feelings. For example, many of us who strongly supported our troops weren't convinced we should be fighting this war at all.

But think of some other curious dynamics:

- When your son first graduates from college, and applies for a good opening in a job some miles away, you may find yourself both hoping he gets that job and afraid that he will, because you won't see him as often.

- Or you are pleased to see your daughter becoming a responsible young woman but are sad because you won't have the little girl around the house any longer.

- Or maybe you are eager to get married and start a family, but concerned that once you do, you won't be able to pursue every whim or opportunity that comes along.

- Imagine what it is like to be one of those people waiting for a heart transplant. On the one hand, you are hoping for a heart to become available, but on the other hand you don't want someone to have to die so that you can get a heart.

- Or how about the fact that Christians have been identified as those waiting expectantly for the Second Coming of Christ, but actually hoping that it doesn't happen in their lifetime.

- Or consider that of all the twelve disciples, Peter always seemed to be the one with the strongest faith. It was he who spoke up when Jesus asked what identity they had seen in him. Peter stated confidently, "You are the Messiah." Later, when Jesus was arrested in the Garden of Gethsemane, Peter was the one who drew his sword and was ready to fight to the death for Jesus. But that same evening, Peter denied Jesus three times. He was one big contradiction. Did he want to stand with Jesus or didn't he?

Well, what are we to make of all these contradictions — these curious dynamics — of life? Do they mean that we are people of weak moral fiber? Do they mean that our faith has fled or that like Peter, it's been overwhelmed with fear or perhaps even sin?

Consider a couple of verses from Lamentations. As you might surmise from the name of that biblical book, it is a collection of funeral dirges — not for individuals but for the city of Jerusalem after it had been destroyed in 586 B.C. by the Babylonians and its citizens forced into exile. But amid the dirges is a short passage that seems a departure from the gloom of the rest of the book. Here it is:

> *But this I call to mind,*
> *and therefore I have hope:*
> *The steadfast love of the LORD never ceases,*
> *his mercies never come to an end;*
> *they are new every morning;*
> *great is your faithfulness.*
> — Lamentations 3:22-23

This eruption of hope in the bleak landscape of defeat and destruction occurred because though the people of Judah and Jerusalem had sinned against God and lost much, God had not forsaken them. They had hope because the prophets had told them that God would yet redeem them.

But beyond all of that, did you notice that there is a curious dynamic in these verses, too? On the one hand, they speak of the *steadfast* love and mercy of God, which of course means that those things are unchanging. On the other hand, they say that these same mercies that do not change are *new every morning*. That's very curious indeed.

In other words, even God himself operates through seeming contradictions — or what we might better describe as paradoxes. The verses are actually saying that the unchanging love of God is a constant element in our existence that is so adaptable that it can helps us through life's curious dynamics.

The author of these lines experienced the undergirding security of God's constant love. He also recognized that with each passing

403

day, his circumstances changed. That which sufficed for yesterday was not always sufficient for today's needs. But the unchanging love of God was fresh with each new day, and that provided him with security amid the vicissitudes of life.

We should also note that Jesus was no stranger to paradoxes and contradictions, too. There is, for example, Jesus' enigmatic comment, "He who finds his life will lose it, and he who loses his life for my sake will find it" (Matthew 10:39). There is also that part of his Sermon on the Mount we call the Beatitudes. They are filled with contradictions. Consider just a couple of them:

- "Blessed are those who mourn, for they will be comforted."
- "Blessed are you when people revile you and persecute you and utter all kinds of evil against you falsely on my account."

And now recall that the word "blessed" is often translated as "happy" or "fortunate." So now you've got: "Happy are those who mourn, for they will be comforted."

Really? Those in grief will be happy?

How about this one: "Fortunate are you when people revile you and persecute you and utter all kinds of evil against you falsely on my account"?

Really? Being slandered and persecuted is a mark of good fortune?

Those statements seem to defy logic!

What we come to understand is that Jesus is talking about the ultimate outcome of people who cling to God in faith. Things that seem to be diametrically opposed, become, under God's hand, the poles of creative tension in which we live out our faith.

You see, faith too has a curious dynamic about it. The language of faith is not all about cheerfulness and certainty. It is not presented in the Bible as a sure thing once acquired. Faith seems to embrace a good deal of ambiguity. I like the definition presented by novelist Doris Betts that faith is "not synonymous with certainty ... [but] is the decision to keep your eyes open."[2]

This is All Saints' Sunday, and one of the things that made those who have gone before us in the faith "saints" is that they were not turned away from God by life's ambiguities. Here's an example: A little less than a century ago, G. K. Chesterton, a British journalist who became widely known for his detective stories and his writings in defense of Christianity, published a book in which he explained how the seeming contradictions about Christianity are actually what convinced him to embrace the faith. By age sixteen, he was an agnostic, and as an adult, he began to read the arguments of many critics of Christianity, writers who were themselves agnostics or atheists. He discovered the oddest thing, however. Instead of cementing him into his position of doubting Christianity, these books actually caused him to doubt his doubts. He said, "As I read and re-read all the non-Christian or anti-Christian accounts of the faith ... a slow and awful impression grew gradually but graphically upon my mind — the impression that Christianity must be a most extraordinary thing." He went on to explain that many of these critics attacked Christianity for opposite things — for contradictory reasons. One attacked Christianity for being too hard on family life and another for forcing family life upon us. Another said it was too pious and another not pious enough. Yet another said it was too pessimistic while another described it as too optimistic, and so on, with accusation after accusation.

At first, this caused him to consider that Christianity must be even weirder than he'd thought, but then one day another explanation altogether occurred to him: "Perhaps, after all, it is Christianity that is sane and all its critics that are mad — in various ways." He gave the following example:

> *Suppose we heard an unknown man spoken of by many men. Suppose we were puzzled to hear that some men said he was too tall and some too short; some objected to his fatness, some lamented his leanness; some thought him too dark, and some too fair. One explanation ... would be that he might be an odd shape. But there is another explanation. He might be the right shape. Outrageously tall men might feel him to be short. Very short men might feel him to be tall. Old bucks who are growing stout might consider him insufficiently filled out;*

old beaux who were growing thin might feel that he
expanded beyond the narrow lines of elegance. Per-
haps Swedes (who have pale hair like tow) called him
a dark man, while [black men] considered him distinctly
blonde. Perhaps (in short) this extraordinary thing is
really the ordinary thing; at least the normal thing, the
center.

"Perhaps, after all, it is Christianity that is sane and all its critics that are mad," Chesterton concluded. The very contradictions that critics thought discounted Christianity actually, as Chesterton saw it, validated it.

Chesterton further explained that Christianity was not merely the sensible thing that stood in the middle of extremes. In the case of pessimism and optimism, for example, it was not that Christianity occupied the compromise position between them, but that it embraced both optimism and pessimism "at the top of their energy, love and wrath both burning." The supreme example of this, Chesterton said, was Christianity's claim about Christ, that he was both fully and completely human and fully and completely God.[3] That's a contradiction if there ever was one, but Christianity's life comes from the tension between those positions, and that's also where faith lives.

Now faith and reason are inexorably linked, and faith does not defy reason or go in an opposite direction. Faith and reason walk together for a good bit of the way and go the same direction, but after a certain point, faith goes on alone, reaching further than reason does. Reason takes us only so far. Faith goes beyond it, but in the direction reason points.

But now, as we talk about the role of contraction in faith, we need to add one more piece to that explanation. As we enter that realm were faith reaches beyond reason, where faith has to go it alone, as it were, and where we are dealing with the deepest questions of life, the operating principles of reason become less useful. God's truth is not limited to what reason can grasp. As author William Johnson writes, "Faith is the breakthrough into that deep realm of the soul which accepts paradox ... with humility."[4]

And so, as we find ourselves both wanting and not wanting the same things, or both believing and doubting the same things, or both wanting explanations and accepting that some things cannot be explained, we can take heart that God too embraces contradiction. In fact, he operates there. The Trappist monk and author Thomas Merton once wrote, "I have become convinced that the very contradictions in my life are in some ways signs of God's mercy to me; if only because someone so complicated and so prone to confusion and self-defeat could hardly survive for long without special mercy."[5]

For us, faith is what's lived between the poles of certainty and doubt. Faith is found in the tension between the opposites. Sometimes we are drawn toward one pole and we are confident in our faith. Other times we are drawn toward the other pole, where we can barely contain our skepticism and doubt, but that's the nature of faith, and contradictions are an integral part of it.

We can only thank God that he too maneuvers in the realm of contradiction, with unchanging love and mercy that is new every morning.

1. Sides was interviewed on *Fresh Air*, broadcast on NPR March 24, 2003. I listened to the interview again on the *Fresh Air* website to get the quote accurately.

2. Quoted by Kathleen Norris, *Amazing Grace* (New York: Riverhead Books, 1998), p. 169.

3. All of the Chesterton material is from the chapter "The Paradoxes of Christianity," from his *Orthodoxy*, (Dodd, Mead & Company, 1908), pp. 81-101 in my 1990 reprint by Image Books.

4. Quoted by Henri Nouwen in the introduction to Parker J. Palmer, *The Promise of Paradox* (Notre Dame, Indiana: Ave Maria Press, 1980), p. 13.

5. *Ibid.*, quoted by Palmer, p. 17.

Stan Purdum

Christ The King
Matthew 25:31-46

Go To Heaven?

Judgment day was the preacher's theme, and he thundered about God's wrath, sin and the day of judgment. A seven-year-old boy listened closely, tugged at his father's sleeve, and asked, "Will they call school off?" He was asking, "What's in it for me?"

Judgment day is on Christ's mind here in Matthew 25:31 and following verses. He is describing that fateful day soon "when the Son of Man comes in his glory" (v. 31). All the angels will be with him. Jesus will sit on a throne (v. 31). And before him will be gathered all the nations of the world (v. 32). There Jesus will divide the sheep from the goats, the righteous from the sinners.

To the righteous Christ will say, "Come" (v. 34). To the wicked he will say, "Depart!" (v. 41). The righteous will enter a "kingdom prepared" (v. 34), "eternal life" (v. 46). But the unredeemed will be "cursed" to "fire" with the "devil and his angels" (v. 41). And this punishment is "eternal" (v. 46).

Hey! I'm not making this up! This is what Jesus said about it! And, yes! They will call school off that day. No one will be discussing weight loss or the weather. None of us will be asking how the stock market is doing. We won't care about the November elections. For all of our attention will be focused on the Judge who is seated upon the throne!

Do We Earn It?

Who is the person that pleases God? How is it one can stand with God's sheep and enter into paradise? Who is the person Christ condemns? On what basis does Jesus say "Come!" to some and "Go!" to others?

At first glance it seems one is favored by good works — feeding the hungry, welcoming the stranger, visiting the sick, and clothing the poor. Indeed, a lot of people believe the deeds we do go into big piles. In the end if our good outweighs our bad we'll go to heaven.

I was talking to a country boy on the dining room steps of East Carolina University. I'd inquired of his philosophy of life. He told me, "It's really very simple. Life is like a trip to the Super Wal-Mart store. Everybody gets a shopping cart and a chance to walk through the aisles of life. On the shelves are all these good things — fishin' lures, shotgun shells, t-shirts, snack foods, and Waylon Jennings CDs. Why, you just go through, pick out what you want, and pay for it at the end.

"If you've been good, you get to go to that 'Big Wal-Mart in the Sky' and shop forever. If you've been bad, God'll sit your butt in a hot car out in the parking lot and you won't get out for all eternity!"

But I remind you, salvation is not a prize we earn. It is the gift of God. Ephesians 2:8-9 clearly states, "For by grace we are saved, by faith, and not that of ourselves. It is the gift of God, not of works, lest any should boast."

Faith In God

Actually, the key to understanding this passage is the phrase, "Come, O blessed of my Father ..." (v. 34). The important word is *blessed*. And to understand it we have to go back to the first of Matthew's Gospel. There, when Jesus first opened his mouth to preach, he said, "Blessed are the poor in spirit ... those who mourn ... blessed are the meek ... and those who hunger and thirst ..." (Matthew 5:1-12). We call these sayings the Beatitudes. And they tell us plainly what sort of person Christ is looking for.

"Blessed are the poor in spirit," that is, those who understand their total spiritual bankruptcy before God. Those who know they are hopeless sinners.

"Blessed are those who mourn." I'm spiritually poor and I care. I wish it weren't so. And I grieve before God.

410

"Blessed are the meek." This means I am approachable by God. He can talk to me and I will listen. He can teach me and I will bend my will to his.

And, "Blessed are those who hunger and thirst for righteousness." When God makes provision for my salvation, when he offers me himself who is become my righteousness, I receive him gladly. I trust him. I do not want a mere nibble, but the whole of what he offers!

These first four attitudes are as fine a description of faith in Christ Jesus as you'll discover in the New Testament. Faith is not just an intellectual consent that Jesus is Savior, but a living relationship, an active attitude that turns from self to God for hope, for provision, for redemption from sin. Faith is trusting Jesus and receiving what he offers.

This is hard for so many. Just go into a bookstore. Check out the topical sections. The biggest one is called the "self-help" section. There you'll find books on feeling good about yourself, how to fix your marriage, on stopping worry, on becoming a dynamic leader, and more. You see, we humans do not want to admit we're spiritually bankrupt and must throw ourselves on God's mercy and provision. We're convinced we can fix things. All we need is a little more time.

But Jesus said those who are "blessed," those to whom God says, "Come!" are those who've turned from self and sin and prideful striving to simple trust in Christ.

Service To Others

In the text, Jesus makes it clear that the best way one can love God is to love the people he makes. "Inasmuch as you have done it unto the least of these my brethren, you have done it unto me."

Look at the second half of the Beatitudes. Matthew 5:7-12 shifts from our faith attitude toward God to our faithful behavior toward people: "Blessed are the merciful ... blessed are the pure in heart ... blessed are the peacemakers ... blessed are those who are persecuted for righteousness sake...."

Be clear about it, if one lives before God poor in spirit, mournful, meekly, and hungrily, then it follows one will live mercifully, pure, and a peacemaker among people.

But be careful to notice that as Christ rewards his saints for their good deeds among men — feeding the poor, ministry to the sick, visiting the prisoner — they seem to be unaware of what they did. "Lord," they argue, "when did we see thee hungry and feed thee, or thirsty and give thee drink?" And Jesus will say, "Truly, I say to you, as you did it to one of the least of these my brethren, you did it to me" (v. 40).

On that day Jesus will say, "Stephen, remember that pastor who publicly slandered you? Remember Howard?" And I'll say, "Yes, Lord, I remember him." Then Jesus will point out, "You were hurt, but you didn't sue him or try to get him fired. You met him with kindness. You just went on with your life, gave him the benefit of the doubt. In short, you were merciful."

"And Stephen," Christ will say, "does the name Mr. Knotts means anything to you? He's the man who came to your church for four years then quit to look around. You read in the paper how he was on cocaine, had raped a waitress, and was in jail. You visited him on Christmas Eve in 1986 in prison. You told him you cared. When he put his hand on the prison glass, you put yours on his and cried, too. Stephen, you were pure in heart. He couldn't pay you back or join your church. Your only motive for going to him was my love."

Then Jesus will say, "Remember that pastors' conference you did in Myrtle Beach, October of '97? You'd just had an award-winning book published and were riding high. You were teaching about fifty clergy couples. There was a one-talent pastor and his wife there laboring in a small rural parish. He was depressed and thinking of quitting. She was overweight and nervous and insecure. You sat to eat with them. You listened. You told her you could see the love of God in her smile and eyes. That meal gave them the hope to carry on. You were being a peacemaker, Stephen."

And I will bow my head and worship Jesus! "Lord, I didn't know what you were doing through me. Blessed art thou, O God! And blessed art people through your Word and Spirit in ministry through your servants!"

For those who are empty, Jesus is our fullness. And for those around us, we are conduits — God pours out his blessings through us. What we receive we pass along — mercy and peace and love.

Conclusion

The sheep and the goats. Those to whom Jesus says, "Come!" and those to whom Jesus says, "Depart!" Those who are so self-absorbed they live without God and with no service to others, and those who in humility become God-aware, trusting, and servants to others: These are the two sorts of person in our world. They are the two who will stand before God at the last day to be judged.

Which person are you?

Suggested Prayer

I am poor before you. And I care. O make me meek and hungry as I trust in your provision. Amen.

Stephen M. Crotts

Once More With Feeling!

It's that holiday season again. Friends and loved ones are making plans for a visit. Christmas decorations are out in the store windows. Once again people's hearts are swelling with optimism. Jack Frost has left his calling card. The smell of wood fires curls from the chimneys, and inside, mothers work their magic as fathers are heard to say, "Make some of those sugar cookies that you made last year, the ones with the sprinkles."

Yes, it's Thanksgiving week, and I'm supposed to preach on gratitude. And you're supposed to be thankful. Ah, but the civil courtesy of gratefulness does not come with the picture-perfection of a Currier and Ives print. The years can be hard. Disappointments crowd in. Thankfulness can be hard to muster.

The text tells us it happened to nine out of ten people in Jesus' day. Remember the story? Ten men. Ten severe cases of leprosy. Chalky skin. Loss of feeling. Highly contagious. Wrapped in rags. Made to dwell apart. Ten different stories of life interrupted. Careers ruined. Families broken. Dreams shattered. Then came Jesus. He healed them all, and pell-mell they began to rush back into the city. Each had an agenda, a thirsty desire to pick up the life they'd had to abandon.

One man, seeing he was healed, returned to fall at Jesus' feet to give gratitude. The other nine? They were "no shows." Perhaps they felt lucky. Or maybe they were just plain impolite. Or could it be they were just in a hurry and didn't have time?

Christ looked at the thankful man at his feet. He looked at the trail over which the others had fled. He said, "Were not ten cleansed? Where are the other nine?"

Since it is the season for great feasts and big family gatherings, I'd like to share one of my recipes with you. It is a recipe for the best Thanksgiving ever! Where did I get this recipe? I got it from God himself. It comes from the Bible.

All you really need is a mixing bowl and several simple ingredients. It is not a very complex recipe. Why, your very life can be the mixing bowl. And here is what you first put in it. 1 Thessalonians 5:18 says, "Give thanks in all circumstances; for this is the will of God in Christ Jesus for you." So the first ingredient in this happy Thanksgiving recipe is *thanksgetting*.

Thanksgetting

Many of you are familiar with the old spiritual that goes, "Count your blessings, name them one by one." Well, this is not such a bad song to be whistling or singing while you mix in several cupfuls of thanksgetting. Just stop and think for a moment! Which of you has gone hungry during the past year? Consider your clothing. How many pairs of shoes do you have in your closet right now? How about that job and your health and your family? My, my! When we count our blessings one by one we just have to thank the Lord! Our list of blessings is longer than your arm! We feel like the country woman who said, "The Lord has blessed me so good He's done filled my cup and run it over into the saucer, too!"

Jesus, while he was here on earth, gave a group of people something to be thankful for. He healed ten men of leprosy. Flesh that had been cancerous was made pure as a baby's skin. And the healed ones were so excited that they ran pell-mell to the village for a reunion with their families. But one of the men took time to stop and thank Jesus for his healing. Now one out of ten is not a very good average. I suppose we still live in that same kind of thankless world today. When you do something nice for somebody else, they are just too busy or too tired or too something to say a sincere thanks. Why, it seems like the words *thank you* are becoming more

416

and more rare. *Thanksgetting* is sort of like an endangered species these days. It may even become extinct like the great whales or the whooping cranes.

Why don't we just stop for a moment and see how much *thanksgetting* we can find. After all, there's no use going on with our recipe if we cannot find all the ingredients. How about you? Can you find any thanksgetting? Is there something for which you would like to say thank you?

Thanksliving

The second ingredient you will need for this happy Thanksgiving recipe is a heaping amount of pure *thanksliving*. You don't have to be particular about it. Just stir it right in there along with the *thanksgetting*. Use the same bowl. It will be big enough to hold it all.

Now it's easy enough to thank God for the healings, the food, the peace, the luxuries he sends our way. But how about the setbacks, the pain and grief? Can we be thankful for them, too? 1 Thessalonians 5:18 says, "Give thanks in all circumstances; for this is the will of God in Christ Jesus for you." This is not just an isolated verse either. The same recipe is taught in Ephesians 5:20. There, God says, "Always and for everything give thanks in the name of our Lord Jesus Christ to God the Father."

What is the first thing we should do when something upsetting happens? When we feel like the blessings have quit flowing? If you are driving down the road and you have a flat tire, do you curse and fume at your delay? What's the first thing you should do when you find out you have cancer or the television is burned out or your in-laws are coming for a two-week visit? You should stop and praise God. You should stop and thank him. "That's ridiculous, Pastor!" you say. "Aw, come on now. We're not really supposed to thank God for our misfortunes, are we?" The text says we should thank God in all circumstances. Not for the woe! But for God who has brought us to this day to show his power.

Last winter, a friend of mine named Roger lost his job in the carpet industry. The recession for him, and his family of four, became a depression. The first thing Roger did was to go home and

417

take a walk with his wife, Heather. And as they were walking, the two of them praised God for shepherding their lives through all this. As the weeks passed, well-meaning friends tried to comfort Roger by saying things like, "Gosh! That's rotten luck, Roger!" Or, "I hear they're hiring workers in Alaska for the pipeline." Nonetheless, Roger kept the faith. He just kept praising God and thanking him. Then, several months later, Roger was hired by another firm in Charlotte in a management position with a much higher salary. The Bible says, "All things work together for good with those who love God, who are called according to his purpose" (Romans 8:28). For the Christian, God has a way of turning setbacks into promotions. This should not surprise us. This same God turned a cross into a crown, a grave into a resurrection! He can transform our hospital beds into blessings, our pain into poetry, and our misfortunes into fortunes. Our only responsibility is to live by faith. Our only task is *thanksliving* and praise.

Consider Saint Paul for a moment. He was the pastor of a growing church. Things were great! He had plenty of food to eat. He was safe, healthy, and quite satisfied. Then came a call to Macedonia. And Paul went. But what should happen? Paul was rejected by the Macedonians. He was brutally beaten and thrown into jail. If that had happened to most of the preachers today, they would have rattled their chains in self-pity and said something like this: "Well, God, you sure didn't know what you were doing this time. Just look at me! I gave up a high-paying job for this!" But that is not the route Paul took. The Bible says that Paul and Silas started singing hymns to God around midnight. Here they were beaten, bloody, and in jail, but they were praising God from thankful hearts. If you read Acts 16, you will see how God received glory by their actions. The Philippian jailer and his family were converted.

So, why be thankful to God during times of misfortune? Because the Bible commands it. "Rejoice always," says 1 Thessalonians 5:16. Why give praise to God continually? Why be thankful at all times? Because gratitude is a powerful healing force. Praise is an acknowledgement of God's goodness. It is faith, pure and simple. *Thanksliving* replaces complaint with satisfaction, self-pity with joy, and whining with creative love. Those who refuse to

418

praise God and live with thanks during difficult times will grow bitter and pessimistic. But those who live thankfully will open themselves up to God's blessing. He can put their faith where it will be seen. Others can be blessed. All things work together for good.

If our recipe for a happy Thanksgiving is going to be complete we have to have some *thanksliving*. Do you have any? Is there some problem or setback or pain that you are willing to praise God for, and thank him for bringing your way? Will you praise him from the prison of some affliction like Paul did? That is real *thanksliving*!

Thanksgiving

Use your life as the bowl and stir in a little *thanksliving* with the *thanksgetting*. Now we need one final ingredient. As we return to the cookbook to see what it is, we find written, "It is more blessed to give than to receive" (Acts 20:35). This is our final ingredient. In with the *thanksgetting* and the *thanksliving* we pour at least a gallon of *thanksgiving*.

Giving is nothing new to the holiday scene. Mothers work hard to give their family the best meal. Fathers work overtime at the plant to buy extra gifts for loved ones. Giving is a joy. It is such a privilege. Why, anytime we catch ourselves feeling really good and warm inside, if we check we will find that we have been giving to others. Jesus promised to bless the giver. If you give a single apple seed to the soil, you will reap an apple tree and thousands of apple seeds. Truly when we give, our blessings are multiplied. As Jesus put it, "It is in giving that you receive."

On the radio a reporter was conducting one of those man-in-the-street interviews. Out among the pedestrians he was asking, "What are you thankful for?" Some were grateful for their health. Some gave thanks because they had good jobs to provide for their families. One lady whispered in broken English, "Much happy to live in America." One man was even thankful because the doctor said he could eat all the turkey he wanted. But the most enchanting remark of all was that of a wee little girl who said, "I'm thankful I'm going to see my grandmother so I can tell her how much I love her." Now that is really *thanksgiving*. It is going beyond mere *thanksgetting* and *thanksliving*. It is taking your eyes off yourself and focusing on another.

This spirit of giving to others from thankful hearts is perhaps the attitude which created the first Thanksgiving anyway. During that first holiday there was no turkey or pumpkin pie or cranberry sauce. The colonists were very poor. Epidemics and a harsh climate had thinned their ranks drastically. It was the Indians who helped them to survive. They had taught them to fish and build winterized huts. They showed them the secrets of fertilizing corn crops with fish. And come harvest time they all sat down for a three-day festival of thanksgetting and thanksliving and thanksgiving. The five surviving women in the settlement provided food for the combined party of 140.

Just as the Colonial era was a time for thankful giving by the Indians, so now is a time for giving on our parts. It is a time for the world of plenty to help the world of need. No! I'm not talking about welfare programs that encourage laziness or social hand-outs that rob incentive. I'm talking about involved, intelligent thanksgiving.

In our world two billion people are hungry. Four hundred fifty million a year face starvation. In the United States there are at least ten million people who are underfed. Many citizens of the third world live on about 27 cents a day.

How do we of plenty react to those in need? Do we say, "It's the fault of the socialists!"? Do we remind them that our ancestors were once hungry, too? Do we write them off as hopeless? Do we say, "I've got mine!? You get yours!"? I suppose we mostly are just overwhelmed. The problem just seems too big for us to deal with. So we ignore it, feeling a bit guilty. Every time we read verses like 1 John 3:17, we sort of cringe. "But if anyone has the world's goods and sees his brother in need, yet closes his heart against him, how does God's love abide in him?" Or how about Jesus' words, "I was hungry and you fed me. I was lonely and you comforted me. I was in prison and you visited me." They cut our consciences like a sharp knife.

420

The first time I ever saw real hunger was during a mission journey in Atotonillco, Mexico. I saw a four-year-old boy eating a dead rat. The next time was in Haiti. There were the hollow eyes of a child staring at me. They still haunt me. There were the bloated bellies. There was the silence. No crying. No sound except the sickening buzz of flies. Both times I emptied my pockets, but it didn't really help. A week later and the money was spent and they were hungry again. Most of our church's giving is like that. It is compassionate giving. It is emotional giving, but it needs to be intelligent giving as well.

A motto of the Peace Corps can be of help here. It says, "If you give a man a fish, you feed him for a day. If you teach him how to fish, you feed him for a lifetime." It does little good to give away a few thousand tons of grain. The hunger will go away for a while but it will return. What we need to give away are know-how, education, and helping hands. We don't need to give away fish. We need to teach them to fish. We need to teach them to farm and manufacture.

The answers to the world's problems are certainly very complex. None of us knows all the answers. But surely we can seek and ask and knock and make things a bit better than they are. Things may look bleak and all but impossible, but they must have looked much the same to those Indians and colonists that first Thanksgiving Day. We don't have to go to Haiti or India or Mexico to begin our work. We can begin helping those close at hand. There are those that don't know Christ here in this county. There are the prisoners, the orphans, the lonely, perhaps the hungry close at hand. Begin to give thankfully here and God will show you ways to give there in Mexico and Haiti or wherever.

Conclusion

What does it take to make a real Thanksgiving recipe? The family all at home? Health? Turkey and dressing? No, not really. All you need for the happiest Thanksgiving of all is a mixing bowl. Your own heart can serve the purpose quite well. Just mix in several heaping cupfuls of *thanksgetting*, an abundance of *thanksliving*, and a large quantity of *thanksgiving*. Then bring it to a boil with all of the warmth and love of our Savior Jesus Christ. You will have the best dish ever served!

You know, friends, traditions can grow very empty over the years. They can be little more than hollow liturgies filled with polite insincerities. People just go through the motions from force of habit. At the Spanish palace in Madrid, it was traditional for two soldiers to guard a certain bench in the palace gardens. No one knew why this was done. All they knew was that guarding it had been the custom for fifty years or more. Finally someone did some investigating, and found that years ago two guards were posted by the bench after it was freshly painted. Their job was to keep the king from sitting on wet paint. Someone forgot to retract the order and soldiers had been guarding it ever since. Is there a legitimate reason for this tradition we will observe this week? Shall we have another Thanksgiving? Oh, sure, it is the traditional thing to do. But is it worth it? Once more? Shall we? Yes! Yes! Once more with real feeling let us have Thanksgiving!

Stephen M. Crotts

Lectionary Preaching After Pentecost

The following index will aid the user of this book in matching the correct Sunday with the appropriate text during Pentecost. All texts in this book are from the series for the Gospel Readings, Revised Common Lectionary. (Note that the ELCA division of Lutheranism is now following the Revised Common Lectionary.) The Lutheran designations indicate days comparable to Sundays on which Revised Common Lectionary Propers or Ordinary Time designations are used.

(Fixed dates do not pertain to Lutheran Lectionary)

Fixed Date Lectionaries *Revised Common (including ELCA) and Roman Catholic*	**Lutheran Lectionary** *Lutheran*
The Day Of Pentecost	The Day Of Pentecost
The Holy Trinity	The Holy Trinity
May 29-June 4 — Proper 4, Ordinary Time 9	Pentecost 2
June 5-11 — Proper 5, Ordinary Time 10	Pentecost 3
June 12-18 — Proper 6, Ordinary Time 11	Pentecost 4
June 19-25 — Proper 7, Ordinary Time 12	Pentecost 5
June 26-July 2 — Proper 8, Ordinary Time 13	Pentecost 6
July 3-9 — Proper 9, Ordinary Time 14	Pentecost 7
July 10-16 — Proper 10, Ordinary Time 15	Pentecost 8
July 17-23 — Proper 11, Ordinary Time 16	Pentecost 9
July 24-30 — Proper 12, Ordinary Time 17	Pentecost 10
July 31-Aug. 6 — Proper 13, Ordinary Time 18	Pentecost 11
Aug. 7-13 — Proper 14, Ordinary Time 19	Pentecost 12
Aug. 14-20 — Proper 15, Ordinary Time 20	Pentecost 13
Aug. 21-27 — Proper 16, Ordinary Time 21	Pentecost 14
Aug. 28-Sept. 3 — Proper 17, Ordinary Time 22	Pentecost 15
Sept. 4-10 — Proper 18, Ordinary Time 23	Pentecost 16
Sept. 11-17 — Proper 19, Ordinary Time 24	Pentecost 17
Sept. 18-24 — Proper 20, Ordinary Time 25	Pentecost 18

Sept. 25-Oct. 1 — Proper 21, Ordinary Time 26	Pentecost 19
Oct. 2-8 — Proper 22, Ordinary Time 27	Pentecost 20
Oct. 9-15 — Proper 23, Ordinary Time 28	Pentecost 21
Oct. 16-22 — Proper 24, Ordinary Time 29	Pentecost 22
Oct. 23-29 — Proper 25, Ordinary Time 30	Pentecost 23
Oct. 30-Nov. 5 — Proper 26, Ordinary Time 31	Pentecost 24
Nov. 6-12 — Proper 27, Ordinary Time 32	Pentecost 25
Nov. 13-19 — Proper 28, Ordinary Time 33	Pentecost 26
	Pentecost 27
Nov. 20-26 — Christ The King	Christ The King

Reformation Day (or last Sunday in October) is October 31 (Revised Common, Lutheran)

All Saints' Day (or first Sunday in November) is November 1 (Revised Common, Lutheran, Roman Catholic)

U.S. / Canadian Lectionary Comparison

The following index shows the correlation between the Sundays and special days of the church year as they are titled or labeled in the Revised Common Lectionary published by the Consultation On Common Texts and used in the United States (the reference used for this book) and the Sundays and special days of the church year as they are titled or labeled in the Revised Common Lectionary used in Canada.

Revised Common Lectionary	Canadian Revised Common Lectionary
Advent 1	Advent 1
Advent 2	Advent 2
Advent 3	Advent 3
Advent 4	Advent 4
Christmas Eve	Christmas Eve
Nativity Of The Lord / Christmas Day	The Nativity Of Our Lord
Christmas 1	Christmas 1
January 1 / Holy Name Of Jesus	January 1 / The Name Of Jesus
Christmas 2	Christmas 2
Epiphany Of The Lord	The Epiphany Of Our Lord
Baptism Of The Lord / Epiphany 1	The Baptism Of Our Lord / Proper 1
Epiphany 2 / Ordinary Time 2	Epiphany 2 / Proper 2
Epiphany 3 / Ordinary Time 3	Epiphany 3 / Proper 3
Epiphany 4 / Ordinary Time 4	Epiphany 4 / Proper 4
Epiphany 5 / Ordinary Time 5	Epiphany 5 / Proper 5
Epiphany 6 / Ordinary Time 6	Epiphany 6 / Proper 6
Epiphany 7 / Ordinary Time 7	Epiphany 7 / Proper 7
Epiphany 8 / Ordinary Time 8	Epiphany 8 / Proper 8
Transfiguration Of The Lord / Last Sunday After Epiphany	The Transfiguration Of Our Lord / Last Sunday After Epiphany
Ash Wednesday	Ash Wednesday
Lent 1	Lent 1
Lent 2	Lent 2
Lent 3	Lent 3
Lent 4	Lent 4
Lent 5	Lent 5
Passion / Palm Sunday (Lent 6)	Passion / Palm Sunday
Holy / Maundy Thursday	Holy / Maundy Thursday
Good Friday	Good Friday
Resurrection Of The Lord / Easter	The Resurrection Of Our Lord

Easter 2	Easter 2
Easter 3	Easter 3
Easter 4	Easter 4
Easter 5	Easter 5
Easter 6	Easter 6
Ascension Of The Lord	The Ascension Of Our Lord
Easter 7	Easter 7
Day Of Pentecost	The Day Of Pentecost
Trinity Sunday	The Holy Trinity
Proper 4 / Pentecost 2 / O T 9*	Proper 9
Proper 5 / Pent 3 / O T 10	Proper 10
Proper 6 / Pent 4 / O T 11	Proper 11
Proper 7 / Pent 5 / O T 12	Proper 12
Proper 8 / Pent 6 / O T 13	Proper 13
Proper 9 / Pent 7 / O T 14	Proper 14
Proper 10 / Pent 8 / O T 15	Proper 15
Proper 11 / Pent 9 / O T 16	Proper 16
Proper 12 / Pent 10 / O T 17	Proper 17
Proper 13 / Pent 11 / O T 18	Proper 18
Proper 14 / Pent 12 / O T 19	Proper 19
Proper 15 / Pent 13 / O T 20	Proper 20
Proper 16 / Pent 14 / O T 21	Proper 21
Proper 17 / Pent 15 / O T 22	Proper 22
Proper 18 / Pent 16 / O T 23	Proper 23
Proper 19 / Pent 17 / O T 24	Proper 24
Proper 20 / Pent 18 / O T 25	Proper 25
Proper 21 / Pent 19 / O T 26	Proper 26
Proper 22 / Pent 20 / O T 27	Proper 27
Proper 23 / Pent 21 / O T 28	Proper 28
Proper 24 / Pent 22 / O T 29	Proper 29
Proper 25 / Pent 23 / O T 30	Proper 30
Proper 26 / Pent 24 / O T 31	Proper 31
Proper 27 / Pent 25 / O T 32	Proper 32
Proper 28 / Pent 26 / O T 33	Proper 33
Christ The King (Proper 29 / O T 34)	Proper 34 / Christ The King / Reign Of Christ

Reformation Day (October 31)	Reformation Day (October 31)
All Saints' Day (November 1 or 1st Sunday in November)	All Saints' Day (November 1)
Thanksgiving Day (4th Thursday of November)	Thanksgiving Day (2nd Monday of October)

*O T = Ordinary Time

426

About The Authors

Susan R. Andrews has been pastor of Bradley Hills Presbyterian Church in Bethesda, Maryland, for fifteen years, and was named Preacher of the Year by *Lectionary Homiletics* in 2000. Active in presbytery and General Assembly ministries, she was elected Moderator of the 215th General Assembly of the Presbyterian Church (USA) in May 2003. Andrews holds degrees from Wellesley College (B.A.), Harvard Divinity School (M.Div.), and McCormick Theological Seminary (D.Min.). A prolific writer, she has been published in *Lectionary Homiletics*, *Christian Century*, and *Christian Ministry*.

Richard E. Gribble, CSC, is an associate professor in the department of religious studies at Stonehill College in North Easton, Massachusetts. The author of fifteen books and over 150 articles, Father Gribble is the former rector/superior of Moreau Seminary at the University of Notre Dame. He is a graduate of the United States Naval Academy and served for five years on nuclear submarines before entering the priesthood. Gribble earned his Ph.D. from The Catholic University of America, and has also earned degrees from the University of Southern California and the Jesuit School of Theology at Berkeley. Among Gribble's previous CSS publications is a three-volume series on *The Parables Of Jesus*.

Stephen M. Crotts is the director of the Carolina Study Center, a campus ministry based in the Chapel Hill, North Carolina, area. A member of the Fellowship of Christian Athletes, Crotts is a popular speaker and a frequent contributor to Christian magazines. Among his many CSS publications are *The Beautiful Attitudes*,

Long Time Coming! and *Heroes Of The Faith Speak.* Crotts received his education at Furman University (B.A.) and Emory University (M.Div.). He is teaching pastor of the Adams Farm Associate Reformed Presbyterian Church in Greensboro, North Carolina.

Stan Purdum is the pastor of Centenary United Methodist Church in Waynesburg, Ohio. He is also the editor of the CSS preaching journal *Emphasis*, and has written extensively for both the religious and secular press. Purdum is the author of *Roll Around Heaven All Day* and *Playing In Traffic*, both accounts of his long-distance bicycle journeys, as well as *New Mercies I See* (CSS).

George L. Murphy is a graduate of Ohio University, Johns Hopkins University (where he earned a Ph.D. in physics), and Wartburg Theological Seminary. An adjunct faculty member at Trinity Lutheran Seminary, Murphy is also a Lutheran pastor who now serves on the staff of St. Paul's Episcopal Church in Akron, Ohio. He has been widely published in both scientific and religious periodicals, and has received two awards from the Templeton Foundation for his papers on science and religion. Murphy is the author of *Toward A Christian View Of A Scientific World* and (with LaVonne Althouse and Russell Willis) *Cosmic Witness* (CSS), *The Trademark of God* (Morehouse-Barlow), and *The Cosmos in the Light of the Cross* (Trinity Press International).